RELINQUISHED

*A Mother's Choice and My 30 Year Journey
to Find My Birth Family*

ROBERT J. YAFFE

Robert J. Yaffe / Relinquished

RJY Publishing - Elkhorn, Nebraska

Printed in the United States of America by Igramspark.

Cover design by Jay Shaw

Library of Congress Cataloguing-In-Publication Data has been Applied For

ISBN 978-1-7324016-8-6

CONTENTS

To my parents

Dorothy and Sol Yaffe

and my wife Rita

AUTHOR'S NOTE

This memoir roughly covers the period 1985-2022. It chronicles the history of my search to discover the nature of my origins and to learn the identities of my birth parents and any siblings that I might have.

As it turned out, there were many new siblings to discover, also many spouses, nieces and nephews along the way. All anecdotes, stories and events recounted in this book are true to the best of my knowledge. Any event described to which I was not present, was related directly to me by a person who was present at the time.

Having said that, I recognize that different people can remember an occurrence differently. Memories are not constant. They can fade and perceptions and perspectives can be altered, with the benefit of hindsight and the passage of time. One may remember an event differently than another, even though both were present and witnessed the same thing. I encountered this phenomenon numerous times early in my career when I served as a prosecutor for the Douglas County Attorney's office in Omaha. It is possible that someone might disagree with an incident or event as I have recounted it. Is this important to me? Yes, however this is my story and I understand that some of my recollections, perceptions, and opinions might meet with disagreement from others, especially in dealing with sensitive and often painful circumstances. I have attempted to ensure this does not happen but I beg the indulgence and understanding of anyone who might have a different perspective regarding any of the stories and events I have recounted in this narrative.

I have sometimes described an occurrence or created dialogue for an event to which I was not present or unable to remember. This is especially apparent in describing my birth and the circumstances leading to my being placed for adoption. However, those events and situations were in every instance, related to me by my birth mother, and in some cases verified by the sons (my brothers) of my birth father. I hope the reader will understand and appreciate the literary license I have taken in describing some of these events. Many recounted facts are related through documents and reports from my adoption files stored with Jewish Family Services in Omaha.

Finally, I have always had an aversion to describing members of my family as stepdaughter, stepson, half-brother, half-sister, etc. Technically, those are the correct terms to describe these relations, but I find terms like half and step seem to diminish their status, especially as my relationship with some of these individuals has grown exponentially over the years. Throughout this book I refer to all as brother, sister, son, daughter. The only exception is that I refer to my adoptive parents as mother and father or mom and dad, and my biological parents as birth mother, birth father, or biological mother and biological father. My reason for this is explained in the narrative.

This is a work of nonfiction. Every event depicted in this book happened. I have tried to relate my personal experience and to chronicle events to which I was witness or as related to me by someone with firsthand knowledge. Details are important, and there are a great many throughout this 30 plus year narrative. Hopefully, the documents, personal notes and tapes I have kept over the years will eliminate or greatly reduce any mistakes or discrepancies. If there are any mistakes, they are mine and mine alone.

FORWARD

GRACE UNIVERSITY
OMAHA, NEBRASKA
2020

Most people know where they were born. I never did. But on a crisp January afternoon in 2017, my wife Rita and I stood outside the former St. Catherine's Hospital in my hometown of Omaha, Nebraska. We had arranged for a tour of the building at this former hospital, the place where I was born. I searched more than 30 years to find it, and I guessed it looked much like it did in December 1949, the year I was born. The building has not functioned as a hospital in more than 50 years and looks much like it did in the late 1940s— a striking four-story dark red brick building with square nondescript style windows atop a hill. An imposing white cross rises the entire four stories, built into a thin vertical window, makes the structure look narrow and overbearing. The towering cross appears out of proportion to the rest of the building.

The building functioned as Grace University, formerly known as Grace Bible College, until the university ceased operations after the 2017-18 school year. As of September 2020, the building had been sold and is scheduled to be renovated into housing for veterans. The former St. Catherine's Hospital, with its storied history, lives on.

Rita and I toured the building shortly before the university closed its doors. Many of the former hospital rooms were dorm rooms and faculty offices. In what was the hospital nursery, visitors could see the now-invisible space where bassinets were once aligned in even rows, displayed in front of a large viewing window. I envisioned the smiling and doting new parents and grandparents, knocking on the glass, trying in vain to attract the attention of their otherwise distracted newborns.

The former nursery is now the music room—the walls adorned with pictures of 18th and 19th century composers. This was, for me, an ironic twist, as much of my life was and is immersed in the study, teaching, and enjoyment of opera and classical music. It seemed somewhat fitting that the room in which I spent my first days, would, 67 years later, be adorned with pictures of composers whose music has done so much to provide beauty, focus, and meaning to my life. There was a certain karma I felt in what was once the newborn ward, with pictures of composers with whom I was all too familiar. I felt comfortable in that room, wondering which space I might have occupied, waiting for Mom and Dad to knock on the viewing window—which, in my case, never happened.

I learned that all of the patient rooms had been transformed into faculty offices decades ago. Rita and I walked the halls looking for Room 325, the place my birth mother would have resided during her short hospital stay. Unfortunately, all of the room numbers had been changed, some more than once over the years, as the hospital was converted into a Bible college.

Upon closer examination, a few of the rooms still bore the faint imprint of what had to be the original room numbers. Those imprints, unobtrusive as they were, seemed like small puffs of memory flashing before my eyes like a bright neon sign blinking in the dark of night. They were a stark reminder that this building had a past, another existence light years away from its purpose in 2017. As I stood outside what might have been the room my birth mother was assigned, I closed my eyes and placed my finger on the almost imperceptible imprint, tracing the numbers with my fingers as if I were reading Braille. I could smell the standard hospital aromas that must have permeated the old building in 1949, the stagnant but antiseptic odors of ether, alcohol, and cleaning compounds. I could envision nurses walking up and down the halls with their carts loaded with medicines and equipment.

Hundreds if not thousands of stories must have unfolded in these rooms and wards. One of them transpired in Room 325. I was the child born in that hospital on December 4, 1949. This book highlights this adoptee's search to ascertain his biological roots. The journey that led me to this building took more than 30 years and is filled with surprising revelations, false leads, detective agencies, and emotional highs and lows. For many years, this search was conducted in secret in fear of the hurt this would cause my adoptive parents should they find out.

This book has provided me a cathartic release, as I relived this life-changing experience that stretched over those long years. During those years, laws and technology changed from closed to open adoptions to private detectives knocking on doors to *Ancestry.com*. Through the pages of this book, you will join me in reliving this journey.

It is an American adoption story. ***It is my story***.

RELINQUISHED

1

CONFRONTATION
OMAHA, NEBRASKA
FALL 1949

Pauline Newman was five months pregnant when she married Ken Karnes in August 1949. They had been together since high school and previously had a child together. Their son was a little over a year old.

Ken was not the father of the child Pauline was now carrying, and he knew this to be true. Ken had been serving in the U.S. Marine Corps in California when the baby was conceived. Initially, Pauline had tried to persuade Ken the baby was his, but he knew better. Stationed in California during March 1949, Ken knew it was not possible that the baby could be his. Pauline eventually broke down and told Ken the truth. Ken, enraged and hurt and already possessed of a short temper, was prepared to terminate their short marriage over the affair and the pregnancy. When Ken became angry, his face would turn red and flushed. There had already been at least one separation in this short marriage, so the relationship was already on tenuous ground.

Earlier that year in Omaha, Pauline met a handsome young man at the local drug store/soda fountain while her husband was training in California. The two became infatuated, and an affair and Pauline's pregnancy ensued. She was desperate to save her young marriage. Ken and Pauline had been romantically involved before this child was conceived. Their son, Ricky Arthur Karnes, was born in August 1948. Pauline's out-of-wedlock and unwanted pregnancy caused great conflict and strain in her marital relationship as it would in most relationships.

After learning of Pauline's affair, Ken made it clear that he would stay in the marriage and together they would raise Ricky Arthur, but there was a condition. He would never agree to raise a child he knew not to be his. Although the letter from the Division of Child Welfare refers to a "mutual" choice, Pauline was delivered this ultimatum.

Ken was willing to put the marriage on the line. He would only remain in the marriage if Pauline turned the child over for adoption. It was a cruel choice, a devil's bargain. If she elected to keep the child, she would face the prospect of raising two young children on her own, a seemingly impossible situation for a young mother in 1949. Pauline made her choice, and that choice was to preserve her marriage. But it was not an easy decision. This affair was not a one-night stand. Their relationship was deep and intense.

When Pauline was in labor, her mind drifted back to an incident three months earlier in September. The young man who had had such an impact on her life, drove to the home in South Omaha where Pauline, Ken, and their son lived. It was an impetuous and foolhardy act. His intention was to persuade Pauline to run away with him. Ken was home on leave at the time, which the man most likely did not know.

Pauline was a curvaceous woman and could wear clothes that would hide her expanding abdomen, and, in her mind, her guilt and shame. Pauline never spoke of her pregnancy and did not believe her lover ever knew she was pregnant. He most likely lived his entire life not knowing that he had a son. She described him as a handsome young fellow, 26, very trim, blue eyes, wavy brown hair, about 145 pounds, and possessing an infectious smile—the kind of smile that could uplift a soul on the darkest of days. He was clearly captivated with Pauline and she with him.

It would have taken great courage to come to the home where Pauline and Ken, recently married, lived. But he was young and obviously deeply in love. Throwing caution to the wind, he decided to make his plea in person. He believed he had found the girl of his dreams. Pauline had been seriously smitten with him as well, to her peril. He had come from somewhere in the Midwest. Pauline could not remember where. He settled temporarily in the Omaha/Council Bluffs, Iowa, area and eventually planned to move on. While in Omaha, he took a job in a corner drug and soda fountain store in South Omaha, just around the corner from where Pauline lived. It was there they found each other.

Their friendship soon became a passionate affair. Pauline became the love of his life. How long he had planned to stay in Omaha is unknown, but he was a determined young man with a purpose. The relationship with Pauline, although short, was intense, and he knew she had impassioned feelings for him as well. He did not know Pauline was carrying his child. She had taken great pains to hide her pregnancy. The man was nothing if not spirited, self-assertive, and determined regarding Pauline. His flaw was that he was lovestruck, and it is unlikely he considered the serious ramifications of what he was about to ask her to do.

If he had known she was pregnant, perhaps things might have taken a different direction, but Pauline was also a determined young woman. She had made a mistake, the consequences of which she would have to live with, but she was determined to save her marriage and raise Ricky Arthur with her husband.

That morning, the impetuous young man drove to the house where she was living with her husband and son, not knowing Ken was actually in Omaha at the time. Ken was stunned when the young man arrived at Pauline's house. Sitting together on the screened-in porch was Pauline and Ken, sitting side by side. Pauline's not-so-secret love drove around the block a couple of times, out of sight of the couple, hoping that Ken would somehow disappear. Finally, throwing all caution to the wind, he stopped the car in front of the house. Seeing Ken on the porch, he froze, hands on the steering wheel, not knowing what to do. This would be his only chance. His life was at a crossroads. He was a young man in love. He knew he could not leave without speaking to Pauline, even though Ken was sitting beside her. He was now acting on impulse, but with audacity and boldness.

Ken immediately suspected it was him, and he was on his feet ready to spring. Pauline was stunned. She never expected him to appear at her home and certainly not to approach her while she was sitting with her husband. Placing her hand on Ken's arm, Pauline assuredly states, "Please, let me handle this." The man gets out of his car, cautiously and nervously standing in the street, on the driver's side, one hand resting nervously on the car, as if the vehicle offered him security and a possible escape. The other hand remained in his pocket, thumb nervously twitching on the outside.

Desperately trying to decide what to do and what to say, the tension between the three individuals continued to build. Pauline's lover had not anticipated Ken's presence. For days, he must have imagined the conversation he would have with Pauline, playing it over and over again in his mind. But in none of those scenarios was Ken in the cast of characters.

Pauline and Ken quietly shared a few more words while the man stood in the street, his arm resting on his car, unsteady and unsure of his next move. Ken's agitation continued to increase by the second. Pauline was somehow able to convince Ken to let her handle this alone. Reluctantly, Ken stormed into the house, his anger about to erupt. He was near his breaking point. He wouldn't stay there long.

As soon as Ken was inside, Pauline nervously approached the car where the man was waiting. "What are you doing here? You can't be here," Pauline mumbled in a low whisper, her eyes peering into his.

"I want you to come away with me," he pleaded. "This is the last chance we have. Come with me; we can make a wonderful life together. I can't stay here without you." She stood next to him speaking in a tone just above a whisper, "I can't go with you, now or ever."

She had also reached a crossroads in her life, her feelings for this man were impassioned and intense, but she had reached her decision. She would remain in the marriage with Ken, she would give up the child she was carrying, and together they would raise Ricky Arthur. The man, beaten down by Pauline's response could barely mumble, "Why not?"

"Because I am married and I have a little boy. Do you expect me to just up and leave them both? I made a mistake, and now I have to do the right thing."

4

"We will figure something out, but I know I want to spend my life with you," he implored.

"But I can't risk losing my son, to say nothing of the fact that I am a newlywed. I love my husband, and I certainly love my son," Pauline calmly replied and just as determined.

"You have to leave now," Pauline implored.

"But I want to spend my life with you. I want you to run away with me," he responded, emphatically and determined as ever. At about this time, Pauline heard what could only be the unmistakable sound of Ken loading a shotgun from behind the front door.

At that moment, Ken appeared at the door, shotgun in hand. "I want you to get off my property, get out of here and never come back." He spoke calmly, but his face was flushed, his rage bubbling just below the surface. Everyone's eyes were fixed on the shotgun.

"Don't you ever come near my wife again. You hear me? Never!" Ken's rage was spilling over; he was furious and indignant.

The man's intense stare quickly shifted between Pauline's eyes and Ken's approaching movement. The situation was rapidly spinning out of control. The man, overwhelmed by fear, jumped into his car, started the ignition, hit the accelerator and drove off, leaving behind the sound of screeching tires. Ken pursued him on foot, chasing the car down the street, shotgun in hand. The car gained distance until it became a speck; the man was gone. The two men would never see each other again. Pauline would never see the father of their son again. Her lover would now become only a memory, a mere reminiscence she would spend a lifetime trying to erase.

2

RELINQUISHED
OMAHA
DECEMBER 4, 1949

Pauline Newman Karnes would have liked to erase December 4, 1949, from her memory, like a dream occurring during a restless sleep that lingers just below the surface, only to vanish within seconds of waking. The memory of that day would return, but not for more than a half century. But return it would, like a wave crashing against a sea wall during a raging storm. Can the birth of a child be erased totally and completely from a birth mother's memory? Pauline attempted to suppress her secrets over the often anguished years.

The story begins on an above average December day in Omaha. The temperature reached nearly 50 degrees. As any Omahan will tell you, a December day in Omaha that reaches 50 degrees is a day to be relished and enjoyed. Nebraska winters are seemingly endless, with snowfall by Halloween covering the city like a soft, downy white blanket and snow that can linger past Easter. December 4 was a brief respite from winter's wrath.

However, the day was not to be a blessing for the attractive, 21-year-old Pauline. Pauline's short brown hair matched her brown eyes. She had a lissome figure and a bright, animated smile. She was buxom by her own description and could turn young men's heads. With one of these men, the attraction was mutual. That attraction had led her to this day.

Pauline entered the hospital early that morning, alone and intent on saving her marriage. Ken was not with her nor was her mother, who had offered her no support during this crisis. Pauline's father had died when she was only eight years old. In fact, for a time leading up to this day, Pauline had been living in a home for unwed mothers across the street from St. Catherine's Hospital, having been banned from her home.

The hospital must have seemed to loom over her as she entered that morning. The seemingly out-of-proportion cross might have appeared awe inspiring to some but must have appeared unwelcoming and even threatening to a young Orthodox Jewish girl, there to give birth to a child she wouldn't keep.

Pauline was alone because her husband had insisted the child was not his. The fact that they had a 16-month-old child at home, admittedly his, only complicated the situation. The decision was made: the child would be placed for adoption.

Pauline was sent to the maternity ward and then to a labor room. I was born a healthy, 8-pound. 4½-ounce baby boy who took his first breaths at 3:40 p.m. Pauline held me once, and then I was taken away. No attachment or emotional bond would be created between mother and newborn son. She was taken to her room, never to see me again. She was released the next day. It would be 53 years before she would set eyes on the "child" again. She would strive to erase the memory of that child from her mind and her conscious thoughts forever. It would be as if her son never existed.

Despite the strain and tension this adoption process would have inevitably caused her, the troubled mother made one request to the authorities who would determine the fate of the baby, the parental rights over which she would immediately relinquish. Her fervent wish, having been born and raised in an Orthodox Jewish family, was that her child be given to Jewish parents and raised in a Jewish home.

A couple of weeks later, she signed a relinquishment order: a cold, legal document that forever changed the course of my life. Her husband signed the order as well.

RELINQUISHMENT

KNOW ALL MEN BY THESE PRESENTS, that we the undersigned, --------------, husband and wife, of the County of Omaha, Douglas County, Nebraska, and parents of -----------------, a minor child, who was born at the City of Omaha, Douglas County, Nebraska, on the 4th day of December, 1949, do hereby voluntarily relinquish all of our right to the custody of and power and control over said minor child to Federation for Jewish Service, a corporation duly organized under the laws of the State of Nebraska and having its office at said City of Omaha, and we, and each of us, do hereby authorize and empower said Federation for Jewish Service to procure the adoption of said minor child by some suitable person or persons. DATED at Omaha, Nebraska this 22 day of December, 1949.

With the document signed and notarized, the child could now be placed for adoption. Custody was transferred to the State of Nebraska, and the adoption was arranged through the Omaha Federation for Jewish Service.

In the following four years, the young woman gave birth to two other children, and the fragile marriage survived. She struggled to put the baby boy out of her mind, out of her conscious thought, and she succeeded in doing so for over 50 years.

Pauline's case was summarized in a letter from Sara Weinberg, executive secretary of the Jewish Welfare Bureau (JWB). JWB, today known as the Jewish Federation of Omaha, was the umbrella organization overseeing most of the Jewish agencies in the community. The following letter summarizes the case. Pauline discussed the state of her troubled marriage, and the "concession" that allowed the marriage to survive. This letter remained in the files of the Federation for Jewish Service (later to be known as Jewish Family Services) for nearly 65 years.

"The mother and her family are well known to our agency and when she learned we wished to help her she said she preferred this and

8

asked that we place the baby. She is married, has a 16 month old child with this man and believes she can make a go of her marriage now. They had some disagreements, resulting in a separation during which time she had an affair with another man. This was only temporary but did result in pregnancy. Her husband was willing to take her back and they mutually agreed to give up the child as soon as it was born, leaving it at the hospital, with an oral agreement for his care. A formal relinquishment was signed by the mother and her husband." December 22, 1949.

The marriage of Pauline and Ken Karnes would survive this marital crisis and they would raise two additional children. In return for giving up the child, Ken agreed he would never bring up the affair, the pregnancy, or the birth. Even in anger or during arguments, Ken solemnly committed he would never hold the affair over Pauline's head, like a concealed weapon, waiting to emerge if desperate measures were needed. He honored this promise until a fatal heart attack took his life in 1977. Ken was only 50 years old. Neither Pauline nor Ken ever shared with their children the secret of their sibling who was relinquished at birth. This would remain a vaulted family secret.

The adoption would be private. Pauline would never know where the child lived or who his adopted parents were—a difficult decision for this young Jewish woman raised as an Orthodox Jew, forced to choose between her marriage and her newborn son.

So Pauline, ever loyal to Ken, relinquished the child that was the result of this disastrous situation. In her mind, her son's only name would forever be "Baby Boy Karnes." I would have been half-brother to little Ricky Arthur, would have been raised by a loving mother, but assuredly unwanted by her husband who was not my father. I was relinquished to the Nebraska State Division of Child Welfare.

The Jewish agency in Omaha assumed responsibility for me on December 12, 1949—eight days after my birth. They arranged for me to remain at St. Catherine's Hospital for several weeks "so as not to expose him to change too early."

I was then placed in a boarding home under the supervision of a case worker and pediatrician. The letter from Sara Weinberg, stated that the child is "a fine, healthy, winsome baby and should be considered for early adoption."

Pauline had been assured at the time of relinquishment that the standard procedure was that a child relinquished to the state would be placed for adoption outside of the State of Nebraska. This would avoid the possibility of the child coming into accidental contact with biological family members during his life, especially in a smaller town. She was told the child would be transferred to Minnesota for adoption.

I was never transferred from the immediate Omaha area. But her request that I be placed in a "good Jewish home" was honored. Within a month, the Federation for Jewish Service was diligently seeking to place me in a Jewish home. That home would be in Omaha.

Pauline and Ken still had their other son to raise together. But fate would intervene in the lives of Pauline and Ken. Within a year, Ricky Arthur would be dead, a tragic victim of meningitis—an unspeakable calamity. A curtain of overwhelming guilt would descend over Pauline that would remain with her the rest of her life.

3

ADOPTED
OMAHA
1949–1950

"Do you know who your real parents are?" I have been asked this ill-mannered question dozens of times in my life. "Yes; yes, I do. My real parents are the parents who raised me from birth, the couple whose last name I share."

Dorothy and Sol Yaffe were my mom and dad. They were and remain the only people I could ever call Mom and Dad. These are the good souls who raised me from birth, nurtured me, ensured that I received the best education from elementary school through law school, while always providing love and support. They instilled within me core ideals and values, a moral code that has served me throughout my life. Like most ideals, I have not always lived up to them, but my parents have always provided me with inspiration. They also nurtured my Judaism, possibly the greatest gift they could have given me. Judaism helped shape the person I am. My core values come from my faith and from both of my parents. I have been blessed to have had the fortune to be raised by two wonderful, kind, and loving parents.

All of this was because of that young woman's fervent desire in 1949 that the son she gave up be placed in a Jewish home. Her decision resulted in my adoption by Dorothy and Sol Yaffe. My biological mother's fervent wish was successful beyond her expectations, and for that I am eternally grateful. For as long as I could remember, I wanted to know who she was. An adoptee's search for roots, for the missing branches on the family tree, is really a search for self. Dorothy and Sol Yaffe became the roots of my family tree. This story details my 33-year journey to discover the missing branches on my family tree.

As a child, I attended Hebrew School at Omaha's Beth El Synagogue. I have vivid memories of contributing money through the Jewish National Fund (JNF) to plant trees in Israel. I had a small poster of a tree with my name on it. Each branch's little circles were for stamps that could be purchased for 10 cents. For every dime contributed, you received a sticker you could place on the tree. When every space on the tree was filled, you had successfully planted a tree in Israel.

During the many years of searching for my biological roots, I often remembered those little posters with the many branches. Just as I could fill in the branches with the stickers of leaves purchased for a dime, I envisioned those posters as my family tree. I had two family trees, one with all the spaces filled with names, my parents at the root, and the branches displaying the names of my sister Jane, grandparents, aunts and uncles, and cousins. The other family tree, my biological parents, grandparents, and all the relatives were blank with no way to fill them in. I desperately wanted to fill in those empty circles. Those branches, filled in, would tell me who I might have been and more importantly, would enable me to know who I am. I needed to know.

In one of our early meetings with Jewish Family Services of Omaha (JFS), formerly the Federation for Jewish Service at the time of my adoption, my wife Rita and I met with Teresa, a JFS caseworker who had access to my original adoption files. She provided us a record of home visits that occurred at the apartment of my mom and dad during my adoption. The purpose of the home visits was to determine Dorothy and Sol's suitability as parents before the adoption could be finalized. This was not an easy document to read. The feeling was akin to going through personal belongings of a deceased loved one immediately after their death. I had intense feelings of guilt reading these pages. I felt I was somehow intruding, invading the privacy of my parents. That feeling did not dissipate when I finished them. Although I always knew I was adopted, my parents never spoke to me about the adoption process. It was a surreal, almost out-of-body experience reading about myself.

The document contained a summary of the caseworker's notes of the home visits made during the period when Dorothy and Sol were being observed to determine their suitability to adopt. Frustratingly, the document was not signed by the JFS caseworker, so there was no way to know who that was. The following are some of the transcribed notes from the unnamed caseworker. They provide deep insight into my parents and just how deeply they desired to have a child they were unable to conceive themselves. Reading these notes, many decades after my adoption and several years after their deaths, was powerful and emotional.

January 1950 - "Mrs. Y came to the office several days previously and spoke about her wish to adopt a child. She said this is something she and her husband have discussed for some time…. They have been married over six years and have consulted a number of doctors, who suggested they should consider adoption." (My parents never discussed with me the reasons why they could not have children of their own.)

"She (my mom) *said, they are not wealthy but enjoy a steady comfortable income…. They want to rear a family too and believe they can provide for a child adequately and enrich their own lives…. Worker believed this is something that has meaning for her."*

What followed was a short description of my mother. That description from January 1950 could just as easily have been written in 2015, the year she died. She was 97 years old.

"Mrs. Y is a small, very trim person. She can be described as petite. Dresses in good taste, is well integrated, (not sure what that meant) *speaks well and is quite self assured. At first, worker had the impression she was overly methodical and precise but upon continued conversation she became more relaxed, though at no time did she talk about anything other than the subject of interest."*

On January 20, 1950, the discussion centered on my parent's inability to conceive. *"This day there was a telephone call to Dr. Margolin,* (an uncle on my father's side). *He provided a reference. He said both are in good health and as is usual the cause (of inability to have children) cannot be easily found; they have been given some medical service and possibility of pregnancy is not entirely ruled out though it is rather remote. Difficulty may be with Mr. Y. He considers them good prospective parents."*

On January 23, the caseworker made a home visit to study the applicants and assess their current status and eligibility.

"They live in a modern 3 room apartment. It was furnished in good taste but modestly as they said they plan to buy a home and then furnish it properly. Mrs. Y was quite a tease and seemed to carry the conversation, though Mr. Y did join in, was well related to the topic and evidenced real interest and sincerity."

"He is of average height and build, of medium coloring, regular features and seems warm and friendly. He said he likes children and had looked forward to being a parent, accepting that as a natural result of marriage."

Both said they are aware of the responsibilities of raising a child and both are willing to make any necessary adjustments in their routines. Regarding finances, they reassured the caseworker that they believed they could provide well for the child and should be able to provide good educational opportunities. According to caseworker notes, *"Both laughingly said they are even willing to give up golfing, as that is their chief interest."* Both of my parents were outstanding golfers and had won many tournaments at the Highland Country Club, Omaha's only Jewish country club at the time. Growing up, we had a basement full of golf trophies. I can accurately report that none of their golf or tennis talent ever rubbed off on me.

In what must have been a personal but revealing moment, they pointed to a huge bottle in the apartment, telling the caseworker this was their bank to save up for a new house. They had been depositing their loose change into it. I was deeply moved by this paragraph in the report. I choked up picturing this jar of coins, which represented how desperately committed they were to my adoption. I wished I had read this report decades earlier. I wanted to hug them and thank them for everything they had ever done for me, for their lifelong commitment to my well-being. I owe them everything.

At the end of the report, Dorothy and Sol showed "*an intense eagerness for this adoption to happen, being unable to conceive a child, they fervently wished for a child that would fulfill their ardent desire to have a child.*"

From the caseworker's notes, "*When told it was a boy, they wanted to see him at once. They questioned if they could take him because they would not have a place in the apartment as it has no separate bedroom. They then asked some questions about parentage and I gave them as much as seemed adequate, but as to be expected they wanted to know more details and kept on asking questions. Mrs. Y particularly wanted to know how safe they would be in taking a child that might be recognized.*"

This was intriguing information. My parents must have known that I was born locally, or they would have had no reason to be concerned over my being "recognized." They were assured by the caseworker that the agency holds all information in strict confidence, and they could not provide them with any further information. Likewise, no information would be given to anyone else. My parents always insisted they knew only that I was born to a Jewish mother and there were no known significant health issues or risks in the birth family.

My mother was and remained until the day of her death both methodical and exacting. Both wanted to accept the child at once but were advised to delay because of a case of chickenpox in the next-door apartment. In the end, they decided not to delay taking the child, but agreed to take him to her mother's house and wait out the chickenpox case there. On February 15, 1950, I was taken to the home of my grandparents (mother's side) until it was safe for my parents to bring me home.

Between February and August 1950, the caseworker regularly visited Dorothy and Sol. One entry, on August 10, 1950, sums up those visits:

"*They, (Dorothy and Sol) wished to thank the worker for bringing them so much happiness as the Y's are just "crazy" about him. From all indications he is a very bright boy. Mr. Y would make some remark about the boy when he saw the worker and most often it was, "Come and see him, he's terrific." On those occasions when the worker was at the home, it was evident they had rearranged their routine, it all centered around "Bobby." Mrs. Y assumed the role of mother rather graciously and spoke with pride of the progress he was making. They soon established a routine for him—moved him to a downstairs apartment, began plans for a house, regular checkups with Dr. Jahr, (Pediatrician), progressed satisfactorily and developed into a large, good natured boy and they were very proud of him."*

The formal adoption took place on September 20, 1950. On that day, I was relinquished for a second time, but this time to the loving arms of my anxious parents. The adoption order, summarized:

IN THE COUNTY COURT OF DOUGLAS COUNTY, NEBRASKA IN THE MATTER OF THE ADOPTION OF ROBERT JOEL YAFFE CONSENT TO ADOPTION

Comes now the FEDERATION FOR JEWISH SERVICE, a duly licensed agency and respectfully shows the court:

That the above named minor child is of the age of nine months having been born on the 4th of December, 1949. That on the 22d day of December, 1949 the parents of said child were the natural guardians thereof and then had the exclusive care, custody and control of said minor child, and did by written instrument duly signed and acknowledged, surrender said child and the control and custody thereof to the aforementioned Federation for Jewish Service, and did thereby relinquish all right and claim to the child.

That said Federation for Jewish Service hereby consents to the adoption of said minor child by Sol Yaffe and Dorothy Ann Yaffe, husband and wife, and voluntarily relinquishes all right to the custody of and power and control over said minor child and all claim and interest in and to the services and wages of said minor child shall be fully adopted by Sol Yaffe and Dorothy Yaffe, residents of the city of Omaha, in Douglas County, Nebraska. Dated in Omaha, Nebraska, this 20th day of September, 1950.

The caseworker, in conversation with Jack Marer (my parents' attorney), noted that the consent form from Jewish Services was sent to the judge along with the relinquishment signed by Pauline and her husband. That document would never be shown to my mom and dad. The birth date would be registered and a new birth certificate issued with Dorothy and Sol Yaffe listed as parents. The original birth certificate would then be sealed, presumably forever. They were never to know the identity of my birth parents or the circumstances of my relinquishment.

Thus it was that on September 20, 1950, I legally became the son of Dorothy and Sol Yaffe. I was officially Robert Joel Yaffe. It would be 1985 before I would begin the long search to seek the answers to the questions my parents never wanted to know.

4

YOU CAN'T KNOW WHERE YOU'RE GOING IF YOU DON'T KNOW WHERE YOU'VE BEEN

My story is really an Omaha story. My childhood, adolescence, and education at the University of Nebraska-Lincoln (UNL) and law school at Creighton University in Omaha, and my years in the Douglas County Attorney's Office—all connected to Omaha. My connection to the Omaha Jewish Community is never-changing throughout my entire life. In 1994, I gave an interview for a book, *Growing Up Jewish in America*, by Myrna and Harvey Frommer.[1] I emphasized my deep-seated Omaha connection. My interview comments were summarized by the Frommers below.

"In the 1950's and 1960's, Omaha was an oasis in the wilderness. Beyond the city line were endless cornfields. Kansas City, the nearest city of any import, was one hundred and eighty miles away. Chicago was a ten hour drive (closer to eight hours today). *The sense of isolation was intensified if you were Jewish. That was one of the factors that solidified the Jewish community and made it unique. Jews lived in a Jewish neighborhood* (called "Bagel" in the '60s) *and had Jewish friends. There was heavy synagogue affiliation in three well attended synagogues. We attended services every Saturday at Beth El Synagogue, the conservative synagogue, even in winter, and winters in Omaha could be pretty bad. At the Sunday morning Junior B'nai B'rith bowling leagues, we filled up all twenty-four lanes. We also had a Sunday basketball league for Jewish kids, which my dad had me join. But I hated it—the smell of the gym, the fact that the other guys were good and I was not."* I was actually terrible, the last guy chosen to be on a team, any team.

"The previous generation had created an infrastructure of Jewish accomplishment in Omaha. One of the largest jewelry stores in America, Borsheims, is an Omaha institution." (The store was

18

founded in 1870, owned by a prominent Jewish family for decades, and became a subsidiary of Berkshire Hathaway, owned by investor Warren Buffett, in 1989).

"Rose Blumkin (1893-1998), a Russian Jewish immigrant, came to Omaha in 1917. A harsh-looking tiny woman who wore her black hair in a bun, she'd drive around her small carpet store in a little scooter cart, pull up beside a customer and offer a deal. That carpet store became the Nebraska Furniture Mart, America's largest furniture store and a multi-million dollar enterprise."

"My grandfather, Nathan Yaffe, came to Omaha from Russia and started the N.S. Yaffe Printing Company in 1906." My grandfather, father, and his brother Irv ran the business for decades. Yaffe Printing remained in business until my dad and Irv sold it in the late 1990's. *"I can still smell the ink, see the printers slab it onto the presses, listen to my father talking over the loud noise of the machinery, giant presses with names such as, "The Heidelberg", as he takes me around and explains the process to me."*

"My parents and most of their friends were successful in business. They were people of accomplishment, and we were expected to accomplish as well." There was always a push in my family for academic excellence. I was expected to become a professional.

"In our community, financial problems were few, and divorce was relatively unheard of. We lived an all-American, upper middle class suburban Jewish life in the middle of nowhere. It was strange, if you thought about it." [2]

From my earliest memories, I knew I was adopted. My parents were always very open about it. I never felt different than anyone else, but I always had a feeling, just a slight uneasiness, lurking just beneath the surface, like the early onset of a toothache. The awareness that I was somehow different was always there, but I never consciously considered it, and often didn't think of it at all. Randomly, thoughts would flood my mind, and I would always search for a solution.

Throughout my childhood and early adulthood, I never really questioned my parents about my adoption. On the rare occasion when I would ask, they would tell me they knew next to nothing. At the time of my adoption, they were told very little, and there were never any names exchanged. They were only told that my birth mother was Jewish and I was born with no known health risks. They told me there was no other information to be had. While growing up, I accepted their answer and tried to move on. But I was haunted by what I did not know about my past. It was not until my mid-thirties that I decided I needed to discover my biological roots.

My search really began in 1985, and it happened in the Douglas County Courthouse where I was working as a deputy county attorney for Douglas County and the State of Nebraska. My search began during the recess of a case I was prosecuting.

The judge and I were acquainted outside of the courtroom, and I had made him aware of my desire to learn of my origins and the identity of my birth parents. During a recess, while in his chambers, he informed me there was a file on his desk that contained my birth certificate. I had never seen it before and could only stare intently at its resting place on his desk. The judge had searched whatever files he could find in the court records regarding my adoption, which was a closed adoption, as they all were in the State of Nebraska at that time. In 1985, I only knew the extremely limited information my parents had given me.

During a court recess, the judge excused himself from his chambers, announcing he had an errand to attend to and would be back in 10 minutes. It was a clear message. He was allowing me to access what was presumably my original birth certificate. My heart pounded as he left the room. Could finding out this information be this easy? I saw the file on his desk with my name on it. When he left the chambers, I nervously picked it up and opened it. The birth certificate was right on top. My parents were listed as Dorothy and Sol Yaffe, my adoptive parents. I knew they were not my birth parents; the birth certificate had been altered to reflect the names of my adoptive parents. My disappointment overcame me like a physical presence in the room. When the judge returned to his chambers, he could read the disappointment on my face. It was at this moment that the need to find answers really hit home.

The spark was lit. I was more determined than ever to find the answers to questions that have tugged at me since childhood. My search truly began that day in the judge's chambers. Having been thwarted by what I immediately knew to be a revised birth certificate, I left the courthouse committed to learning the secrets of my origins.

I would have been dismayed to know the search would stretch more than 30 years. Three decades represents a good portion of a lifetime. Why would anyone want to spend that length of time searching for answers to one's past? What relevance does it have to the present or to the future? How does any of this affect the way I live my life? These were all pertinent questions; questions most likely faced by every adoptee searching for their origins, regardless of the motivation for their search. But I would forge on. There had to be an original birth certificate, not the altered one I saw on the Judge's desk. I was more determined than ever.

There can be many reasons why an adoptee might search for his biological roots. These can include a search for medical and genetic information, religious issues, or perhaps some deep-seated problems with the adoptive family or a myriad of psychological issues. Maybe it's just a desire to see if there is someone in the universe who looks and acts like you—a doppelgänger who shares your DNA. All these valid reasons can be of less or more importance, depending upon circumstances and needs of the adoptee seeking the information.

I can tell you my search was not about finding an alternate or a substitute family. The search was about resolving my questions to fill in the branches on that empty side of my family tree. It was not about Dorothy and Sol. It was my need to learn of my medical history so I could fill out a form in the doctor's office. It was discovering whether there were siblings out there who might share my physical features and the tantalizing prospect of meeting them. It was about discovering the roots and branches that exist in my biological family. It was about meeting the birth parents who gave me the gift of life and understanding why they made their decision to place me for adoption. It is not only about who I am, but who I might have been.

There was no specific eureka moment when I decided I needed to discover my biological origins. I can best describe myself as methodical and intellectually curious. To have no knowledge of the identity of my birth parents, the circumstances of my birth and subsequent adoption, my medical history, my siblings (if any), was too much for me to accept. From my earliest memories, I wanted to know. I demanded answers. My friends had answers. I had none. By 1985, at age 36, I knew the time had come. Either I commence an extensive search, or I move on. I began the search that day in the judge's chambers at the Douglas County Courthouse.

A slight digression. When talking about adoption, terminology is important. Asking an adoptee who his real parents are is annoying if not inappropriate. If asked, "Do you know who your birth parents are?" is a very different question. The terms birth mother/father, parents, stepparents, Mom and Dad, carry a myriad of connotations. To be clear, I have only one mom and dad. There is no birth mother or birth father who could ever take their place. The fragile emotions attached to these monikers would become painful issues I had to confront from both my adoptive parents and my birth mother.

So why conduct a search? "The need to search isn't related to whether a person loves his or her adoptive family," explains Linda Yellin, MSW, ACSW, a therapist specializing in adoption services in Farmington Hills, Michigan. She continues:

"No matter how loving and close a family is, no one can provide the missing pieces to the puzzle for the adopted person that the birth family can. This is a hard concept to explain, especially to people who were not adopted."

"There are two different cups that need to be filled. The adoptive parents feel that there's something wrong with their relationship with their child if they don't fill that cup. But they can't fill it; it isn't theirs to fill. Their cup may be overflowing, but the other cup remains empty."[3]

The other cup is the one I had set out to fill. Others know their origins, medical history, and family trees. Why shouldn't I have the same information regarding my origins? The argument is often put forward that the right to privacy of the birth parents should be respected at all costs. If the adoption was a closed adoption, as were most adoptions in the 1940s and '50s, then the birth parents should have the absolute right to decide if the information they possess, especially their identity, should ever be released to the child they gave up for adoption. Closed case.

The agreement the birth parents entered into with the state created a contract that ensured their identities and the circumstances of the adoption would remain secret forever. When I have been confronted with this argument, my response has always been consistent. I was never party to this agreement. My birth parents' contract with the state does not obviate my right to know the origins of my birth. Access to my original birth certificate and to learn of my origins is a basic human right.

Of course, anyone has the right to decline contact with or associate with anyone they wish. No one has the right to force themselves on anyone. If after contact is made with the birth parent and those individuals make it clear they do not wish to meet or have any relationship with the child, then the adoptee must walk away, as onerous as that might be. My right to know did not mean a right to a relationship. I was prepared to walk away, if, after locating one or both of my birth parents, they, for whatever reason, did not want to meet me. Both parties also could discover an ongoing relationship will not work. It might even be possible for the adoptee to feel closer to their adoptive family than ever after a reunion with their biological family. I knew all of these were real possibilities and I had to be emotionally and intellectually prepared for whatever unfolded. I was determined to pursue this path, no matter where it led.

I thought I had the moral justification to pursue the identity of my birth parents. I was also determined that if I learned of their identity, I was morally justified to seek out a meeting with them. A personal encounter was the only way to truly receive the answers and the information I desired, and I was determined to pursue this path as far as I possibly could. I understood that I was obligated to honor my birth parents' wishes and cease contact if they refused to meet with me. I would still persistently exhaust every possible attempt without harassing and hopefully not creating indignation or anger.

Although many adoptees vehemently deny ever thinking about adoption (my sister Jane, also adopted, until very recently being one of them), I clearly was not one of them. The curiosity, inquisitiveness, and need to find the source of my origins grew and festered. Sometimes that curiosity would rise to the surface, like when handed a medical history to fill out, whose questions I could never answer. The few details my parents were given at the time of my adoption were all they ever wanted to know, and they were content. They thought this was all I needed to know as well. But I felt that I had the absolute right to know my back story and origins. No one else has the right to say that my biological roots are not important to me. Knowing my biological roots were important to me, and I was willing to devote as much time and effort as I possibly could to unlock those secrets.

Some may argue that one's history, heritage, and the love of one's adoptive parents should be enough, and the rest is irrelevant. Those comments usually come from people who were not adopted. Psychotherapist Annette Baran, MSW, one of the authors of *Adoption Triangle*, wrote:

"Adoptees are not looking for a mom and dad. Birth parents may be genetically connected, but are strangers. **The parents who raised a person are the parents,** *(emphasis added). If adoptive parents are open and patient, the adoptive family is strengthened, not weakened, by a search and reunion."*[4]

I only hoped that would be the case as I embarked on my search. No matter what the results, Dorothy and Sol would always be my only mom and dad, not to be replaced by biological parents.

I found it interesting and informative to examine Jewish sources as to what our sages had to say about adoption. The concept of adoption is reinforced many times.

One who raises a child is as if they gave birth to that child. From where do we learn this? From the book of Ruth. A child was born to

Naomi. Did Naomi really give birth? Didn't Ruth? Yes. Ruth gave birth but Naomi raised him, therefore he is considered as a child of Naomi. (Sanhedrin 19b)

There are other examples as well.

A person who raises an orphan in his home and writes on a contract "my son" or the orphan wrote "my father or mother," it is not considered fake. It has been Kosher since they raised him. (Shulchan Aruch Choshen Mishpat 42:19)

Even the obligation to honor the adoptive parent could not be clearer.

At the time when God commanded Moses to go and save the Jewish people in Egypt, Moses responded, "I must first get permission from Yitro (Jethro) who is like my father. One who raises someone and takes care of him deserves honor and respect more than a father or mother." (Shmot Rabah)

Chapter 16 of the Book of Genesis records the story of Sarai, Abram's wife, who had borne Abram no children. (Sarai and Abram's names were later changed to Abraham and Sarah). Sarai had an Egyptian maidservant whose name was Hagar. Sarai told Abram that the Lord had prevented her from bearing children. She told him to consort with her maid, and perhaps he would have a son through her. Abram heeded her request.

Dennis Prager wrote the following in his excellent commentary to the Book of Genesis:

"According to the Laws of Hammurabi and other ancient Near Eastern legal documents, it was common for an infertile wife to provide her husband with a concubine in order to bear children for the couple. Those children were considered the wife's children as much as biological children would be."[5]

In Chapter 30 of Genesis, we read that Jacob became incensed at his wife, Rachel, who was unable to bear him children. She said to him:

"Here is my maid Bilhah. Consort with her, that she may bear on my knees and that through her I too may have children." (Genesis, Chapter 30, verse 3)

According to Prager, in the ancient world, *"Placing the newborn on someone's knees was a gesture of adoption."*[6]

"Bilhah conceived and bore Jacob a son. And Rachel said, God has vindicated me: indeed, He has heeded my plea and given me a son." (Genesis, Chapter 30, 5-6)

Actually, four of Jacob's 12 sons were born through concubines. Prager points out that those sons were considered every bit as much tribes of Israel as the sons born of Rachel and Leah, his wives. The fact that some were born to concubines rather than wives is irrelevant. Like an adoptive mother today, Rachel was considered their mother.[7]

The most famous adoption in the Bible is the story of Moses. When Pharaoh ordered the killing of the first born of the Hebrews, Moses's mother placed her infant in a wicker basket and placed it among the reeds by the banks of the Nile River. His sister hid herself to learn what would befall him. Exodus, Chapter 2, 5-6, tells us that the daughter of Pharaoh came down to bathe in the Nile. She spied the basket amont the reeds and sent her slave girl to go and get it. When she opened it, she saw it was a baby boy. She took pity on the child and said, 'This must be a Hebrew child.'

In verse 10, we learn that when the child grew up, the wet nurse brought him to Pharaoh's daughter, who made him her son. She named him Moses, meaning, 'I drew him out of the water.'

The daughter of Pharoah only raised the young Moses. She was not his birth mother. It is telling that so many Jewish sources regard the ones who raises an orphan boy or girl in his house, is given credit as if he/she gave birth to the child. These ancient Jewish sources emphasize that it is the nurturing and raising of the child that renders them the parents, not necessarily the accident of birth.

Simply stated, I needed to know where I came from, to learn of my origins. My existence was a "who am I?" puzzle, and I needed to fill in the pieces of the puzzle and view the finished tapestry. Who might I have been and how might my life have been different? How might other lives have been different had I lived with different parents under different circumstances? These were questions inflaming my passion and driving my desire to find the answers. I wanted to learn the reason behind my adoption and how my birth parents felt about the monumental decision they made.

I never had any doubts about my identity. I was Jewish because my adoptive parents told me I was Jewish, and I was raised Jewish from birth. From my earliest memories, Judaism played a significant religious and cultural role in my life. My closest friends were Jewish, and we all attended Hebrew school, I had my *bar mitzvah* (the Jewish religious initiation ceremony) at 13, and I have always felt at home at Beth El Synagogue in Omaha.

Both the Orthodox and Conservative movements in Judaism recognize matrilineal descent in determining whether a person is Jewish. The mother determines whether the child is Jewish. I was never told the religion of my birth father, but I assumed he was not Jewish, otherwise my parents would have been told both my biological parents were Jewish, not just that I was born of a Jewish mother.

In 1983, the Central Conference of American Rabbis (CCAR), the reform movement's body of rabbis, passed a resolution, known as the Patrilineal Descent Resolution. This recognized patrilineal and matrilineal descent in answering the question, "Who is a Jew?" The point is whichever position one accepts, bloodline is still a crucial factor in determining who is Jewish. I was aware of this as I searched for my biological origins.

My Jewish heritage is important to me. I have been privileged to serve as both synagogue and JCC executive director, prayer leader and part-time "High Holiday Cantor." I never doubted my Judaism. Issues of conversion, marriage, and the questions of one's own religious identity are just a few of the challenges many adoptees of different faiths must confront during their lives. All those factors played a role in deciding to search for my biological family. It would be intriguing to learn about my birth mother's Jewish background and understanding the reason why a young woman in 1949 was willing to give me up for adoption yet insist that I be placed in a Jewish home.

The health information provided to me by my parents meant I knew I was born healthy and with no serious health issues in my birth family. This was sufficient knowledge as I grew up, but inadequate as I entered middle age. I wanted more. This was a result of all those years of never being able to answer the most-routine medical questions. This became even more frustrating when I had children of my own. "What am I passing on to them?" Who knows?

This was a forceful reminder that I was different from others and did not have the answers most people take for granted. The information I lacked could possibly provide lifesaving information to my children or grandchildren. By the time I reached my mid-thirties, my frustration level was high.

When I opened the file in the judge's chambers and saw my adoptive parents' names on the revised birth certificate, I knew I had to see this journey through, no matter where it took me or how long it took.

My parents told me that my adoption was processed through a Jewish agency. I naturally assumed I was relinquished to that agency by my birth mother. I was eternally grateful to her for insisting I be placed in a Jewish home, but I desperately wanted to know why she made this decision that has been of defining importance in my life.

Shortly after looking at my file in the courthouse, I wrote a letter to the State of Nebraska Bureau of Vital Statistics, inquiring about how I could obtain my original birth certificate. I received a disappointing response in November 1985. All they could tell me, in formal legalese, was that my adoption was granted by the Douglas County Court, which I already knew, and that Jewish Family Services of Omaha had served as the placement agency, which I also knew. I could obtain the original birth certificate, but I would need signed consent forms from my birth parents, or in the alternative, certified copies of their death records. Of course, I could not provide this information because I did not have it. This was a dead end. The first of many.

The next logical step was to approach Jewish Family Services of Omaha (JFS). I surmised that JFS must have some record of the adoption, even if it was a closed adoption. Enter Rabbi Allan M. Gonsher (Allan).

Sue, my first wife, and I (we divorced in 1988 and I married Rita in 1990) had been friends with Rabbi Gonsher and his wife, Rini. He was the Executive Director of JFS in 1985. I called him to discuss my desire to find my birth parents and to seek his assistance. Perhaps this would not be such a difficult process. I could not have been more wrong.

*****

1   Myrna Katz Frommer, and Harvey Frommer, *Growing Up Jewish in America*, Harcourt Brace & Company, 1995. pp. 60-61

2   *Ibid.*, pp. 60-61

3   Shelley Kapnek Rosenberg, *Adoption and the Jewish Family*, Jewish Publication Society, 1998. Quoting Linda Yellin, MSW, ACSW. pp. 52-53

4   Shelley Kapnek Rosenberg, *Adoption and the Jewish Family*, Jewish Publication Society, 1998. Quoting Annette Baran, MSW. p. 69

5   Dennis Prager, *The Rational Bible: Genesis, God, Creation, and Destruction: The Alperson Edition*, Regnery Faith, An imprint of Regnery Publishing, A Division of Salem Media Group, 2019. p. 187

6   Dennis Prager, *ibid.* p. 355

7   Dennis Prager, *ibid.* p. 355

5

THE BEGINNING
OMAHA 1985

In addition to serving as Jewish Family Service Director in Omaha, Rabbi Gonsher is an Orthodox rabbi, an experienced family therapist, and a published author. He is a clinician trained in psychology, with a master's degree in social work from Columbia University.

To understand my relationship with Gonsher, a bit of background is in order. Sue (Kully) Yaffe and I were married in June 1971. By today's standards, we married early. I was 21 years old and had just finished my junior year at the University of Nebraska-Lincoln. Sue was 20 and had finished her sophomore year at UNL. Sue was born and raised in Hastings, a small town in central Nebraska. After graduation in 1972, we moved to Omaha, where I attended law school at Creighton University in Omaha, graduating in December 1974. Sue had graduated with a degree in elementary and special education, and had secured a teaching position at the Glenwood, Iowa, State Hospital School about 20 miles east of Omaha. We left Omaha in 1974, after I had received my law degree from Creighton. I accepted a commission with the U.S. Army as a captain in the Judge Advocate General's Corps (JAG) and would spend the next three years as trial counsel (prosecutor) and Chief of Military Justice at Fort Lee, Virginia.

This is where our two daughters were born: Angela in 1975 and Alicia in 1978. After my three-year tour of duty, I left the army and accepted a position as a deputy county attorney with the Douglas County Attorney's office in Omaha.

Sue was both interested in and supportive of my search for biological roots. We socialized with Rabbi Gonsher and his wife, Rini, on many occasions, enjoying Jewish holidays together and sharing common friends. After the failure to discover any useful information thus far, we both agreed that discussing the matter with the rabbi in his capacity as JFS director was the best place to start.

When we met, I explained that I wanted to locate my biological parents, if possible, and learn anything I could regarding the circumstances of my adoption. I suspected and hoped there might be useful information concerning my adoption in the JFS files. He told me he would search through old files and see what, if anything, might still exist.

He called me at my office a couple of days later. I had recently left the County Attorney's Office and was working in a small private law firm. I was thinking of changing career fields and entering Jewish communal service. I had spent 8 years as a deputy county attorney, serving most of those years on the felony trial staff. I enjoyed my years in the prosecutor's office, but did not want to end my career there. I also did not have any interest continuing in private practice.

My involvement in the Omaha Jewish community was a powerful draw. I had been an active volunteer in the Jewish community for several years, having served in many leadership positions. I envisioned myself as an executive director of a Jewish community center or perhaps a synagogue. I was determined to make that vision a reality. By the winter of 1985, I was ready to make a life-changing career move. This was my status when Gonsher called me on a brisk December morning in 1985.

"Bob, I have found your adoption file. It does have information regarding your biological roots," he said somewhat somberly.

"Are there names? Do you really have this information?" I sputtered. I was genuinely shocked. This was a bombshell.

"Yes, I do have this information. You understand I can't just release the information to you without permission from both sides. I can try to establish contact, but there has to be a mutual agreement between the biological parent and the adoptee. This is the law in the State of Nebraska," he explained.

He then asked me to send him a letter granting permission to represent me in this matter. After he received the letter, we would proceed.

On December 6, two days after my 36th birthday, I sent Rabbi Gonsher a letter granting him authorization to conduct an adoption search. The letter reads in part:

Dear Rabbi Gonsher,

This letter will serve to grant you complete authorization to conduct an investigation to determine the whereabouts of my natural parents.... I hereby give you complete authority to use the information from my adoption file in conducting the above stated investigation. Further, it is my desire that, if necessary, you continue to conduct this investigation after your employment with Jewish Family Services has been terminated. If this requires photocopying or removing any files or information from the agency you have my express permission to do so....

If you are successful in making contact with these individuals, or any member of their family, it would be my eventual desire to set up a very private meeting with them.... If contact is made with these people, you must assure them that any meeting would remain strictly confidential. It would be my suggestion that you could serve as an intermediary in any negotiations between the parties involved. Regardless of the outcome of your investigation I request permission to obtain certain information that is contained within those files. I would like to know the following:

1. *The exact date and time of my birth.*

2. *The location of my birth.*

3. *Any medical information contained within those files concerning either my medical condition or the condition of the natural parents.*

4. *The marital status of the natural parents.*

5. *The religion of the natural parents, if determinable.*

Finally, if such individuals or members of their family are located and are not willing to disclose information or to have such a meeting, it would be my desire to determine whether they would be willing to answer various questions to a third party such as yourself without having any names disclosed....

Thank you for taking this investigation into your hands. It is a matter of importance to me and I am more than confident that you will handle this delicately, professionally, and discreetly.

The rabbi was given complete authorization to begin seeking a reunion between my birth parents and me. He had located my original adoption file with lightning speed. That file, now in his hands, contained all the information, the missing pieces to the puzzle I had wanted to solve since the time of my earliest memories. Gonsher reiterated to me that under Nebraska law, he could not release any information without consent from both parties. I took the time to review the pertinent Nebraska statutes, and they were crystal clear that both the adoptee and the biological parent must agree before names could be exchanged. He nervously pointed out that this was the first time he had ever been involved in a case of this nature. As this process continued, I knew he would periodically consult with the local attorney representing JFS before taking action on his own.

Suddenly, it felt frustratingly close—this could be life changing. Various scenarios raced through my mind. Was I emotionally and psychologically prepared to meet my biological mother and father? Were they prepared to meet the son they gave away 36 years ago? And what about siblings? How might they react to me? A hundred questions flooded my brain as I imagined every conceivable scenario and situation. At this point, I wasn't even thinking about my mom and dad and how they might react to this. It was all happening so quickly. Little did I know, the one scenario I did not conjure up was that the search would drag on for 17 long and tedious years.

Two days later, Gonsher called me. It was an astonishing conversation, burned into my memory like a tattoo branded on your skin. I was alone in my office when he called.

"I spoke to her," Allan said in a matter-of-fact voice.

"Who?" I asked.

"Your mother," he replied.

"My mother?" I responded. My first reaction was that he had spoken to Dorothy, my adoptive mother. Why would he be speaking to her? She was the last person I wanted to know about this.

The rabbi was silent. Then it hit me like a sucker punch to the stomach. "Oh my God, you spoke to my *biological* mother. Are you telling me you actually spoke to her? Are you sure?" I asked. I was desperately trying to process what I had just heard.

"Yes," he replied.

"Does she want to meet? Can we arrange a meeting?"

"She really does not want to meet you." I was stunned by that answer. It never suggested itself to me that when I made myself known to my biological family members, that they would not immediately want to meet me and learn as much about me as I wanted to learn about them.

"Why does she not want to meet?" I asked, trying to mask my disappointment and hurt.

"She has put all of this out of her mind for many years and does not want it brought up now." Another sucker punch.

This was not what I had hoped to hear. My emotions had plunged from elation to dismay, in a matter of seconds.

The rabbi then told me that he had not had a lengthy conversation with her. By the end of his conversation, it seemed clear to him she did not want to be disturbed. The rabbi's voice was very quiet and subdued throughout this conversation. It was as if *he* had experienced an emotionally wrenching experience and was trying to come to grips with it.

"Can you tell me anything at all, where she lives, are there siblings, what about my father?" I was searching for any possible clues that could lead me to her identity.

"Her husband died several years ago," he explained.

Yet one more punch to the gut. My biological father was dead. I would only be dealing with my birth mother, who clearly did not want to meet me. When did he die? How did he die? I was engulfed with a whole new set of questions.

The rabbi seemed nervous with my questions, rattled off one after the other. He reminded me again that under Nebraska law, laws that I was well familiar with, he could not release identifying information to me unless *both* parties agreed, and it now appeared one of the parties had not agreed.

Near the end of this harrowing conversation, Rabbi Gonsher opened the door, ever so slightly. The woman did agree to talk to him again.

"This could have been much worse," he added. "She could have said that she never wanted to speak to me again and slammed the phone down. That didn't happen. There is a possibility she could change her mind if she is interested enough to stay in contact with me. Had she hung up, there would have been nothing I could do, the search might have ended then and there."

Perhaps the door was open, if only but a crack.

Gonsher said he would contact her again in a couple of days, giving her time to overcome the initial shock of the conversation. I again had to continue to wait and practice patience.

A couple of days later, I received a second call from the rabbi. My biological mother would not agree to meet me, but she would meet with Gonsher.

The door had opened a little wider.

She was at least interested in on-going dialogue with Gonsher. I was frustrated, but somewhat encouraged. I wanted Allan to share information with me—at least some clues if not her identity. What he did share only managed to frustrate me more.

"Can you at least tell me where she lives?" I asked.

"No, but I can tell you that she lives close by," he would answer.

"In Omaha?"

"No, outside of Omaha."

"Is it within a day's drive?"

"Yes," he replied.

"Nebraska or Iowa?" The eastern Nebraska-Iowa border is the Missouri River. One can leave Omaha and cross into Iowa in a matter of minutes.

"I don't want to say more," the rabbi said.

The information Gonsher would provide me was both intriguing and exasperating. The answer to one question would only lead to other questions. This process led to a spiral of emotions, now centering on the rabbi. He had information I desperately wanted but insisted he could not share.

As a lawyer, I knew he was trying to act within the bounds of Nebraska law, but it was nevertheless disheartening and dispiriting. Yet at the same time, he would release limited information in bits and pieces. It was like being handed small pieces from a jigsaw puzzle with the knowledge that you might never get all the pieces and never know what the finished puzzle will look like. I had a prescient feeling that this situation, this triangular relationship between Gonsher, my birth mother, and me could eventually strain our friendship.

My biological mother agreed to meet with the rabbi on December 17, 1985. He would not disclose the location of the meeting. I took his suggestion to write a letter that he could take with him to let her read. Perhaps I could ease her fears and let her know I did not have ulterior motives. Maybe this letter could push open the door a bit more. I sat down one evening, took a deep breath, and wrote a letter to my birth mother. Perhaps my words could convince her to agree to a meeting between us.

I knew several years ago that perhaps I someday might be writing such a letter as this. Yet neither the passage of time nor reflecting on the events of the past week makes it any easier as I attempt to write this letter.

I will preface this by saying that I do not, under any circumstances, wish to cause you any pain. If I am, then I am deeply sorry and I sincerely regret the situation I have set in motion. Perhaps if the initial shock of the discovery has abated, then maybe you can understand the way I feel and why I asked Rabbi Gonsher to conduct this search.

I tried to assure her that I had absolute trust in Gonsher and I thought him to be the best person in the community to speak with her. I then told her a bit about me, my marriage, children, career, and my commitment to the Jewish community.

I have known for as long as I can remember that I was adopted. My parents never kept it a secret from me. For the majority of my life, I had no more than a strong curiosity as to my background. Over the years, I would often contemplate my past, "Where did I come from? Who are my natural parents? Are they alive? Are they happy? Do they ever wonder what has become of me, as I do of them? As I entered my thirties, my desire to know my origins became more important, especially as my commitment to Judaism grew. As I enter middle age, and I see my own children growing up, I have become more acutely conscious of the unanswered questions in my life. As a person, a father, a Jew, I feel that I must know my heritage, my origins, my genetic makeup. I must learn the circumstances under which I was brought into this world. When I can answer these questions, a part of my life will be fulfilled. That is why I asked Rabbi Gonsher to help me.

I am aware that the circumstances involving placing a child up for adoption can invoke memories that one might not want to remember. Yet sometimes the distance of time makes it easier to reflect upon the past.

I tried to assure her that any discussion or meeting would remain confidential.

Your privacy will always be respected. I can assure you from the depth of my heart, that whatever comes of our communications will remain confidential forever.

I would very much like to meet you. It would mean a great deal to me and would serve to fill a void in my life.... Rabbi Gonsher has told me you don't favor a meeting right now and I can truly understand your fears and reluctance. I only hope you can eventually see clear to allow a meeting to take place. I am willing to communicate with you on whatever terms you wish.

Please be willing to communicate with me. It does not have to be forever. Perhaps in the end we may both be more understanding of our own lives. It will fill a void in my life, and enable me to continue my life and face my future, with a knowledge of my origins. This is crucial to me. I thank you from the bottom of my heart for reading this. Until that time, I wish you happiness, and I hope we can communicate soon. I hope I have not caused you pain.

December 15, 1985, 11:30 p.m.

I thought I had covered the salient points. I wanted her to hear from me directly. Gonsher would meet with her on December 17, two days later.

I anticipated the rabbi's call with bated breath. When he called late in the afternoon, I could immediately hear the disappointment in his voice and knew the meeting did not go well. She would still not agree to meet me. The letter did not seem to move her. However, Gonsher was able to elicit some information from her, which he felt comfortable passing on to me.

Thus began a slow release of information, like a steady drip from a leaky faucet. Some of this information would later provide the impetus for our search independent of Gonsher's contacts with my birth mother. This search occurred years later at a time when we began to question whether Rabbi Gonsher would ever successfully bring my biological mother and me together.

This is some of the relevant information he obtained from her that he was willing to relate to me from his meeting. According to Gonsher, she was a first-generation, American-born Jew. Her husband died of an aneurysm the Saturday after Thanksgiving 1977 at age 50.

This, of course, was alarming and a source of real anxiety. Did my birth father die at age 50? What diseases could be laying dormant in my DNA, waiting for the right moment to spring forth and wreak havoc in my life? I had no other details about his health.

My father was not Jewish. There was diabetes in the family. My birth mother was raised in an Orthodox Jewish home by her mother and grandmother. Her mother worked at the Dr. Sher home, which was known as the Jewish Old People's Home in Omaha during the 1950s. They weren't called assisted-living facilities back then.

Rabbi Gonsher learned that her family was very poor despite that they were from a prominent Omaha Jewish family. This revelation was startling. What prominent family? Did I know them?

"Is there any way you could tell me the name of the family?" I asked.

"No, I don't feel comfortable doing that," he replied.

"Do you think I would recognize the family name if I heard it?" I continued.

"Yes, I believe you would."

End of discussion. I was left flat and began to feel an overwhelming sense of frustration. He was holding the information I so wanted to learn, and only releasing bits and pieces, small clues, but never enough to really fill in the blanks. It seemed unfair that he possessed this information I had been seeking for most of my life, while at the same time I understood his concerns about privacy and Nebraska law. He was in a dilemma, but it didn't make me feel any better.

Although my birth mother was raised in an Orthodox Jewish family, by her adolescence the family was out of the mainstream Jewish community. She attended Hebrew school, but never finished high school. She described growing up as a struggle. Her family was very poor. She told Gonsher that her mother, while working at the

Dr. Sher home, would often sneak out food from the facility to feed her family. How did this make sense after being told her family was from a prominent Jewish family in the community? What happened? Always more questions.

The woman revealed to Gonsher that she married a Catholic neighbor who lived across the street from their house. She had known him since she was 17 years old. Her mother and grandmother effectively disowned her over the marriage. She worked for a Jewish-owned company in Omaha for 18-plus years. Gonsher did not disclose the name of the company, only that she worked "in a factory setting."

She revealed that her husband had served in the Korean War. She had problems with his family's antisemitism. Her husband "drank a little." She also harbored deep resentment toward the Omaha Jewish community, which she claimed offered her no support during her pregnancy. In 1949, she went to California to visit her husband, who was serving in the military and stationed there. She had one son with this man, although it was unclear if they were married at the time.

Her husband had worked for ADT Security as a security guard and then as a truck driver for an Omaha company called Bee Line. He eventually went to work for Union Pacific Railroad, which has headquarters in Omaha, in the shipping department. He worked there for the remainder of his life. He died at age 50 of a massive heart attack, a "widowmaker," the weekend after thanksgiving, 1977. Her life was devastated by this tragic loss.

My mind went numb as I listened to this narrative. If this man was my father, I just learned he dropped dead at 50. I was 36 years old at the time and could not get my fantasized image of this man out of my head. This was the medical information I most feared. I also felt intense sorrow, sympathy and commiseration for this woman I had never met. I wanted to meet her if only to offer solace and support for her husband, the birth father I would never meet.

She became pregnant with me about a year and a half after her first son was born. While in California, her husband accused her of being pregnant by another man. She denied this, but he didn't believe her.

"My husband could be a very jealous and angry man," she told Goshner. She thought it was better to relinquish the child and save her marriage. She told the rabbi that if she had not done so, I would have been hated by her husband. I asked myself what kind of a person is this? How could he despise the child, even if he was the product of an illicit union? How could he have made her give the child up? This must have been excruciatingly painful for her. Has she spent decades wondering what happened to me? Yet she has shown no desire to meet me. After hearing this narrative, I wanted to meet her more than ever.

She also told the rabbi no one else knew of her pregnancy except her immediate family including her younger sister. She told Gonsher she was told that after the birth, the baby would be sent to Minnesota for placement. One of the reasons she agreed to give up the baby was because she did not want the child to grow up like she did. She related to Gonsher that after all these years, her sister is the only person who knows of her pregnancy, birth, and the subsequent placing of the baby for adoption. Even her children have never been told anything.

This was a lot to take in. First, I had just learned I had siblings. I suspected I did, but now it was confirmed. My thirst for information and a meeting with her increased tenfold. The lack of my siblings' knowledge of my existence was deeply disturbing and even depressing. What if they would want to meet me, even if she did not? What gives her the right to make that decision for them? Is it acceptable that they might never have the opportunity to meet their brother? These questions weighed heavily on me.

I thought Gonsher might be providing me clues that, with a little research, might lead me to the identity of my birth father, which in turn would enable me to identify my surviving birth mother and her family.

The woman described herself as a stay-at-home mom. Her husband did not allow her to drive. Yes, he did not *allow* her to drive. "There was never any physical abuse, but when he became angry, he "had a temper," she told the rabbi. She described "a white streak across his face when he was irritated."

There was no practice of religion in the family home. She told Gonsher that her mother-in-law once shrieked at her, "You are a Christ killer!" Her husband, however, never exhibited any antisemitism toward her. She felt the Jewish community was of no help to her, and she lost much of her faith in Judaism because of the lack of empathy from the local Jewish community. As a result, she described tremendous anger at the Jewish community for not supporting her. She only agreed to speak to Gonsher because as a young rabbi, she felt he could understand her anger. It would seem that she received no spiritual support from either side of the family.

She told Gonsher that she and her daughter lived less than a block from each other. Her daughter is married with three children. The woman also has a son living in another state. Neither of her children know of my existence, and it is her fervent desire that it remain this way.

Gonsher had provided me with significant information. I knew my birth father's place of employment as well as the exact date of his death. Accessing Union Pacific employment records and looking for obituaries might bear fruitful results. It was extremely frustrating that Gonsher knew the identity of my birth mother, yet he could not release it to me. I sensed he was conflicted and suspected this situation was taking a toll on him while definitely affecting me. He agreed to keep in continual contact with her and thought that if she was speaking to him, the door was still open.

This was the best I could hope for as 1985 came to an end. But 1986 and the five years following were to be momentous and life changing. There would be tremendous upheaval in my personal life. The search would grind to a slow, frustrating crawl.

6

LIFE CHANGES
OMAHA | COLUMBUS | TOLEDO, OHIO
1986–1989

There are moments in our lives we remember forever, sandblasted in our minds like old photos. The moments might be associated with pivotal events in our lives: getting married, deaths of loved ones or friends, birth of children, a career promotion, or a first date. In my life, one momentous personal decision juxtaposed with a national historical event. In this case, a tragedy.

I made a decision that became a major turning point in my life. The day was Tuesday, January 28, 1986. My decision was to propel my life in a new direction. I was alone that morning in our living room. I had just returned from a job interview in Columbus, Ohio, and was about to unpack my clothes. The job interview was for a middle-level management position at the Jewish Community Center in Columbus.

I turned on CNN (a regular habit to this day) and watched the Space Shuttle Challenger with seven crew members aboard take off. This was particularly significant because it was the first time a civilian, a teacher, was on board. Seventy-three seconds into the flight, the Challenger exploded, and all seven crew members plunged to a fiery death captured live on television. Like millions of others, I was riveted to the TV, and the moment of that explosion would remain with me forever, like words chiseled into marble.

I watched this tragedy unfold only minutes after having returned from the airport following the Columbus interview. For the previous two years, I had contemplated leaving law practice altogether and entering the professional world of Jewish communal service. I had been serving as a deputy county attorney for several years since returning to Omaha after serving in the Army JAG Corps. My volunteer involvement in the Jewish community was extensive. I had served on any number of boards and committees from the synagogue to the Jewish Federation. In 1986, I won a coveted Young Leadership Award from the Omaha Jewish Federation. The selection of each year's recipient was selected by all past award recipients. This was a meaningful accolade and a great honor. At some point, I decided I did not want to go into the private practice of law, but instead wanted a second career as a Jewish communal service professional.

After two years of soul searching, I had a serious conversation with a friend who also happened to be the executive director of Omaha's Jewish Community Center (JCC). He knew I wanted to pursue a new career and had set up an interview for me with the executive director of the JCC in Columbus. I returned from that interview on the fateful morning of January 28. I had been offered a mid-level management position. I knew I would have to earn credibility and gain experience before I could secure a position as an executive director.

On this day of national tragedy, I would make a life-changing decision. I would change my career, move the family to Columbus, and give up law practice. The decision meant Sue would also have to give up her teaching job. My parents were against it. They felt I was making a mistake, wasting my hard earned law degree. Understandable. Sue was, at best, ambivalent. The Challenger disaster and the incredible commitment these brave astronauts made and died for provided me inspiration and motivation in arriving at this momentous decision.

At about the same time, a significant change in Rabbi Allan Gonsher's career occurred as well. In January 1986, he left JFS and opened a business called Kids Inc. The website describes his company as one dedicated to "helping children develop." The description continues:

Kids Inc. is pleased to offer parents, children and families therapeutic support in a friendly setting. Play therapy is the art of understanding, interpreting, engaging, and enjoying play with children. Children's play is the most natural way that children express their feelings, thoughts, and emotions."

As I recognized major changes in both of our lives, I did not want my adoption search to end. At the time, Gonsher held all my trust, and he expressed a willingness to continue his contacts with my biological mother through periodic phone calls and holiday greeting cards. He would continue to encourage her to open herself up for a face-to-face meeting.

It seemed this was the best that could be hoped for. Gonsher asked for written permission to continue in effect "working for me" or keeping me as a client, depending upon how one interprets the relationship. I sent him the following document on January 20, 1986, edited for length:

I hereby unconditionally authorize Mr. Allan Gonsher of KIDS, INC. to retain any and all records pertaining to the circumstances of my birth, and subsequent adoption in December, 1949.... It is my express desire that Mr. Gonsher continue to represent my interests regarding the above adoption and subsequent search.

I am fully aware that Mr. Gonsher is no longer employed by Jewish Family Service of Omaha, Nebraska.... This authorization expressly allows Mr. Gonsher to continue to make contact with the natural mother, or anyone else on my behalf. Authorization shall remain in effect unless revoked in writing.

(Gonsher had asked me to use Mr. instead of Rabbi).

I could not have known or anticipated the conflicts and turmoil which would arise from the many contacts he had with my birth mother over the years. Nor could I have imagined a time when I would, in writing, revoke that authorization. But it would be 16 years before that action occurred. By then, Gonsher would have moved his family from Omaha to Kansas City, Missouri, and opened a Kids Inc. office there while maintaining his Omaha office.

In April 1986, my family moved from Omaha to Columbus, where I embarked on a new career at the Columbus JCC. I had a three-year contract and was responsible for cultural programming, including managing a community theater program that was a component of the JCC.

In 1989, a job opening in nearby Toledo caught my attention. It was for assistant executive director of the Toledo JCC, a move that would represent a clear step up in the Jewish professional world. I applied for the job and was hired. I moved to Toledo and began my new position in April 1989. The plan was that Sue would remain in Columbus for the duration of the school year with the girls, and then relocate with the children to Toledo.

The next several years would see major changes in my life, my career, and my marriage.

7

Endings & Beginnings
Toledo
1989–1992

Why would a man, at age 37, give up his hard-earned career in law, relocate his family to another city, and take on a middle-management position for which he has had no formal training? Perhaps an early midlife crisis? I don't think so, or at least I didn't at the time. The reason was simple—my passionate commitment to Judaism, which was reinforced through my strong connection to Omaha's Beth El Synagogue, the conservative congregation in which I grew up.

From an early age, I was fascinated by the rituals, liturgy, and music of my faith. Judaism was a central component of my life since I was old enough to remember. Jewish books for children, Friday night candles, wine, and *challah* were all elements of my childhood, building blocks of my life that stuck in my soul as I reached adulthood. Sitting through long Passover seders at my grandparents included the rituals I may not have understood (all of it was in Hebrew), yet the solemnity and holiness of the evening resonated for me.

At the beginning, I and most of my friends growing up were regular Hebrew school comedians. Almost every Jewish child attends Hebrew school beginning in second or third grade and attends regularly until they become bar or bat mitzvah at age 13. The committed ones carry on after their bar or bat mitzvah, but most of us ended our Jewish education as soon as the bar mitzvah was over. During the years I attended, my parents received many calls regarding my less-than-stellar behavior. I could be a wise guy, and I had much help and support from many of my friends who were just like me.

I remember sitting with my friends during a Sabbath morning service at Beth El. It was also *Sukkot*, a holiday commemorating the wandering of the Jews after the exodus from Egypt and during their 40-year search for the promised land. I was 10 or 11 years old. After services, certain blessings are recited inside the *sukkah* (a booth outside the synagogue festively decorated for the holiday) followed by cookies, cakes, and other sweets, which was the primary reason most of us were there in the first place. That particular day, my buddies and I must have been noisy or just horsing around. At the end of the service, but while the congregation was still seated, the rabbi called us out from the *bimah* (pulpit). He asked us by name to remain in our seats after the service was concluded and after everyone else had left the sanctuary.

We watched the congregation file out, while remaining glued to our seats, looking straight ahead, afraid to look to the left or right. We were no longer brave and unruly children. We had been called out by name in front of the entire congregation.

When the pews were cleared, it was just us and Rabbi Myer S. Kripke, a noted Rabbinic scholar who was strict and severe. We were still sitting when everyone else had left the synagogue. We received a scolding I remember to this day. Then came the coup de grâce—we would not be allowed to enter the *sukkah*, no sweets, nothing. We could just stand at the corner and wait for our parents to pick us up. It was a walk of shame for a bunch of 10-year-old rambunctious kids.

When I got home, I confessed my crime to my parents and was promptly grounded for an indefinite period of time. I did not appreciate having my freedom restricted, but I understood, even at that age, my conduct in the synagogue had been inappropriate. I felt shame and guilt because I actually enjoyed spending time in the synagogue, often at my parents' side, following the chants and learning the rituals that made us different from our Christian neighbors. The seeds had been planted.

My attitude began to change when I started to prepare for my bar mitzvah. Mr. Alex Katz, who trained me, provided me with a new perspective. It wasn't until years later that I learned Mr. Katz was actually Rabbi Katz. He felt there should only be one "senior" rabbi in the synagogue, so he preferred to use the title mister—a truly humble man. What turned me around was the chanting. I had one of the better voices and took my preparation very seriously. I really enjoyed the musical aspect of the bar mitzvah ceremony, the ancient tropes and beautiful melodies that affected me deeply. I decided I wanted to lead the entire service, start to finish. Many of the melodies were tunes universally recognized in most of the world's synagogues. Many others were "Beth El melodies," or other melodies which had been adapted by our synagogue cantor, reflecting his training and individual style. I also wanted to impress and earn the respect of Rabbi Katz. It seemed that all of the Hebrew teachers were fair game for goofing on and playing pranks. But not Rabbi Katz. Never Rabbi Katz. It was as if the respect and awe in which I (and others) held him, granted him an invisible shield of respectability that protected him from the shenanigans we engaged in every day of Hebrew school. Although I didn't know it at the time, Rabbi Katz influenced my life in a most positive way throughout my career in Jewish communal service. But on my Bar Mitzvah day, November 22, 1962, I led the entire service, a very proud day for me.

Years later, I became a *Shaliach Tzibbur* (prayer leader). I was fortunate to serve as the High Holiday Cantor for 12 years at Temple B'nai Abraham, a conservative (later, reform) congregation just southwest of Cleveland in Elyria, Ohio. I often led services in many of the communities where we lived over the years.

What I lacked in athleticism, I hopefully made up for with the gift of a good voice, some even said a beautiful tenor voice. I was, from an early age, singing in other venues besides the synagogue. Beginning with my lessons with Rabbi Katz, I was determined to develop and use my voice in the synagogue as well as other venues. By the time of my bar mitzvah, my behavior had improved, and I was proud to lead the Shabbat morning service from beginning to end.

One of my earliest memories was of singing in the children's chorus of the Omaha Opera Company. I can remember a particular performance of "Carmen" where after the children's marching chorus in Act 1, I stood in the wings, just feet away from the beautiful soprano performing Carmen, and watched her sing the beguiling "Habanera." It felt like she was singing to me as well as the hapless tenor-singing Don José. That moment backstage cemented my lifelong love of singing and, most importantly, a lifelong connection with opera.

Through the years, I would often be asked to lead various portions of the service at Beth El as well as several other synagogues in cities where we lived. A few years ago, after having chanted the *Haftarah*, (words from the books of The Prophets, always following and thematically linked to the Torah portion just completed), I was approached by Rabbi Katz's daughter, a longtime member of Beth El.

"When I listen to you, I hear my father."

By this time, the Rabbi had been dead for many years. Her comment meant a great deal to me, more than she knew. The rabbi was one of those mentors who helped shape my love of Judaism and music.

During the late 1970s through the mid-'80s, while working in the Douglas County Attorney's Office, I was hired to be the part-time assistant ritual director at Beth El. I would often read the morning Torah portions on Monday and Thursday (these are the weekdays when the Torah is traditionally read in orthodox and conservative synagogues). This was actually a paid position with a title that gave me pride.

During the years I spent in Jewish communal work, as a JCC director and as a synagogue director, I cultivated relationships with rabbis, cantors, and other Jewish leaders from whom I hoped to gain Jewish insights and an education I could pass down to my children and from them to their children. *L'Dor Va-Dor*, an oft-used Hebrew phrase meaning "from generation to generation," is one of the basic and most important tenets of our faith. *"You shall teach them diligently to your children, and shall talk of them when you sit in your house, and when you walk by the way, and when you lie down, and when you rise up."* (Deuteronomy. 6:7). I have tried to pass our rituals and traditions to my own children and grandchildren.

I owe both my biological mother and my adoptive parents' eternal gratitude for giving me the wonderful gift of Judaism, my biological mother for insisting I be placed in a Jewish home, and my adoptive parents for raising me in a rich, loving Jewish environment. They instilled in me a love of Judaism, its teachings, rituals, liturgy, ethical teachings, and music. I have tried, not always successfully, to live out the very values I strove to pass on to my children. I wanted to believe in something larger than myself and to live a life that improves the lives of others while working in a Jewish environment. That's why I left the field of law, uprooted my family to Columbus, and entered the world of Jewish communal service.

Sue had secured a solid teaching position in Marysville, Ohio a small town outside of Columbus. She loved being an elementary school teacher but was not excited about the prospect of moving to Toledo and probably other locations to advance my career. In addition, our daughters Angela, 13, and Alicia, 11, were doing fine in the Bexley (suburb of Columbus) public schools. As expected of any young children, they were not eager to change schools, cities, or friends. The plan was for them to move to Toledo after the school year ended.

But the goalposts moved. The family would not move after the school year but instead relocate to Toledo at the beginning of the new school year. During this time, I made many weekend visits to Columbus, a five-hour round trip from Toledo. Not unexpectedly, this was a difficult period for all of us. The trips back and forth between Columbus and Toledo, uprooting the girls weekend after weekend, became long and tedious.

During these months, Sue and I began to drift apart. I was no longer the young prosecutor living with his family in Omaha; I was an embedded professional invested in Jewish communal service. I had made sweeping changes in my life—changes Sue had not signed up for. Leaving Omaha was difficult for Sue and the kids. We had been well established there, and had become part of the fabric of the Jewish community. Another move, from Columbus to Toledo, just three years after settling in Columbus, was just too much, and our marriage did not survive. The temporary separation became permanent, and by the end of the year we were divorced. Sue and I had been married for 18 years before the marriage ended in 1989.

The divorce was amicable, as divorces go. Sue stayed with her teaching job, remaining in Columbus. Leaving my two young daughters in Columbus was emotionally draining and very difficult. I drove back and forth on most weekends so I could spend as much time with the girls as possible. One of my daughters, Angela, who would later play an integral role in my search process, has remained in Columbus with her Israeli husband and two children. My other daughter Alicia, also married to an Israeli, currently lives just outside of Tel Aviv, with three children. Alicia made *Aliyah* (immigration to Israel) several years ago. Both girls regard Judaism as integral parts of their lives. Sue, now retired from her teaching position, still lives in Columbus.

I began my new position as assistant executive director of the Toledo JCC in April 1989. Within the first week on the job, I set aside time to interview all the staff I would be directly supervising. One of those staffers, Rita Scheer, was then serving as the Center's program director. Rita, from Bloomington, Illinois, had a strong family background, one sister and a brother. She was a journalism major from Drake University in Des Moines, Iowa. Rita was also recently divorced.

The first time I met Rita, she informed me that she had applied for the assistant director's position as well and was not happy I had been given the job. She also didn't care much for me either. How do I know that? She told me, right there during our first meeting. Probably not the best start to a professional relationship. However, once my divorce was finalized, Rita and I developed a personal relationship.

In November 1990, Rita and I were married at Toledo's only Orthodox synagogue, Congregation Etz Chaim. My daughters were present at the ceremony, as were Rita's two children, Marc, 13, and Abby, 9, from her previous marriage. Sue and I shared custody with Angela and Alicia living in Columbus with their mother. We became a blended family, and at the time of this writing Rita and I have been married for over 30 years. Our four kids, all married, have given us nine grandchildren.

To me this was all *bashert*, one of those hard-to-define Yiddish words, which can best be characterized as finding a soulmate, a predestined marriage partner. Rita has been my driving force, the motivation and inspiration in my life for over 30 years. On Friday evenings, as the Sabbath is ushered in, many Jews recite *Eshet Chayil*. This poem from Proverbs 31:10 describes a woman of "worth, valor, and strength." Rita is all of that, and she has enriched my life and has given me strength to become a better person. She has not only been my strength, but my best friend and, above all, my soulmate.

In 1992, I was promoted to executive director of the Toledo JCC after the departure of the current director, who was my boss. In 1996 I accepted a two year position as executive director of the Winnipeg JCC in Canada. There I oversaw the construction of a new facility in that city. Near the end of my second year, I was offered a wonderful opportunity to become executive director of one of the Chicago JCCs. Chicago had one of the largest most prestigious Jewish Community Center systems in the country. We moved to Chicago in the spring of 1998, where we lived for the next 16 years. After several years as JCC executive director, I transitioned to executive director of a large conservative synagogue in Chicago. Throughout those years, Rita was employed in Chicago as a human resources director for a packaging firm. We both retired in 2014 and moved to Omaha the same year. But I get ahead of myself.

During those years, 1989-1992, after I moved first to Columbus, then Toledo, divorced, remarried, and settled into a new career, the adoption search was put on the back burner. This was in part because of my extraordinary life changes, and in part because the search process had stalled. Throughout these years, Rabbi Gonsher and I kept in periodic contact. He was still having conversations with my birth mother, but those contacts had become sporadic. There was never any real progress made toward a reunion. He thought that keeping the door open a crack still meant there was a possibility she might be convinced to identify herself to me and allow a face-to-face meeting to take place.

I cannot pinpoint the moment or even the conversation when I first made Rita aware of my adoption and subsequent search for my biological family. But when I did, she was immediately intrigued and captivated by everything in the search process which had preceded her. My quest had gone on for nearly six years by the time we were married, and she thought we should step up the process.

By 1992, there had still been nothing new from Gonsher other than periodic phone calls and Jewish holiday cards he mailed to my birth mother. Rita and I were gradually becoming disillusioned and frustrated with his lack of progress. In spite of his periodic contacts with her, I received no new information from him during the first two years of my marriage to Rita. Rita had been encouraging me to not give up the search. It was her motivation and encouragement that kickstarted my search. I had a spouse who would be a constant partner in this process. I was invigorated as we went forward together as a team.

We discussed the real possibility that these periodic conversations between my birth mother and Gonsher could go on indefinitely, with the only result being that *he* had established a relationship with my birth mother, and I would never meet her or her children whom I assumed had no knowledge of my existence. I felt a growing frustration toward my birth mother as well. I had tried everything to convince her we were only interested in a meeting, nothing else. The letters I had written, the many conversations with Gonsher, the numerous contacts he had with her had all been to no avail.

How much longer would this go on? On one of the many occasions we discussed this situation, an equally frustrated Rita suggested the time had come to try to locate my biological family on our own. She thought we might have amassed enough information to find them. We knew there were clues, such as her husband's employment, his death the weekend after Thanksgiving 1977 while working for Union Pacific Railroad in Omaha, and probably more if we just put our heads together. We agreed we would start there and then begin to look for outside agencies, perhaps a private detective agency to help us. Although the road would be long, it was Rita's commitment and persistence that would lead the way.

8

FRUSTRATION
TOLEDO | WINNIPEG | CHICAGO
1992–2002

The first step was a letter to Rabbi Gonsher authorizing him to speak to Rita as well as to me about this matter. The following letter is undated but would have been sent in 1992.

> *Dear Allan,*
>
> *I appreciated your return phone call and your continued support in working with me over the years regarding this matter. Please consider this letter to be authorization for you to speak with my wife, Rita, regarding any matter considering this adoption that you would discuss with me. I have made Rita a partner in this endeavor in every way. She is committed, as I am, to resolving this matter.*
>
> *Our ultimate goal is to discover the name of my biological mother.*
>
> *We will in no way contact her without her consent to such contact.*
>
> *In addition, I will be contacting my attorney regarding the rights of all parties in this matter. I will advise you of my findings.*
>
> *I have enclosed a letter for you to forward to her.*
>
> *Sincerely,*
>
> *Robert Yaffe*

The tone of this letter was severe and legalistic, clearly expressing my increasing frustration with the lack of progress after seven years. The process had stagnated. Nevertheless, the attorney I consulted was insistent: under Nebraska law, *both* parties must agree before names can be exchanged. Gonsher told us that if he gave us the name he could be breaking the law and possibly putting his license and career in jeopardy. Despite this, Rita and I were convinced he was just not doing enough. We thought he must find a way to convince her that meeting with us was the right thing to do. The fact that she had voluntarily maintained communication with Gonsher for seven years was encouraging, but the very length of time these conversations had gone on was equally discouraging and demoralizing.

And perhaps, *I* had not done enough. Together, Rita and I decided another letter to her couldn't hurt and might just convince her that one private meeting would not threaten her or her relationship with her children.

Rita and I drafted two letters, one to Gonsher, the other to my birth mother. The letter to the rabbi, although addressed to him, was in reality to her, and it was our expectation both letters would be delivered to her. One of his suggestions had been that we write a letter to her that would reinforce my feelings. Writing these letters was difficult. The tone was different from the first letter I had written to her in 1985. This time, I revealed more of myself hoping that if she understood me better, she would be encouraged to open up in return. The letter to Gonsher (edited for length), was a plea to her to agree to a meeting.

> *Dear Allan,*
>
> *Please understand that I would rather be meeting face to face instead of through written correspondence. I hope you can help her to understand that I am trying to fill a void in my life. I wish that she would put the trust in me that she has put in you over the past years.*

… Please try to help her understand the importance of at least a one-time contact. You have known me for years, and know that I am honest and sincere. The fact that seven years have passed since my initial letter attests to my patience and understanding of her feelings. I hope we don't have to see more years pass before she realizes that I am not a threat to her or her family, or that I am in any way sitting in judgment…. Thanks again for all your help. You have my heartfelt appreciation.

Bob,

June 17, 1992

I revealed more of myself to her in my letter written directly to her, which was written at the same time as the letter to Gonsher.

For the past six and a half years, I hoped, prayed, and wished that you would agree to make some contact. As my life has changed radically and time becomes more precious to us all, I ask you to please reconsider some of my wishes. I by no means wish to harm you in any way. I am more than willing to let you set guidelines for some type of discussion. It would mean the world to me to hear your voice or be able to talk to you face to face.

I was trying to tell her that a compromise might be a phone conversation as opposed to the face-to-face meeting I had been pushing so hard for, which might feel too threatening to her.

The conversation or meeting could come to an immediate end if that is your desire.

I have questions that only you can answer…. Simple questions of heredity and family history are important to me, especially knowing my biological father passed away at a relatively early age….

I am counting on the fact that you feel something for the child you gave birth to. I am not asking for love, but only peace of mind. Please help me to close this chapter, even if in your mind it is already a closed book.

When I last wrote, we were living in Omaha. A lot has happened in the last seven years. I have divorced and remarried. My family has expanded to include two beautiful stepchildren. Recently, I was promoted to Executive Director of a social service agency in the East. My wife and I work together in the same agency....

I was trying to give her specific information about me in the hope that if she saw I was putting my trust in her, her comfort level would increase, and she would be likely to reciprocate.

I understand from Rabbi Gonsher that you have given this more thought due to recent illnesses. I hope this letter finds you well and that the passage of years since my initial letter has demonstrated my sincerity and honesty towards you and our meeting together. I realize that forty-two years ago you made a difficult and painful decision.

I know that it would be difficult to discuss this decision four decades later. However, I believe that through the years you have wondered about my life, my safety, my happiness. I hope you have come to terms with the reality of my birth. Please help me to do the same, as only you can.

I closed the letter by crossing another line. For the first time, I shared photographs of my family. She was under no obligation to reciprocate. I was uncomfortable with this, but I wanted that meeting perhaps more than I realized at the time.

I have enclosed pictures of my family. My girls are 16 and 14. My stepchildren are 15 and 10. The beard has been with me for 7 years.

I had now provided her with pictures of myself and my family. Although I did not reveal my name, she could, with little effort, easily learn my identity. If she received the Jewish Press, Omaha's weekly newspaper for the Jewish community, she would have seen coverage of our departure from Omaha and our move to Columbus. My hope was that opening up to her with personal information would demonstrate my trust in her, thereby encouraging her to reciprocate. I hoped this might be the step to finally convince her that a face-to-face meeting was deserved. I had no other way to convince her.

It was a few weeks later when Gonsher called me and informed me that my birth mother had finally agreed to speak with me. She had agreed to drive to Omaha with her sister Esther and allow the rabbi to set up a phone call so we would speak. Rita would be on the call as well. The meeting would take place in the rabbi's Kids Inc. office in Omaha.

At long last, I would speak to this woman who had proven so disappointedly elusive. My emotions were palpable. I was euphoric. Finally, this was really going to happen. I had waited seven long years. Was it the letter I sent? The photos? Who knew? It didn't matter. I was going to speak to my birth mother. A phone call from Omaha to Toledo was a monumental step.

Rita and I discussed many scenarios we might encounter during this call. We discussed everything, including which questions to ask, which ones not to ask, should we have notes or be spontaneous, how to greet her, and more. We discussed my parents as well. I felt the now familiar guilt, but the anticipation I felt about finally speaking to my birth mother trumped those feelings. I knew there would come a day when I would have to confront all of this with my parents, but that day was not today.

Our anticipation was over the top as we waited for the call. My heart was racing. We conjured up various scenarios. What would be my first words to her? There was no handbook on this. My heart told me that my parents would not be pleased with my actions. that somehow they would see this was an act of betrayal. Like Scarlett O'Hara, I told myself I would think about this tomorrow and pushed it from my mind.

On the morning of the call, I was as eager as a buzzing bee hovering over a sunflower. After what seemed like an inordinate time, the phone rang. It was Gonsher.

"I have some very bad news," he said.

"What?" was all I could say, although I had an immediate premonition of what was coming.

"She called and canceled the meeting," he somberly answered.

My heart sank like an anchor. "What do you mean she canceled the meeting? Why?" I demanded to know. I was immediately angry, an emotion I never felt over the past seven years of this search. How could she do this to me? Hadn't I proved my sincerity over the past seven years?

She never gave Gonsher an answer—perhaps cold feet, perhaps something else. According to the rabbi, they had driven within a short distance of Omaha and she just changed her mind. He did not know why, and she offered no explanation.

This was yet another unexpected and dreadful blow. After seven years, we had come so close, only to be sent back to square one. The frustration rose in me like a high fever. I was dismayed. This was the closest we had come to a conversation, and it was canceled at the last second. What did she have to fear? What could be the risk of one telephone conversation? I had no answers. I had to accept the possibility that I was never going to meet my birth mother or my siblings. I was angry, disappointed, frustrated, and defeated.

Gonsher promised he would continue to pursue his relationship with her. He thought if she continued to be willing to communicate with him, the door was still open. I could not understand why she would continue her relationship with the rabbi if she had no interest in ever speaking to or laying eyes on me. I could make no sense of any of it.

Everything ground to a halt. Gonsher continued to communicate with her periodically, but there was no further movement toward a meeting. When all was said and done, I still only possessed the knowledge I had back in 1985.

Rita never wavered in her commitment and drive to bring together my biological family and me. Nevertheless, my eagerness to see this through began to wane. Although I continued to keep in contact with Gonsher, our communication became less frequent and life intervened. Weeks turned to months, and months turned to years.

Nevertheless, in August 1995, through Rita's persistence, I made a further attempt to effectuate a meeting with my birth mother. Gonsher suggested I write yet another letter to her that he would deliver. Reading this letter today, I sense the frustration and anger I was experiencing at the time. One can also find an element of pleading. A decade had passed since the first contact with her had been made. The frustration and the setbacks were truly discouraging and dispiriting.

> *August 30, 1995*
>
> *Once again I am writing in hopes of making you understand my needs. I do not want to hurt you or your children. I am an honest and hard-working individual simply trying to answer questions that will be with me forever. I have concerns that go beyond you. My understanding of your husband's death is vague. The fact that he died at age 50 is very upsetting to me. I would like to know more about him.*
>
> *Once in my life, I would like to meet the person who brought me into this world. I have no desire to make this public in any way. I am a private person with no desire to draw any attention to this matter. It would not benefit anyone. I have seen far too many of those crazy TV shows that sensationalize adoption reunions. This is not my way.*
>
> *We have abided by your wishes and desires. Given the information I have obtained nine years ago* (actually 10 years ago), *I could have done more to find you. I believe that would be possible. However, it is not the way I want*

this contact to be made. I cannot make you believe in me. Please think about the way in which I have handled myself. I am not your enemy or someone for you to fear. Please show me the respect I believe I have earned from you.

I would like you to call me. Allan Gonsher has my number. He will give it to you if you like.

As you are aware, I would very much like for this contact to happen. In spite of whatever reason or circumstance led to my adoption, you are the individual who gave me life. I have had a good life. I have children, a professional career, and I am happily married. The void I feel can only be completed by a contact with you.

I hope that after nearly ten years since my first correspondence with you, that you will allow this contact to take place.

The letter was sent to Gonsher, who assumedly sent it to my birth mother. The letter was forceful, determined, and tough. I am uncomfortable reading it today and can only wonder what she might have thought when she read it.

Why, after ten years, did I not just leave it alone? After ten years, maybe it was time to move on. There was one factor, however, that would not allow me to end this search. Rabbi Gonsher was still maintaining a relationship with her. He was speaking to her. He was even sending her Jewish holiday cards. This meant to me that the door was still open. I had written several letters to her through the rabbi. I had to assume she had at least read them. I believed she had pictures of my family. I thought this must have affected her. She had to know I was only asking for one very private face-to-face meeting. If she was communicating with Gonsher, and I was communicating with her (albeit only one way) through my letters, there had to be interest and a reunion might still take place.

When I began my search that day in the Douglas County Courthouse, I became determined to see the search through, as far as I possibly could. I felt then as I did now. I had the moral justification to learn the identity of my birth parents and to seek out a private encounter with them. My stipulation was I should never create a situation in which I am harassing them or creating, at least intentionally, anger or indignation. At this point, I had no reason to suspect that I had invaded her privacy or was harassing her in any way. To date, it was only Gonsher who had spoken to her. To the best of my knowledge, she was keeping the door open, at least with the rabbi. Had I reason to believe she unequivocally did not want to meet me I would have cut off the search on the spot. But her willingness to communicate with Gonsher convinced me she was hesitant to cutting off all contact and that I should continue.

The last letter, like the others, did not convince her to meet with me. I was continuing to lose faith in Gonsher's ability to make this happen. I do not know what else he could have done, but what he had been doing over the last ten years was not working. Maintaining a relationship with her for a decade, his face-to-face meetings, numerous calls and letters, were not enough. It was about this time that Rita and I decided it was time to look for new alternatives.

Just before we moved to Winnipeg, Manitoba in 1996, we contacted JASA Investigations, a private investigative service in Des Moines, Iowa. We hired the firm with the task of obtaining any information they could find that might help us in our quest. In a letter to the agency in June 1996, we summarized some of the clues we had learned from my discussions with Gonsher.

1. A family member, either the mother or grandmother, had worked at the Dr. Sher Home in Omaha.

2. The family had a land interest in property where the former Richard Young Hospital in Omaha had stood. It was property the family could not afford to keep.

3. My birth mother went to Omaha Technical High School. She did not graduate because she married at age 17. (This later turned out to be incorrect).

4. My biological father fought in the Korean War, after which he returned to Omaha and worked as a truck driver and security guard. His last known job was in shipping at Union Pacific Railroad. Not sure whether he was working at the time of his

death, which was the Saturday after Thanksgiving in 1977. He died of a massive coronary.

5.   The family, mother and daughter, lived in a small Iowa community, about a one-hour drive from Omaha. She has a son currently living in Texas.

6.   My biological mother worked in a Jewish-owned "factory setting" for 18 to 20 years. We were told we would recognize the company name, but Gonsher would not name the company.

7.   Mother, Jewish; father, Catholic.

We paid JASA a retainer and hoped they could find some answers. We received our disappointing reply in October. We were living in Winnipeg by then. Apparently the investigation had been delayed by the closing of one of their offices and an investigator who had failed to identify our case as uncompleted. The results, in short:

Property records were reviewed but their chaotic state prevented the obtaining of any useful information. There was no provision in Nebraska law allowing for the perusing of birth records. High School records prior to 1949 in Omaha were not complete. Tech High School no longer exists. Omaha World-Herald and Council Bluffs, Iowa, newspapers were checked for a male in his 50s, who died the weekend of Thanksgiving 1977. Daily obituaries were checked. No individuals matching the information provided were found.

That was it. We never contacted JASA Investigations again. Another dead end.

We had moved to Chicago in April 1998 with the search once again on hiatus. I was both aggravated and discouraged with the whole situation. Conversations with Rabbi Gonsher were becoming much less frequent. Throughout the years he had provided clues, little bits and pieces here and there, released to us like water seeping through cracks in a dam. With our move to Chicago, my concentration was focused on my new position. Rita had taken a job with a company called The Packaging House (today called TPH Global Solutions). Rita was the human resources director and the assistant to the CEO. She was as sharply focused on her new position as I was with mine.

She would remain with the company for the next 14 years. We were both focused on our careers and life in the Windy City. I was the new executive director of the Mayer Kaplan JCC, one of several JCC's in the city.

Chicago, only an eight-hour drive from Omaha, was a great location for us. It allowed us to make many trips back and forth to Omaha, to visit my parents, and attend University of Nebraska football games and College World Series baseball games in June. My biological family lived somewhere in Iowa. I was determined to find them. Since JASA did not work out, we decided to examine the clues and see if we could find the answer.

After we moved to Chicago, my sister Jane and her husband Dorand had expressed interest in helping us with the search. Jane is eight years younger than me. We were not particularly close growing up, but we have always maintained a bond that has continued throughout adulthood. Dorand was a truly good-hearted and kind person, a *mensch*. An avid bike rider, he would participate each year in the famous Iowa RAGBRAI, a bike ride across Iowa. Dorand sadly passed away in 2002, after suffering a massive coronary. He was only 50, a tragic loss for Jane, her two children, and everyone who knew him.

During our visits to Omaha, we would occasionally meet up with Jane and Dorand. That's when they took an interest in my adoption search. I was very concerned about how my parents would react if they found out, a concern that later turned out to be only too real. I was glad we shared the story with Jane and Dorand. Dorand had become very interested in the search and was more than willing to jump in and help in any way he could.

We shared with them the information we had received over the years from Gonsher. We revisited the notes I took in 1985, notes from the first time Gonsher shared information with me that he had obtained from my biological mother. Those notes included the important information that my biological father died in 1977 the Saturday after Thanksgiving, that he had worked in the Union Pacific shipping department until the time of his death, and the other clues we had shared with JASA. Armed with this information, it seemed the local obituaries would be a good place to start, even though JASA had failed to find any such relevant information.

Rita and Dorand spent hours in the Omaha Public Library, pouring over obituaries, both from Omaha and Council Bluffs. Nothing. Not a single death notice listed anyone who had or was working at Union Pacific at the time. Another dead end.

My earliest notes from Gonsher indicated the family (the information somewhat vague) had at one time owned some or all the land currently occupied by Richard Young Hospital in Omaha. Richard Young was a psychiatric hospital once located on South 26th Street and served the Omaha area for 72 years before closing its doors in 1987. By the mid-'90s, the hospital had been torn down, and the land stood vacant. With this information, as tenuous as it was, we spent hours at the Omaha Public Library searching through dozens of pages of public records, looking at land plots comprising where the hospital stood, looking for any name that might connect somehow. Another dead end.

Three years went by quickly. During this time, I can remember only sporadic conversations with Gonsher. There just seemed to be nothing left for us to do. He was still talking to my biological mother on occasion. Apparently, he was also sending her *Rosh Hashanah* (Jewish New Year) cards. The clues he provided had evaporated like an oasis in the desert. As the 20th century became the 21st, it seemed inevitable that I would never know the identity or have an opportunity to meet my biological family.

Circa 2000, I told my story to one of my JCC colleagues. She mentioned it to an Illinois state senator who was involved with adoption legislation. The issue of closed versus open adoptions was a hot topic at the time, and the senator wanted to propose legislation that would make it easier for adoptees to locate their biological parents. I was invited to address a legislative committee tasked with looking into the issue of open adoptions. I declined out of respect and concern that my parents might hear of my search.

Even after 15 years, I was constantly concerned my parents might hear that I had been searching for my biological family and be deeply hurt by my actions. Protecting their feelings had been a high priority for me and only a few close friends and my sister and her husband knew about the search. Nevertheless, this was a missed opportunity, one that might have influenced lawmakers to ease the closed adoption restrictions. I regret not participating in those hearings.

These years were a busy time for our family. Our focus was on our careers and family. I had also become a lecturer on matters of opera and classical music and had begun to build a following in the Chicago area. I was teaching classes in opera and opera history at a local community college.

I also began to get requests to lecture to various chapters of the Lyric Opera of Chicago. Each summer, I spent a week in the Wisconsin Dells teaching courses on opera, opera history, and classical music.

Rita and I would often drive to Nebraska on fall weekends for University of Nebraska football games. Yes, we did drive eight hours for a home football game. This might seem inexplicable to many, the notion that one would drive eight hours each way to attend a weekend football game, but trust me, for a devoted Cornhusker fan, it's a no-brainer.

In 2000, my daughter Angela had graduated from The Ohio State University, and was working as a parole officer for the State of Ohio. Alicia had graduated from the University of Kansas and was contemplating a move to Israel, where she would eventually make *aliyah* (become a citizen), marry and have three kids. My stepson, Marc, 23, secured an internship with the Al Gore presidential campaign in 2000 and was assigned to the Secret Service. He had a front-row seat to that historic election. My stepdaughter, Abby, was attending Indiana University to pursue a teaching degree.

All of this served as a distraction from the search. Life was good in spite of the disappointing results. My search had been going on for 15 years and had begun to fade into the background of our lives. But it did not fade away entirely. Rita, as always, the stalwart champion of the cause, never let go. Sometime around the end of 2001 or the beginning of 2002, she discovered an organization in

Chicago called "Truth Seekers in Adoption." This was encouraging. The mission on their website stated:

We are a group that invites everyone involved in the adoption triad (adoptees, birth parents, adoptive parents) to come together to support each other in the sometimes very emotional and confusing aspects of adoption reunions.

I was not really looking for a support group. We had already been disappointed in the results from JASA. But I was intrigued by this organization. I was hoping to establish contacts, perhaps to learn how others found their families, maybe someone had used a method we had not considered. It couldn't hurt to seek them out. The representative we spoke to indicated that they might be able to offer assistance in conducting an adoption search, but first I was required to attend their seminar on adoption. I signed up for the $30 seminar.[1]

The seminar's subject matter involved adopted children and reunions with biological relatives. The meeting took place on a bitterly cold, wintry Chicago day in February 2002. Eight to ten people attended the three-hour seminar at Lutheran General Hospital in Chicago. The facilitator spoke of many of the difficult and conflicting emotional issues faced by adoptees, birth parents, and adoptive parents. Most of these issues I was well aware of, many of them discussed in the pages of this book. My level of frustration was high. I had spent $30 only to hear nearly everything I already knew.

Some of the attendees had met their biological families already. There was no discussion or words of wisdom on how to deal with the frustration of having undergone a 17-year search thus far proven fruitless, while a close friend and former head of a social service agency has been maintaining communication with my birth mother the entire time.

At the end of the session, I was introduced to a gentleman whose name I no longer remember. He was either an active or a retired detective with the Chicago Police Department. I filled him in on all the information I had received from Gonsher, the same information I had been repeating over and over for years. He said he would check things out and call us in a couple of days to let us know whether or not he could help me.

When he called, the news was discouraging. He told us he was unable to help us because the adoption took place out of state, and he had no way to examine Nebraska adoption files, which were closed as tight as a drum. Disappointment again. The mere fact the adoption took place out of the State of Illinois should not have dealt a death blow to any adoption search. Furthermore, he knew going in that my adoption took place in Nebraska. He could have saved me the disappointment I now felt. Add to this the fact I had to sit through a seminar that was of no value to me, exacerbated my aggravation. Another dead end. But sometimes great events hinge on the thinnest of threads.

At the end of our conversation, the man offered a suggestion. He told us he was aware of a North Carolina-based private detective firm that specializes in adoption searches. This firm had a reputation of success in matching adoptees to birth families. The company's name was Kinsolving, a rather clever name given their business. He apologized for not being able to give us any further help. He needn't have apologized. A new door was about to open. Enter Kinsolving.

*****

1   While researching this book, we unsuccessfully attempted to reach out to Truth Seekers in Adoption. A church where the organization conducted their seminars indicated they had not been meeting there for several years. It is possible they are no longer in business.

9

KINSOLVING INVESTIGATIONS
MATTHEWS, NORTH CAROLINA | CHICAGO
MARCH 2002

A series of serendipitous encounters led the way to Kinsolving. We did not know it, but a pivotal moment had arrived—the most momentous in 17 long years.

Rita and I first looked at the Kinsolving website[1]:

If you are searching and have not been successful, then Kinsolving Investigations may be your key to unlocking that door.

That message hit home.

Kinsolving Investigations charges NO MONEY UPFRONT. Kinsolving also does not require that you know a name. If you feel you have reached a dead end in your search or are just beginning, Kinsolving Investigations will review your case for no fee!

We certainly were not just beginning and were hoping we had not reached a dead end, at least not yet. It got even better as we explored the website:

Kinsolving Investigations is owned and operated by Christine Lee. First and foremost, Chris is a reunited birth mother having found her daughter 17 years ago. Secondly, she is a private investigator. Every person involved in Kinsolving is a member of the adoption triad and therefore has very strong ties to the adoption community.

This was followed by several pages of questions and answers of which two were of particular importance to us. First, the cost:

Each case is looked at individually. Once the cost is determined, you will be sent our quote along with a contract.

Second, they answered the question about how long the search would take. Of course, this was the hardest question to answer. They would strive to finish each case as quickly as possible. Some cases could take from six months up to a year before they could even obtain a name. An honest answer. I wondered if any of their searches have dragged on for 17 years. Doubtful.

We called Kinsolving on March 7 and spoke to Chris Lee. We explained our situation and provided some of the facts of our case, including the dates and my birthplace, the birth father's connection to Union Pacific when he died, the fact that the biological family lives within an hour drive of Omaha, etc.

This time the response was extraordinary. In the most nondescript manner the voice on the line replied, "This doesn't sound too complicated of a case. We should be able to handle it."

"Wait a minute," I replied. "We've been at this for 17 years, asked questions, checked library records and more. We have had no luck whatsoever." We were assigned to a Kinsolving investigator, Scott. We told Scott about Rabbi Gonsher, his now long-term relationship with my birth mother, and his inability to share information with us. We provided Kinsolving all of the clues the rabbi had shared with us so many years ago. He listened carefully, and his response was simple yet astonishing.

"We have handled tougher cases than this," he answered matter-of-factly. "I believe we can handle it." The topic of discussion could just as well have been about determining a location for lunch.

It sounded too good to be true, but we had nothing to lose. We proceeded with caution. They sent us a client information sheet and a payment agreement that we signed and returned on March 11, 2002.

I was nervous, but we were not yet risking anything. The payment was $3,500, an impressive amount in 2002 (and still is). The money was due and payable within three days of notification that the search had been completed. The key provision:

The client understands and agrees that no information will be received until the entire amount agreed upon in this contract is paid in full. When full payment is received for the completed search the investigator will provide the client with the current name and address of the person being sought. The telephone number will be provided if available.

We would pay nothing if the investigation was fruitless, as we assumed it would be. I could already hear the expected response, "Nebraska adoption records are sealed, and we can't access them." In the unlikely event the search wasn't fruitless, well, we would cross that bridge when we came to it. We filled out the client information form, signed the payment agreement and that was that.

Here is a summary of the information we provided Kinsolving:

Birthmother, born 1928, married, Jewish, never graduated from High School.

Married at 17. One boy and one girl from this marriage. Her husband, Catholic, was in the military (1949), and also served in the Korean War. She became pregnant. Her husband (presumptively my birth father) is known to have worked for ADT as a security guard, a local trucking company, and for Union Pacific, where he was working at the time of his death. He died the weekend after thanksgiving, 1977, the result of a massive heart attack."

Kinsolving emailed me on March 14:

Robert,
Your case has been completed. Per your contract you need to send a cashier's check for $3,500.00 made payable to Chris Lee-Kinsolving Investigations.

Following mailing instructions, there was a final sentence.

Upon receipt of your payment your information will be mailed to you the day it is received."

Could this be true? My skepticism immediately kicked in, full gear. This has to be a scam! Sending $3,500 to a company I had only read about on a website was an action I would never have advised a client to do. Rita and I have been searching for years, encountering dead end after dead end.

How could this company, a company I knew truly little about, have completed this search so quickly? Was I so desperate to resolve this search that I would take such a reckless and ill-advised action? The Kinsolving agent had seemed so nonchalant about the whole thing. My head was telling me that I was about to part with $3,500 with nothing to show for it. Yet Chris Lee and Scott had seemed so convincing regarding the information they received and were ready to share. My brain told me I was getting scammed. My heart told me I was going to send the money. The decision was made. We would roll the dice, risk the money.

On March 14, a certified check for $3,500 was sent to Kinsolving Investigations.

Rita and I thought it would be best to receive the information from Kinsolving together since we had spent so many years conducting the search together. We were a two-person search team after all. The plan was that Rita and I, both in our respective offices would open the email simultaneously so we would be together at least figuratively when the email arrived. Nothing doing. It appeared that the investigator assigned to our case, "Scott the Investigator," had court appearances on the 15th and could not guarantee a time when he would be available. In addition, he informed us that the standard operating procedure for Kinsolving was for the recipient to receive the information first, digest it, and then ask questions of the Kinsolving investigator. OK, we could live with that. The check was sent to Kinsolving by FedEx.

And then, the check went missing. We waited.

We received a call late in the day. Kinsolving had not received our check. This bump in the road took several hours to resolve while we tracked it down. Somewhere along the way, it was misdirected by FedEx. Eventually, the issue was resolved, and the FedEx check was received by Kinsolving. That night, lying in bed, sleep eluded me. I wondered if we had been scammed or if this would be just another dead end, but this time a dead end that cost us $3,500. After a long and restless night, we both awoke, sleep deprived.

It was a mild, late winter morning in Chicago on Friday, March 15. It reached 59 degrees, a preview of the coming spring. Rita and I went to our respective offices to await the results, if there were to be any. We decided that we would suffer through the morning, continuing to check our emails. If information came through to one of us, we would call the other so we would at least open the email together, each of us in our respective offices.

By mid-morning, nothing. A feeling of skepticism began creeping through my brain like a slowly intensive pounding headache. The only way to curb this inner turmoil was to call Kinsolving and get the matter resolved. Rita and I made the conference call together. As I dialed, I wondered how I would react if the number had been disconnected. It wasn't. The friendly receptionist connected us to "Scott the Investigator," the sobriquet we had given him.

"I was just wondering (greatly understated) when we can expect the information regarding my search," I asked. "I believe you have our check for $3,500?"

"Hold on, please." Minutes went by as Rita and I waited in our respective offices, holding our respective breaths.

After what seemed like 45 minutes but was in reality about two minutes, Scott the Investigator was back on the line.

"Yes, we have received your check," he said, in a very businesslike tone.

"And our information?" I asked. "Were you able to find results?"

"Yes, it's all right there, in the email. I sent it to both of your email addresses. Read it and then we can talk about it," he added.

We could only describe our emotions at that moment as incredulous.

We checked our email inboxes at the same time. There it was. The message from Kinsolving. Could the answers be just a mouse click away?

It was surreal to sit in my office on a normal workday, people routinely going about their business while I was about to receive the information I had been searching for nearly half of my life.

"Well, Rita," I said, "Let's see what they have to say." Even now, I was skeptical that this whole search could have been successfully completed in just a few days.

My finger lingered over the enter button.

"Let's do it together," I said, my voice shaking slightly.

"One … two … three."

And there it was. Answers. Kinsolving and "Scott the Investigator" had come through. This was not a scam. What I could now see I could never unsee. Somehow I knew the information I was looking at was correct. After what had seemed like a lifetime, Kinsolving had solved the riddle in a matter of a couple of days. My heart was pounding.

After a review of all the information Rita and I had provided Kinsolving, my actual birth name appeared on page two.

Baby Boy Karnes aka. Baby Boy Stahl.

Mother - Pauline Stahl Karnes, Caucasian, 21 years old, born Omaha, Nebraska. NOTE: Used the fictitious middle or maiden name of Stahl."

Already a mystery; she used an alias?

The next paragraph gave a brief family narrative:

Pauline Newman was born 08/12/1928 in Omaha, Nebraska. The eldest daughter of a Jewish grocer. Her father sold his business to what later became known as "Hinky Dinky."

Hinky Dinky was a large supermarket chain in Omaha. The name was a spinoff from the national chain, Piggly Wiggly, and the song "Hinky Dinky Parlez-Vous." The name would be familiar to anyone living in the Omaha area when the stores were still in business. The store chain was sold in 1972. At one point, there were approximately 50 Hinky Dinky stores operating.

She was married in 1949 to Lawrence Kenneth Karnes, dob. 1928.

We learned many years later that they were not actually married until August 1949, just a few months before my birth.[2]

His family was Irish Catholic. They had three children; a. Ricky Arthur (died 2-4 years old); b. Lawrence Kenneth, jr. dob 1950; c. Linda, dob 1953. The family resided in Omaha, Neb. until they relocated to Council Bluffs, Iowa. It is known that Lawrence Kenneth Karnes, Sr. served in the Marine Corp. and was stationed in Panama. His date of death was November 26, 1978. The family had relocated from Omaha to Council Bluffs in 1960.

The immediate takeaway was that Pauline's maiden name was Newman. The information from Kinsolving connected her to the "Hinky Dinky" Newmans of Omaha, one of Omaha's more prominent families, both then and now. The other takeaway was that Kenneth Karnes, presumably my birth father, had **not** died the weekend after Thanksgiving in 1977. All this time, Rita and I thought he had died the weekend after Thanksgiving in 1977. In fact, he died the weekend after Thanksgiving in 1978. We had been a year off, and had used that year in our extensive search through obituaries, and other public records. It never occurred to us to search a year ahead or a year behind. That entire process had been a waste of time. Either I wrote down the wrong year when I spoke to Rabbi Gonsher back in 1985, or he mistakenly gave me the incorrect year. The takeaway was I now knew my original last name, "Karnes." Most important of all, monumental in fact was the entry on page three of the report.

BIRTHMOTHER

Pauline (Newman) Karnes

DOB 8/12/28 Omaha, Nebraska

CURRENT RESIDENCE:

------------ Street, Atlantic, Iowa 50022 PHONE # 712-XXXXXX (actual address and phone number included in the email).

We now knew where the family lived: Atlantic, Iowa. Gonsher had told us it was a city within a "reasonable" driving distance from Omaha. Atlantic is about 75 miles east of Omaha off Interstate 80.

As mentioned, the Kinsolving report stated that Kenneth Karnes had passed away on Sunday, November 26, 1978. He was a long-time resident of Council Bluffs, Iowa. The email also mentioned Pauline's sister, Esther, living in Council Bluffs.

We spoke with Chris Lee that evening from our home. We thanked her profusely for the information provided. The only question remaining was about Pauline's daughter—my sister! The information indicated she lived near her mother, perhaps in Atlantic. The information was somewhat vague. It listed a last-known address as Council Bluffs. The address and phone number of her son (my brother!) were also included. He was living in Carrollton, Texas. His phone number was listed in the report. Ms. Lee indicated she would see what they could find regarding Pauline's daughter, Linda.

Once again, Kinsolving came through. The next morning, we received an official addendum to the report. My sister's name was Linda Sage; her spouse, William Sage. Their address was in Atlantic, and phone number was included.

The closing paragraph on the addendum stated:

We wish you both the best in your reunion. Hopefully Bob's birth mother will be receptive (KEEP THINKING POSITIVE ATTITUDE). If not, then he can try to contact his siblings. Kinsolving Investigations

At long last, we possessed the information and the ball was in our court. The next moves would be ours.

1   If you are interested in pursuing the Kinsolving website, you will be in for a disappointment. While conducting research for this book, we learned from the Private Protective Services Board of North Carolina, the agency that licenses private detective agencies in that state, that Kinsolving Investigations went out of business in 2013. They could offer no explanation, but one can speculate that the popularity over the past few years of companies such as *Ancestry.com* and *23andMe* have made the search process much easier and eliminated much of the need for private detective agencies.

2   Although the actual marriage certificate of Pauline Newman and Ken Karnes has not been located, an Omaha World-Herald wedding announcement (which we later obtained) indicates the wedding took place in 1949, which would make Pauline 21 years old at the time of the wedding. The earlier report from JFS indicated she had married at 17. The discrepancy is unexplainable.

10

PLAYING DETECTIVE
ATLANTIC, IOWA
2002

In hindsight, the decision to establish contact with the Karnes and Sage families was inevitable. After 17 long years of searching, the names, addresses, and phone numbers of the people we had sought out were staring back at us. Yet Rita and I spent the next two weeks deciding what to do and how to do it, the decision to go forward and contact these people or remain silent.

I spent several sleepless nights tormented over this excruciatingly difficult dilemma. Did we have the right to make phone calls, calls which would most assuredly alter the existence of the people whose lives we would touch? Would we be accepted or rejected out of hand? Would we be told to leave them alone? Would we be revealing a secret that might cause insufferable and irreparable pain to Pauline, a secret she had buried for over half a century?

Our initial decision was to not call Rabbi Gonsher. We weren't sure whether if after we told him, he would feel he needed to call Pauline. We also didn't know for sure if Linda or Ken had any inkling of my birth and subsequent adoption. We decided from this point on we would leave Gonsher out of the conversation. We also assumed he already had most of the same information that we now possessed. The only information he was lacking was that we now possessed the names as well. I would decide on whether or not to involve Gonsher at a later time.

We called a support group counselor from Truth Seekers in Adoption to seek out his guidance. After congratulating us on our successful search results, he offered advice:

1. Let a third party make the initial contact. Avoid the "Hi, I'm the son you gave away 52 years ago." I knew this could be extremely

damaging and could also close off communications. A third party might be less threatening to both parties.

2. Ease into things slowly. Ask some identifying questions first. Make sure it is a good time to talk. It's possible other family members might be present during the call. No matter what, I did not want Pauline to be angry or annoyed. That could end things in a hurry.

It seemed like sound advice. Of course, Gonsher would have been the ideal intermediary, but Rita and I remained strong in our decision to leave him out of the equation. Pauline might have suspected that he gave us their personal information without her permission, and the conversation could be shut down before I even had the opportunity to speak to her.

I decided Rita would be the choice to make the initial contact. She would be effective yet empathetic, and she had been involved in this process from nearly the beginning. I also thought Rita deserved to be the first person to speak with any of them. It was through her perseverance and determination that we had finally located my biological family. Besides, it could have been intimidating and frightening for Pauline to receive the call directly from me.

We also entertained another idea. We had previously planned a trip to Omaha on March 27 for Passover, a major Jewish festival commemorating the liberation of the Israelites from Egyptian slavery. We would be with my parents for the Passover Seder, the ritual feast that marks the beginning of the holiday. What if we left Chicago early and drove the 15 miles or so off Interstate 80 to visit Atlantic? We had the addresses, we could check out the houses, maybe catch someone coming or going. What was the downside? We were really just driving through town. It would give us the chance to see where they lived and who knows what else.

We were about to find out what else. Rita and I concluded we would not initiate direct contact before we made this excursion to Atlantic to check things out and get the lay of the land.

On March 27, we left Chicago for Omaha to celebrate Passover with my parents. Because of the lateness of our departure, we would have to delay our trip to Atlantic until the return trip to Chicago.

After the holiday we left for Chicago, via Atlantic, on Sunday, March 31. I felt anxious and on edge as we left Omaha early that morning. We told my parents we were driving back to Chicago. Of course, they had no inkling about our planned detour.

I tried to bury at least some of the guilt I felt as we set out. This would not be the last time I left Omaha with a guilty conscience after visiting my parents. I knew they would never approve of what we were doing, and the feelings of guilt would only intensify as we moved forward. But moving forward was the only option. I was close to learning the secret of my very existence, my birthright. I was convinced I had an absolute right to know who my birth parents were. Searching for and making contact with them would never diminish my love for my parents. Yet I also knew I would eventually have to tell them what I had done. Until that morning, the search, all 17 years of it, had been an abstract. But today, the moment we veered off into Atlantic, it became real—a real place with real people who had answers to my adoption questions. For the first time, we would be on their turf. I was drawn to Atlantic like a bee to honey.

This anticipatory feeling did not negate the great guilt that flooded my soul that weekend, all for lying to my parents. It wasn't a direct lie; on Sunday, we would in fact be driving back to Chicago. But we would leave earlier than we normally would to afford us plenty of time to check out Atlantic. It was a lie by omission, but a lie just the same. These situations would occur many times in the months to come, and the guilty feelings never dissipated.

Atlantic, Iowa is located just off Interstate 80 at the junction of Highway 71 and Highway 6, situated between Des Moines and Omaha. The population is about 7,500. No one seems to know how the town got its name, but there is a charming local legend of Atlantic's founding fathers estimating that the town was about halfway between the Pacific and the Atlantic oceans. The men were considering the advancing railroad and thought that once the rail line was complete the town would be a connecting link between the two oceans and become a major trade center. According to a 1999 publication by the Atlantic Chamber of Commerce:

Which ocean would provide the proper name? Atlantic? Pacific? It is said that a quarter provided the answer. "Heads, Atlantic, tails, Pacific," was the shout as the piece of silver cut through the humid summer air and made its way toward the ceiling of the small office. The men's eyes focused on the coin as it began its descent and then gathered around the place where it fell with a clatter, against the board flooring .... With a shout of, "Heads it is!" the search for a town name ended. Atlantic was born, and an ocean of opportunity opened up for those who came to call Atlantic "home." [1]

I've often asked myself why we felt the need to visit Atlantic to scope things out before we made the final decision about whether to make contact. Of course, the obvious answer was that it was convenient, literally on the way to and from Omaha. The ability to check out the surroundings, to see their homes, to view their community, all without their knowing of our existence, gave us an advantage in what could be a difficult encounter.

By the time we would make contact, we would know a great deal about them, even though they would know nothing of us. I was not doing this to gain an upper hand. I wanted to have a clear picture of the town they lived in, the streets where they lived, the homes they occupied.

Looking back, the side trip to Atlantic seems somewhat surreptitious. I could not resist turning off the highway and driving the 15 miles to view the town whose existence I had conjured in my imagination all these years. All of those emotions and feelings of guilt swirled around in my brain and accounted for the skittishness I felt as we approached Atlantic.

We arrived in town around noon. I was as nervous as a cat up a tree. It was about 50 degrees. Atlantic is a typical small-town USA, situated in Cass County, Iowa. When entering town, we found ourselves in the heart of downtown, which consists of several streets, somewhat lackluster in appearance. Well kept, but drab-looking businesses and offices line the streets. There didn't seem to be more than two or three traffic signals, and traffic was practically nonexistent on a Sunday morning. Hair salons, a Fairway and a Hy-Vee grocery store were visible as we drove through town. A gas station had been converted into a restaurant with the memorable name "Oinkers Lounge & Grill." Atlantic is a farming community with some industrial companies having made their home there, including the Coca-Cola Bottling Company and Skyjack, a company that builds industrial lifts. It is also home to a campus of Iowa Western Community College. All in all, Atlantic is just small-town America, functional and clean.

We immediately drove to the address of Linda and Bill Sage. It seemed many of the streets in Atlantic were named after trees, as was theirs. We knew it was very close to Pauline's home. As it turned out, the two homes were only a block from each other. I was uneasy and apprehensive as we approached the Sage home. We drove around the block a couple of times before we stopped. The house was one of several on a small incline. Rita was driving. As we passed the house our car slowed, I snapped a few pictures.

"What if someone comes outside while we are taking pictures? What if someone calls the police?"

"Relax," Rita told me. Compared to me, she had nerves of steel. I had never surveilled anyone before, and I can best describe the experience as unnerving.

The house itself was an unremarkable light green two-story structure. Dark green wood trim provided an accent to the lighter green siding. The house gave the appearance of a warm, middle-class family living in middle America. Pauline's house was just up the street, not even a minute's walk from the Sages. From the close proximity of the homes, it seemed inevitable that Pauline and her daughter Linda must have a close relationship. This close proximity gave me a good feeling about them, but where would I fit in? And what about Kenny, who lives in Carrollton, Texas? How does he fit in?

Pauline's single-story house was like the Sage home and most of the other homes in the immediate neighborhood. This home seemed older and smaller than the Sage home, like a place where someone's grandparents might live. There was no attached garage but an older vehicle off to the side. There was an attached porch off the front entrance with easy soft-cushioned chairs.

While driving around the block a couple more times, we pulled over so Rita could take a few pictures. We felt like a couple of private detectives on a stakeout! My heart leaped to my throat every time we drove past either house. Every time we passed Pauline's house, I peered onto the porch, hoping that perhaps someone would appear, affording me a tantalizing glimpse of my own flesh and blood. Maybe I could get a picture of her. We never saw anyone from either home. We never even saw a neighbor or a child outside any home on the block.

We took pictures of the homes before deciding we had seen enough. I felt I had experienced what an undercover detective might feel like and was ready to leave town and get back on the road to Chicago. Rita wanted to stop at the local McDonald's on the way out of town. We only bought something to drink because it was Passover, and Rita and I observed the holiday's food restrictions. I was really anxious to leave, which was kind of irrational, seeing that no one could possibly know who we were.

My nervousness dissipated as we worked our way to the counter during the lunchtime rush.

Suddenly, Rita, acting as if through some uncontrollable impulse, decided to ask the couple waiting in front of her whether they knew the Sage family. My heart was in my throat, and I held my breath. Why did she have to ask this question? The last thing I wanted to do was draw attention to us. I stared straight ahead, waiting to hear their answer. The answer was not what I wanted to hear.

"Oh, sure, that would be *Sheriff* Sage. He is the deputy sheriff of Cass County."

That was all I had to hear. I felt as if I stood out like the Empire State Building. I left the line and made a beeline out the nearest exit. The very house we had staked out and photographed was occupied by none other than the deputy county sheriff. An irrational thought went through my mind. "We could have ended up in jail. Wouldn't that have been a hell of a way to meet my new family?" My cell phone rang. It was Rita. "Get back in here and have your drink. You're acting like an idiot! We're not leaving yet." Reluctantly, I returned.

We sat in the corner of the restaurant with our Diet Cokes. "Did they ask why you were asking? Did they want to know who we are?" I asked. "No and no," Rita replied. I didn't see the people Rita had spoken to anywhere in the restaurant. They were probably out calling the County Sheriff's office reporting suspicious people in the McDonald's asking questions about Sheriff Sage. I was thinking and acting irrationally and out of character, but I was extremely anxious, to say the least. It wasn't over.

After sitting for a few minutes, we overheard a couple at a table nearby talking about being at the Jewish Community Center in Omaha a couple of days earlier. I looked over to see if it was possible that I knew who they were. I did not want to have to explain to friends of my parents what I was doing in Atlantic Iowa when I should have been halfway to Chicago. I didn't know them but I had heard enough. I insisted we needed to leave, and leave we did.

I do not really know why I reacted the way I did that morning. I guess it was a stew of feeling guilt about betraying my parents, acting behind their backs, anticipation, the excitement of being near my birth family, nervousness over having basically stalked two houses, one of them occupied by the deputy county sheriff, all contributed to the restless, worked-up feelings I had that day.

When we reached Chicago, we both realized we had reached a crossroads. The search was over. We knew the names, addresses, and phone numbers. We knew where they lived. We knew what their homes looked like. The next move was ours. At long last, I would make contact, and let them know I exist. We would contact Pauline. What would be her reaction? We were about to find out.

*****

1   *Atlantic Iowa Magazine*, published for the City of Atlantic and the Atlantic Chamber of Commerce, 1999

11

FIRST CONTACT
CHICAGO
APRIL 2002

From the beginning of my search so many years ago, I had believed that finding out everything I could about my birth parents would mean finding out about myself. This was of utmost importance, but the risks were monumental. I could be utterly rejected by Pauline and her children. Although I had two loving parents who raised me well, the prospect of an immediate rejection would be painful. It could all come crashing to an end with a phone hang-up. If it proceeded and she wanted to begin a relationship, I could risk my relationship with my mom and dad. Would I constantly worry about my parents finding out? Would I feel like a cheating spouse carrying on a clandestine relationship living in daily fear of being discovered?

On April 1, 2002, Rita and I discussed these possibilities, plus that we would be disrupting the lives of Pauline and the families of her children. Clichés such as "leave well enough alone" and "let sleeping dogs lie" came to mind. I was reminded of a quote by Holly van Gulden from her book, *Real Parents, Real Children: Parenting the Adopted Child*: "The overriding objective of search is 'to heal: to grieve the loss, find resolution, and come out of it with a positive sense of self."[1]

I wasn't sure about the healing or grieving the loss, but I was sure about the need for resolution. My positive sense of self drove me throughout all of this. I knew that I would make contact. I was determined to see this through.

Truth Seekers in Adoption had advised us to use a third party to make the initial contact. Rita was not exactly a third party, but she was the perfect person. We decided we would call the next evening. We would go to Rita's office at the Packaging House after closing. This would ensure there would be no one there to disturb us. The office phones also can record conversations.

This seemed like a good idea. We could listen to the conversation afterwards, pick up any information we might have missed in the excitement of the initial call as well as any meaningful nuances or inflections. At that time, there was no way to place the phone on speaker, which meant I would be able to hear only Rita's half of the conversation. Listening to the tape after the call would enable me to hear everything. We didn't really consider the legality or the morality of recording the phone call. Of course, it would be recorded without the knowledge or consent of Pauline.

Although we agreed the call should be recorded, there was an uncomfortable feeling, the same feeling we had while scoping out and photographing the homes in Atlantic. I thought I was invading her privacy without her consent, and it made me feel dishonest. It felt deceptive then and feels deceptive today, but I thought this was the best way to get the answers I had been seeking for so long.

We arrived at Rita's empty office at 7 p.m. The sun was already down, with a little light remaining in the sky, as dusk would soon turn to night. Rita worked in an enclosed cubicle directly across from the CEO's office. Her desk was positioned to see directly into the large glass window of her boss's office facing her cubicle. Adjacent to Rita's desk was just enough room for the chair where I would sit during the call. Her desk was strewn with documents. There were several family pictures on the desk as well. One shelf had several boxes and containers of candy and gum, which Rita made available to co-workers. I would listen to as much of the phone call as I could hear from my chair. I often found myself pacing in and out of the cubicle, the frustration of not hearing the whole conversation adding to my trepidation. I would not participate in the call unless Pauline wanted to speak to me. We were ready. Rita dialed Pauline's phone number listed on the Kinsolving report.

A woman answered almost immediately. We both knew it was Pauline. I listened. It didn't take but a few minutes to realize the conversation was not going well. If the reader is anticipating a joyful woman anxious at long last to hear news of the son she gave

88

away and had been longing to hear about for decades, you will be disappointed. Actually, the call was a debacle, although Rita tried her utmost.

The conversation began with a firm denial that she was who we knew she was. Rita spent some time discussing my situation, the search over many years, Rabbi Gonsher—all of it leading to this phone call. The woman firmly insisted we had the wrong person.

At the seminar, we learned that when phone contact was made, the longer you could keep the party on the phone, the better the chance of a successful reunion. Throughout the entire call, Rita spoke very calmly and tried to persuade her that she could be trusted. Pauline did stay on the phone—for almost an hour. That was positive and offered us a glimmer of hope. It was obvious in the first three minutes that we had found the right person. Rita was speaking to my birth mother. The conversation summarized below is taken directly from the call transcripts.

"My husband is a good man and has had a wonderful childhood, a professional in the community. He asked me to talk to you to lessen the shock," Rita declared, trying to tell her that she had nothing to fear. She explained to Pauline that I would like to know the circumstances leading up to my adoption. We had a written list of questions: will she agree to a very private meeting? Can we involve her children, what were the circumstances leading to my adoption, and what were the circumstances surrounding the death of her husband, Lawrence Kenneth Karnes? Those answers were not forthcoming. She again denied she was who we knew her to be.

"I'm really sorry to see this end this way, but there's nothing I can do. Nothing I can do."

Rita asked if she could just put me on the phone. Pauline responded in what can be described as a stream of consciousness.

"No, please. I'm not as bad as you think I am. He should thank God it all worked out well. Things are better left. I don't want to get involved. My rights have been violated. YOU HAVE NO IDEA HOW MY RIGHTS HAVE BEEN VIOLATED. You have to go back 52 years— things were done, THEY WERE DONE. Your mind can't be brought back. Can't go public. If you (Rita) can't help him, nobody can. That is your place. Tell him to let it go."

It was disturbing and heartbreaking to listen to.

"We don't want it public. We want to keep this private. Bob wants it private," Rita added, trying to assure her that her privacy would be respected.

"So do I. If I have to see an attorney, I will. Forget it. It's over, done. Nothing's going to change."

She said the "A" word, attorney. That changed the whole tone of the conversation. We never expected to hear that. Three minutes on the phone, and she has invoked an attorney.

"I understand. Bob wants a resolution. Bob just wants to talk." Rita was trying to diffuse the situation.

"I'm not the right person. Nothing that bad—it just happened. It is something done and over with. I'm not going to go through this weekly."

"Bob wants to end this," Rita stated firmly.

"Honey, the only way you're going to put an end to it is to find the right one (still denying she was the right person) or have her put a gun to her head," Pauline ominously replied. Lawyers and talk of suicide. This could not be worse.

Rita attempted to move the subject away from her comment about putting a gun to her head. She had kept her on the phone so far, but the conversation was turning ominous and it could end at any moment. Rita asked about her relationship with Gonsher.

Pauline opened up like floodgates in a dam. She said she was terribly upset with Gonsher and had never given him permission to tell us anything. Rita carefully explained that the information we received that led us to discover her identity came from the private agency we hired, not from the rabbi.

She told us about one call with the rabbi. Her daughter Linda answered the phone. She had to come up with an explanation as to why a rabbi would be calling her from Omaha. She made up some reason and told Linda he was calling to raise money. She also claimed the rabbi had told her that everything could all come out after her death, regardless of whether she had given permission to contact her children. She said she had once hung up on the rabbi during one of their many conversations. She was emphatic that she had never agreed to speak with or meet with me at any time. I remembered the meeting Gonsher had scheduled with her and then told me she backed out at the last minute. She also told us she had never received any letters or pictures from us. Very perplexing and unexpected.

Rita told her we would speak to the rabbi. Apparently, Pauline was terrified her children would find out about my birth and adoption. The phone calls from Gonsher, as well as periodic holiday cards that kept her running to the mailbox ahead of her kids only served to increase her fear. This must have been the opposite of what Gonsher intended. All of this had made her life difficult over these many years, and it broke my heart to hear it.

Rita reassured her we would discuss all of this with the rabbi and ask that he not contact her anymore.

The conversation continued:

"I don't want to be an open book. Isn't that awful?" Pauline said.

"Help me close it," Rita responded.

"What is there to know?"

"Is Ken Karnes the father of my husband?"

"He is not here. I can't speak for him. My mind is spinning." A nonanswer. Evasive. Neither a confirmation nor a denial.

"Did you ever go to Rabbi Gonsher's office?"

"Once. About 15 years ago (this would have been around 1987-88), I cried like a 13-year-old girl. I asked to be left alone."

Gonsher still maintained contact with her, calling her every year and sending holiday cards. She insisted that she never agreed to talk or to participate in any conference calls.

"Once, when you were sick, did you agree to talk to Bob by phone?"

"No, never."

Pauline kept returning to what I presume were references to my birth.

"What I did is over. Over. I knew he would be brought up by a Jewish family. I insisted that the baby be given to the JCC." (She most likely was referring to Jewish Family Services, not the Jewish Community Center). "They wouldn't even let you see the baby back then. I left the hospital the next day. That was unheard of back then. That's all I knew." By now, she had tacitly admitted she was my birth mother.

She seemed to be deeply ashamed about the circumstances of my birth and was desperate that her kids never learn of what she did.

Rita asked if she could meet Pauline somewhere. Pauline replied that she had recently had her hip replaced. Driving would be hard. She mentioned she did not learn to drive a car until immediately after her husband died.

Pauline asked Rita when she would next be in Omaha. A spark of interest. She seemed to not want to end the phone call. Rita told her we would be there in a couple of weeks.

One revealing moment during the conversation occurred when Rita told Pauline about our daughter, Alicia, who was living in Israel at the time.

"You know, you have a granddaughter in Israel."

Silence from Pauline, then, "Now I have someone else to worry about." It was a poignant comment. We had moved away from talk of lawyers and suicide. The door seemed to be opening, if just a little.

During much of the entire conversation, I found myself frantically jotting notes to put in front of Rita: IS IT HER? splashed across the front of a manila folder. Will she talk to me if you are on the line? Did she give up a kid in 1949? Meet us once and we can put this to rest.

Rita mostly ignored these notes as she was focused on Pauline and keeping her on the line. If this was a sign of progress, then Rita succeeded. The call was already 40 minutes and counting.

Pauline spoke of her young son, Ricky, who had died of meningitis. "He was two when he died in 1950. Would have been three in October that year."

Rita expressed her sorrow over this tragedy. Silence.

"Can I call you again in a few days?"

"If you want. Please tell your husband that I am asking on bended knee that he doesn't tell my kids." She was desperately worried that if Linda and her brother found out it would destroy her.

"I can promise short term."

"What does he want?"

"Is Ken Bob's dad?"

"Ken is dead, and there's nothing to be gained. No way to meet his father, the man is gone."

"But was he Bob's father?"

"He signed all the papers." Pauline seemed strangely evasive about my paternity.

The call ended a couple of minutes later. Pauline seemed to have struck a rapport with Rita, and it seemed clear she wanted Rita to call her again. We were both emotionally drained. It certainly did not go as we had wished and most assuredly did not point to the reunion we had eagerly hoped for.

I felt remorse after listening to the playback of the call. Pauline seemed to be devastated from years of contact by Rabbi Gonsher, as innocent and well intentioned as those contacts might have been. I have to believe that he did not realize the effects his regular calls and holiday cards had had on her. I believed he was acting in good faith all these years and always acting on my behalf. But it was now apparent that he had had the opposite effect on her.

But it was worse than that. I was her deepest secret she had taken great pains to keep from her children. It was a secret she never wanted them to know and had asked us "on bended knee" to please not call them.

I asked myself what have I accomplished over these years? I harbored years of guilt over lying and deceiving my own parents, and now I had disrupted Pauline's life, unleashed her personal Pandora's box of trouble. This is where my search led. I knew the names and addresses of my birth mother and sister and brother. I would never meet any of these people, and my sister and brother would never know they had a sibling who had spent the better part of two decades looking for them. My birth father had died at age 50, although Pauline's evasive answers had left the question of whether Ken Karnes was my biological father up in the air. The only glimmer of light came from the fact that Rita and Pauline seemed to have established a rapport during that one-hour call.

Rita and I agreed that Pauline seemed open to hearing from Rita again. She told Pauline that we would not contact her son or daughter without speaking to her again first. We agreed we would wait a couple of days, hoping Pauline might change her mind about a reunion and allow me to contact my newly discovered siblings. Rita would call her back, and if she had not changed her mind, she would tell Pauline we would never call her again, and we would never contact her children.

We would also let the rabbi know our search was over and that there was no need for him to continue any further contact with her. Hopefully, we could then extricate ourselves from this completely. Pauline could live the rest of her life knowing her secret was safe, and I would have to accept that the information I had received was the end of the line. Search over. Just a call from Rita to bring closure to Pauline.

————

Three days later, on Friday, April 5, Rita made what we anticipated would be our final call to Pauline. We were back in Rita's office around 7 p.m. feeling disheartened, but ready to record this conversation as we did the last. Pauline answered on the second or third ring. As soon as Rita identified herself, Pauline threw us what can only be described as a bombshell:

"I told my kids." she stated, calmly and resolutely.

"What?" was Rita's immediate response.

"I told my kids. Everything. They know. I cried when I told them. I told them I had done something bad. That I had been paying a price for the last 17 years." She did not say she had paid a price for the 50 years since she had given me up for adoption, but was referring to the 17 years since she was first contacted by Rabbi Gonsher, at my direction.

"You told them everything?" Rita asked incredulously.

"Yes. They know."

"But why? We told you that we would not contact them until or unless we spoke. What made you want to tell them?"

"I figured it was better to hear it from me, not anyone else. My sister knows. So if you want to call them, they already know."

"Bob decided he would never have called your children."

"Well, I told them, and I cried when I did. Linda (her daughter) thought that I should meet with Bob. I don't have two heads you know! When I told my sister she said, 'now it's out, you don't have to worry about this anymore.' I replied, 'I'm free.'"

"Bob only wanted to ask you a couple of questions."

"I know, but I talked to a lawyer and he told me I don't have to answer anything. I have been petrified for 17 years." Rita reiterated that we received the information regarding the identities of her family from the private detective agency we had hired for that purpose.

Pauline returned the conversation to my birth and told us the baby was taken away from her, and that was it. She repeated that she was sent home from the hospital the next day. She signed away her rights. "I was told I would never see the baby again."

It seemed that despite all she was saying, she wanted to talk with Rita. She wanted Rita and me to know the pain she has endured over the years and for both of us to understand what she had been through.

"I had no feelings (for Bob) whatsoever. But it does bother me," Pauline told Rita. This was perhaps the most gut-wrenching statement I had heard from her. She had not really given me much thought over the past half-century. Yet it bothered her that she did not have feelings, which suggested she did have feelings, if that makes sense. Whatever feelings she had for me were suppressed feelings until Rabbi Gonsher made his contact with her in 1985.

By now, I knew in my heart Pauline was a sensitive individual who had been living for nearly two decades knowing someone was seeking her out. She now has been located and her secret revealed. These conversations must have been both tiring and grueling for her. My heart ached, and we knew Pauline's life would never be the same after we contacted her and changed the lives of several families forever. We had ripped the scab off and left an open wound. It didn't seem there was much left to say.

Pauline's sister was no help. Pauline had described conversations she had with Esther regarding me contacting her. Esther was extremely suspicious, wondering what it was we "wanted" from her sister, and why a grown adult would even be engaging in this search. She suggested that Pauline call my mother and "lay her out every which way." She described me to Pauline as a maniac. Pauline said she would not do this.

Esther told her she had received a phone call recently from someone who asked her questions about her relation to the Newman family in Omaha. These are the "Hinky Dinky" Newmans to whom Pauline and Esther were related. She was unsettled by the call as no one had asked her about this in more than 50 years. (The call probably came from a detective from Kinsolving). I could sympathize with her feelings. She had maintained Pauline's secret for decades, then the long-lost son shows up at the door and everything is out in the open. Who wouldn't be suspicious?

Regarding my adoptive mother, Pauline indicated Gonsher told her that my mother had given her blessing to me searching for my biological roots. Either she was confused, or Gonsher had been mistaken about my mother. My mother knew nothing of any of this, and I was sure beyond any doubt whatsoever that she never would have approved and given her blessing to my search. In fact, I had taken every precaution to ensure she would never learn of this search.

My parents and I were polar opposites regarding the subject of adoption. Any time I ever mentioned the subject of my adoption to them, the response was always the same. "We knew you were born healthy and of a Jewish mother. We never asked for more, and we do not want to know anything about it." Period. End of discussion.

Rita again asked Pauline if her husband Ken was my father. She explained that this was a genuine concern since he died at age 50, and I was already older than 50. Her answer was that she had a son who was also 50 and health issues were a concern to him as well. When asked again whether Kenneth Karnes was my father, she regressed to the weekend of his death, Thanksgiving weekend in 1978.

"Ken spent seven years in the Marine Corps. He died after he had just had a good physical the month before. The doctor offered no explanation, except that he drank too much beer and smoked. We had a big Thanksgiving dinner, 35 people. He died that Sunday," Pauline reminisced. She then told us his full name, as if she were reading an obituary. "His full name was Lawrence Kenneth Karnes, but everyone called him Ken."

Making one last attempt, Rita again asked if Ken Karnes was my father:

"Well, he signed the papers. I can't speak for him." This was a peculiar answer. Logically, of course, she could speak for him. Who would know the father if not her? I would most likely never know if Ken Karnes was my biological father. She did tell Rita that there were no diseases in the family I needed to worry about.

"I served my time in hell. I could be the poster child for abortions. Tell Bob I am really, really sorry," Pauline said quietly and somberly.

"Bob wanted you to know that he would be there for Pauline or the kids if they ever needed him. Bob has said that he won't call his sister or brother."

"Tell him to go with God and that he's lucky to have you." The conversation was over.

On the one hand, this call was devastating. In our minds, the search had now ended. We had agreed long ago that if the other party or parties did not want to be contacted, we would respect their decision. This is now what happened, and we would indeed respect this woman's right to privacy. We would not call her again. Linda and Ken knew they had a brother, but I also knew I would never meet them. The whole 17-year search had come to a screeching halt. From both conversations, we could infer that Pauline was a decent, respectable woman who had made a difficult life-changing decision and had spent decades suppressing it, seemingly protecting her family as well.

She had suffered over the past 17 years even though Rabbi Gonsher must have thought he was acting reasonably and professionally in trying to affect a reunion on my behalf. I think of the years of miscommunication and misunderstanding. Our phone call had brought back memories she had tried to suppress for over 50 years. My actions from the very beginning had seemed to have caused great pain. I would have to live with that. The fact that Linda and Ken now knew who I was made the entire situation even more painful. I could never betray my word and call them.

I still felt justified in every action I had taken. I am reminded of the expression, "I didn't ask to be brought into this world." I felt fully entitled to ask the questions I asked, to seek the information I sought, and to know all there is to know about my birthright. Regarding the guilt I felt about not telling my parents about this, I know that in the Jewish tradition it is acceptable to not say something that will cause pain or hurt someone's feelings if there is no evil intent or harm done in not telling them.

That Pauline decided to tell her children after we had said we wouldn't call them was her choice. When she hung up after our first phone call, she was so sure we were going to call her children that she launched a preemptive strike and told them herself. She miscalculated our intentions. That was her choice and her choice alone.

It was over. Pauline said, "Now I am free." She could now let go of the secret she had kept from everyone for over 50 years. "I didn't want to tell them I had done something bad," Pauline had said. Well, the secret was out, like a genie released from a bottle. Closure for Pauline. For me, acceptance that this was as far as the search would go. I knew all I was ever going to know.

Over the weekend, Rita and I listened to the two phone conversations several times. The unanswered question remained. Was Ken Karnes my biological father? No answer.

On Tuesday, April 9, we both went to our respective jobs, and went out for dinner that evening. When we returned, there was a surprise awaiting us.

*****

1   Holly van Gulden and Lisa M. Bartels-Rabb, *Real Parents, Real Children, Parenting the Adopted Child*, The Crossroad Publishing Company 1993, 2000. p. 229

12

PHONE CALLS
CHICAGO
APRIL 2002

My birth mother had been crystal clear on one point—she wanted no part of me. After nearly two decades, several letters and capped by two phone conversations with Rita in which Pauline was promised I was only interested in one face-to-face meeting and would never call her kids, she would not agree to one meeting. The woman had brought me into the world, gave me the gift of life, yet she could not find it in her heart to meet with me.

Over the next couple of days, I tried to force myself not to think about Pauline. I was particularly frustrated because I was never able to get a direct answer about whether Kenneth Karnes Sr. was my biological father. This was one of the most crucial questions. Did my biological father die at age 50 of a massive coronary? Pauline seemed to dance around this question like a politician avoiding a reporter's question.

It was harder not to think about Linda and Lawrence Kenneth Jr., the siblings listed in the Kinsolving report we had received. On her own initiative, she had told them about me, including the circumstances of my birth. Her secret was out. How would they have reacted? Wouldn't they have wanted to meet the sibling who had spent 17 years seeking them out? Had they no curiosity as to how I looked, what I sounded like, or what I was like? Were they sitting around the kitchen table discussing us? Perhaps not.

They, like Pauline, might very well have seen our calls as invasive. It stood to reason Linda would be defensive of her mother. Linda lived practically next door to her after all. That had to be an intense relationship. I had no right to expect anything from her. I knew that if the situation were reversed, I would want to meet my brother or sister no matter what the circumstances. Rita had done her best with Pauline. She had made it clear that we were not looking to be on a segment of Oprah Winfrey's show. Rita had clearly established a rapport, or at least a mutual understanding. Apparently, it was not enough.

I was angry, hurt, and indignant. Pauline had our phone number if she ever wanted to speak to us. I wasn't holding my breath.

My anger continued as Friday turned to Saturday, and Saturday rolled into Sunday. Monday was back to work for both of us and a return to "normalcy." The search was over. I decided the contact between Rabbi Gonsher and Pauline should end. As well intentioned as he might have been, it was now evident that his continual contact with Pauline had caused her great anguish.

Rita had told Pauline I would not contact her or her family and I intended to honor that promise. Since Pauline was never going to agree to a face-to-face meeting, there was no further purpose in Rabbi Gonsher maintaining contact with her. Rita had told Pauline during her conversation that we would let the rabbi know that further contact from him would not be welcome. The following letter (edited for length) was sent on April 2, 2002.

> *Dear Rabbi Gonsher,*
>
> *This letter will serve to revoke my authorization to continue the investigation to determine the existence and whereabouts of my biological parents and/or family members. Please cease any and all contact with any individual or individuals you may have contacted over the past 17 years on my behalf regarding the circumstances of my birth and subsequent adoption.*
>
> *If you make any further contact with any individual you may have discovered as a result of this investigation, you will not be representing me and will be making such contact against my express wishes. I hope that you will honor my wishes and terminate the investigation at this time.*

> *I thank you for your efforts over the past 17 years. Many questions have been answered and I am convinced that there is no purpose to be served by further investigation.*

There was also a paragraph expressing my desire that the entire matter remain confidential. After all, both of my parents were still alive, and I did not want any of this to ever reach them.

The letter was harsh. I was deeply discouraged that there would be no meeting, no opportunity to ask any questions. In the end, the seemingly well-intentioned rabbi did not help matters and may have inadvertently made the situation worse. I wanted to end this entire search process knowing I had done the right thing.

First, I promised we would not contact Linda or Ken without Pauline's permission. Second, I promised I would ask Rabbi Gonsher to stop contacting her. Third, I wanted to ensure my parents never learned of any of this. This could best be accomplished by just breaking it off. I felt then as I feel today—that an adoptee has a right to know who his birth parents are. However, this right does not extend to a right to a relationship.

Looking back, I believe I should have called the rabbi and explained the situation to him. He deserved an explanation. After all, he had also put 17 years into the search without compensation. He deserved a phone call, and instead I sent him a formal legal document. For that I am deeply sorry. It was wrong, but I was frustrated. He had handled this search for 17 years, and through Kinsolving, I was able to obtain the answers in less than a week.

My mindset on that day was to move on. No more contact meant no more contact. I would honor the commitment we made to Pauline, including ensuring that she would not receive any more calls or cards from the rabbi. So the letter was written. Nevertheless, I was wrong in not contacting him. He deserved an explanation.

Tuesday, April 9, was an uneventful workday for Rita and me. We met after work for dinner, as we often did during the week, and didn't get home until sometime after 8 p.m. We were tired, ready to unwind in front of the TV before going to bed. I sat down in the family room, and Rita went into the bedroom.

Within a minute she shouted to me, "Bob, get in here. You've got to see this!"

"What is it?" I asked, not really wanting to get off the chair.

"You have to come in here and see what is on our phone."

That got my attention. Our phone had one of those Caller ID boxes attached to it. It did not show phone numbers like Caller ID does today, but it did reflect the area where the call was coming from and the time it was placed. There was no message machine. You had to scroll the box to see where the calls were coming from and the frequency of the calls. There must have been a dozen calls over the past couple of hours, the box reporting they all originated from "Western Iowa." This was a total shock that struck me like a thunderbolt on a sunny day.

"What do you think? Do you think Pauline is calling us? Maybe it's Linda?" I asked, somewhat incredulously.

"I don't know, but we don't know anyone from western Iowa. It has to be someone from the Sage or Karnes family," Rita replied.

In the back of my mind, I knew it could not be Pauline. After the two phone conversations, it didn't seem possible that she could have had a change of heart and had decided to call us and set up a reunion. I thought it could be Linda or Ken calling to tell us in no uncertain terms how we had disrupted their families and upset their mother. I didn't know what else to think so I thought the very worst. We did not have time to speculate. Within two minutes of scrolling the caller box, the phone rang, startling both of us. The box immediately showed the words "Western Iowa."

We looked at each other. The phone rang again. Rita answered. We had no idea who was on the other end of the phone or what to expect. "Hello ..."

"This is Carla. I'm Linda's daughter. Did you call my grandma?"

"Yes."

"My mom would like to talk to you. Can I put her on?"

"Yes. We did not call to cause your mother to be upset or to hurt her," Rita replied, anticipating the worst.

"Hold on, I'm going to put my mother on." This was moving fast. A pause on the phone.

A moment later, "Hi, this is Linda."

"This is Rita Yaffe. As you probably know, our information shows that Pauline is my husband's biological mother."

Linda confirmed that Pauline had told her and her brother that it was true.

"I told her we were not going to call her again, or you either."

"I know that," said Linda.

Rita asked, "Does she know you are calling us?"

"No," Linda answered.

"Did she give you our number?

"She told me that you had given her the number, and she had written it down and kept it."

"I made her repeat the number back to me so I would know that she was actually recording the number," Rita added.

Rita asked the obvious, "How did you get the number?"

"I sent my husband over to her house to look for it. We live about a block from her house (we were aware of this). He looked all over but could not find it. My husband the sheriff couldn't find it, so I went over to the house and looked for it. It was posted right on her refrigerator for all to see."

Pauline had hidden our telephone number in plain sight.

Several minutes of small talk followed. Linda told Rita that her mother had always been very proud of her kids. They never dreamed their mom had given up a child. This was all a complete shock—out of character for her mother.

Finally, Rita said, "I'm guessing you didn't call to talk to me. Would you like me to put Bob on the phone?"

"Yes, I'd like that."

For the first time in my life, I was speaking to a blood relative, my biological sister Linda. I could not help but wonder what it was like for Linda to find out, after nearly 50 years, that her mother had another child and to find out she had a brother and was speaking to him for the first time. It was a surreal feeling, like when you are on vacation and you visit some iconic location you have only read about your whole life, but now you are standing right there.

We spoke for a couple of hours that evening. Today, most of the conversation is a haze. How does one "catch up" on 50 years during a relatively brief phone conversation. I learned that she very much wanted to talk to her new brother and actually wrote down our phone number. Pauline had no idea Linda had done this or was contacting us. She had told Linda about the pregnancy, her decision to give up the child, and my placement for adoption.

Linda then told me a bit about her own life. She talked about growing up in Council Bluffs and her education, which ended after high school. There was a short marriage that ended in divorce, then her subsequent marriage to Bill (who searched for our phone number) the deputy sheriff of Cass County and the love of her life. She has two other kids besides Carla: Denise and Matt. I told her about my background, education, my first marriage, then my marriage to Rita, kids, etc. She told me how much Pauline liked talking to Rita. Linda knew she was Jewish but hadn't really been raised in the faith. She was interested in learning about Judaism from me.

When this extraordinary conversation was over, I was elated and unaware we had been talking for two hours. It didn't escape me that Linda and I were now both engaging in a deception, her mother and my parents. This helped to establish an immediate bond and for that I felt grateful. When the call ended, I choked with emotion.

We spoke again the next day—another long conversation as we continued our journey of discovery. She told us she was going out of town April 12-15. She called again on the 15th and asked me to call her brother, Ken, who lives in Texas. He was expecting the call since Linda had told him about her conversations with me.

I called Ken that evening. He was living in Carrollton, about 19 miles from Dallas. We spoke for about an hour and a half. Ken was a Dallas Deputy Precinct 3 Lieutenant. Law enforcement seemed to be a common theme in both our families. Ken seemed very excited to speak with me as well. He had announced to his office that he had a big brother! He spoke of his sometimes cloudy relationship with his father. He left home at an early age, joined the Army and served in Army Intelligence. Ken also served a tour in Vietnam.

Although he was not raised Jewish, he considered himself a Jew, even though he had accepted Christianity some years before. He characterized himself as "born again." Years later, in one of his Facebook posts. he called himself a Jew by birth, a Christian by choice.

By today's vernacular, he would be called a Messianic Jew, formerly Jews for Jesus, a denomination not recognized by any of the traditional branches of Judaism. But we established a rapport and a bond during this initial call, although I thought there might be more differences than similarities between us. We would soon discover that in the world of religion and politics, we could not have been further apart. These profound differences would in many ways shape the future of our relationship.

Soon after these calls, we received family photos from Carla, Linda's daughter who had made the first telephone contact with us. The photos included a picture of Pauline taken seven or eight years earlier. This was the first glance I had of Pauline. In many ways, she was as I had pictured her for all those years—curly black hair and a kind but stern expression. Her eyes were dark, her eyebrows furrowed. She carried a bit of a gloomy appearance, but yet there was a sense of compassion as she sat at the kitchen table among her family. She might possess a sense of humor, but it would take a while to capture her heart.

The last sentence of Carla's note she sent with the photos was heartwarming:

I hope you enjoy your meeting with mom and Kenny. They are both good people. I'm just sorry about grandma. Just remember it is her loss! See ya soon, Carla

On April 16, Linda and I spoke again. It seemed inevitable we would meet. Everything seemed to be spiraling quickly. We agreed we would meet at a hotel in Davenport, which is located on Iowa's eastern border with Illinois. The city is about halfway between Atlantic and Chicago.

Pauline would know nothing of this trip. Now we all would share a secret, none of us wanting to hurt our respective parents. We chose Saturday, May 11, to meet in Davenport. We would all drive there in the morning, stay overnight and return home on Sunday. Linda and Ken needed to be back in Atlantic on Sunday. It was Mother's Day, after all.

13

MOTHER'S DAY WEEKEND
DAVENPORT, IOWA
MAY 2002

May 11 arrived. The crisp, clear Saturday in Davenport was made for light jackets as the temperature only reached the lower 50s. We made the drive from Chicago, arriving at the hotel with time to spare. We stayed at a hotel called Jumers (no longer in existence). This was our agreed upon rendezvous point. Ken and his wife Dee had driven to Davenport from Dallas, and he had taken every precaution to make sure Pauline did not know they were going to Davenport, much less to meet their new brother. Our three-and-a-half-hour drive seemed like ten hours.

Along the way, I wondered if I was emotionally and psychologically prepared to meet my biological siblings. I wondered what was going through their minds as they travelled to meet a brother who, as of six weeks ago, they didn't know existed. I also thought of my parents, Dorothy and Sol. What would they think if they knew I was on my way to this rendezvous, an end to a seemingly endless journey? I deeply felt the nagging guilt that had plagued me for years, like a bad cold that lingers.

In my heart, I could never escape the feeling of betraying them. My mother would be angry, and my father would be hurt. Both would question why I was risking messing up these people's lives. But this trip to Davenport was an irrevocable step about to alter all of our lives, regardless of the outcome. I wondered if Linda and Ken felt my same guilt for having "outed" their mother, who it seemed would never have wanted them to even know about me, much less to ever lay eyes on me. The secrets each of us were keeping formed a strange kind of alliance between us.

We checked in at the hotel just after noon, intentionally early. We unpacked and then went downstairs to the lobby to wait. The lobby had rustic decor, complete with a fireplace, grandfather clock, and heavy overstuffed chairs. The subdued lighting created an overall feeling of a country lodge where one might sit and relax with a book in hand.

I immediately found myself pacing around the lobby in circles, like a boxer waiting nervously in his corner for the bell to sound. The parking lot was visible from the lobby, and I found myself glancing expectantly toward the parking lot. I gaped at every group of people getting out of cars.

"Are they here? Rita, do you think it could be them?" My mind raced back and forth between two possibilities. First, we would meet and at the end of the weekend come to the decision that we would all go our separate ways. In the second scenario, we would meet, and it would lead to the beginning of a long and beautiful relationship. Which way would it go? My eyes were glued to the parking lot, watching people exiting their vehicles, wondering every time a door opened if it could be them.

Finally, it was them. How did I know? I just knew. They glanced in different directions with the same nervous energy Rita and I felt. They walked into the lobby. I was nervous, but knew that the initial greetings would not be mere handshakes. "Linda?" I asked. Smiling broadly, she extended her arms, and we gently hugged. It was as if we were close friends who had not seen each other for many years. I had wondered for days how this moment might play out. My biggest fear would be that we would meet, spend an evening together, then return to our lives as if nothing had happened, like two trains passing in the night. But I knew during that embrace that scenario would not play out. I knew at that moment this day would be a new beginning, the next chapter in my long journey to discover my origins. Ken and I gave each other a warm hug as well, and we were then introduced to Linda's husband, Bill, and Ken's wife, Dee.

We eyeballed each other looking for physical similarities. There were none, but Linda and Ken also did not really resemble each other. Linda is average height with shoulder-length blonde hair, blue eyes, a warm smile, and a deep voice. She wore a bright yellow jacket and white shorts. Ken wore a blue jacket with a law enforcement star and an earpiece in his left ear, the headphone wire connected to a large cellular phone he wore on his waist. He wore blue jeans and a blue baseball-style cap on his shaved head.

We snapped pictures in the lobby and marveled at the path that brought us together. One of the spouses (I don't remember which one) snapped a picture of the three of us, our first family portrait. Linda, with a look of contentment, looked ahead while Ken (I learned he goes by Kenny) smiled with an arm around my shoulder. I stood in the middle, broadly smiling and looking too thin, as I must have been on one of the many diets I have tried. There is another photo of the three of us standing in front of the fireplace in the hotel lobby, Linda wore a bright yellow jacket, in the center, this time her arms casually wrapped around the waist of both Kenny and me. Above the fireplace was a faux painting of some Victorian-looking lady, gazing over us contentedly, pleased about the homecoming taking place in her lobby.

Rita and I had decided earlier while preparing for the trip that we should bring gifts for Linda and Kenny to memorialize the occasion. We thought the gifts should be the same for Linda and Kenny. Rita and I stressed over which gifts would be appropriate for such an occasion. Finally, Abby suggested a memory box. Perfect. So later that afternoon, we presented both of them with an identical cherry wood box with a gold plate. Engraved on the plates, the words "New Beginnings, May 11, 2002."

Linda and Kenny also brought gifts. From Kenny, I received a miniature NASCAR vehicle (Jeff Gordon, Pepsi, No. 24). I knew absolutely nothing about NASCAR, but I knew this was a gift from the heart. Ken could be described as Texan through and through, which might help to explain his love for NASCAR. From Linda, it was a wristwatch, representing to me the passage of time, time we had missed, the new watch symbolizing a new start, a future together. The gifts poignantly represented the emotions Rita and I felt and believed that Linda and Kenny did as well.

We spent the rest of the day getting to know each other, filling in details about our backgrounds, marriages, children, professions, and just about anything we could think of, trying to pack 50 years of our histories into one evening's discussion. We made a valiant effort. Linda told us how she had found our phone number on her mother's refrigerator and took it home, and how her husband was unable to locate the number that was hidden in plain sight. She was very excited to meet her new brother in spite of knowing her mother would never have wanted the meeting to occur. She told us her mother was deeply ashamed of what she had done but was now glad that everything was out in the open.

Linda reiterated her mother had spoken highly of her conversations with Rita. As I suspected, Rita had established an empathetic bond with Pauline during those phone calls. I knew Linda felt guilty about meeting us behind her mother's back, but the very idea of meeting a new sibling overpowered her remorsefulness. Underlying all of this was the knowledge that Pauline had no idea where Linda was that weekend and no idea Kenny was anywhere but Texas. My parents had no idea I was meeting my birth siblings for the first time. In an odd way, the fact we were all engaging in parental deceptions, served to strengthen the newly formed bond between us. It did not alleviate the underlying feeling of guilt over deceiving my parents.

Nevertheless, the questions remained. Would I ever meet Pauline? According to Linda, the prospects were grim.

The hotel's fire alarm awakened us sometime after 2 a.m. A fire in the kitchen could not be contained by the kitchen staff. A loudspeaker announcement told everyone to evacuate the building. We went down to the lobby and met Linda, Bill, Kenny, and Dee. There we were, somewhat bewildered, in our pajamas along with the other guests, many looking mystified, some annoyed and angry their sleep had been interrupted. Equally startled hotel staff mingled in the lobby with the guests. We watched the firemen in full gear—overcoats, helmets, the works—coming in and out of the kitchen.

Most patrons exited the hotel and waited in the parking lot. We hung back near the entrance but remained in the lobby.

When we finally got the all-clear, it was a few hours into Sunday morning, Mother's Day. I wanted to put all of this into perspective. Rita and I had initiated contact with Pauline. She begged us not to tell her kids. We agreed we would not. She contacted them on her own, and told them what had happened. Linda snuck the phone number out of her mother's house and contacted us. Today we met, and it went beautifully. The hotel fire added drama to the weekend. So many questions remained, racing through my mind as sleep evaded me.

Would I be satisfied with having now met my biological brother and sister? Was Ken Karnes Sr. my biological father? That question lingered but I strongly suspected he was not. As much as Pauline would not want to disclose to her children that she and her husband had given away a child, how much more so would she not want them to know the child was the result of an illicit affair. I did not feel comfortable discussing this with Linda and Kenny so soon after meeting them for the first time. How would I ever know for sure if Pauline refuses to meet me? Will Linda and Kenny ever tell her we met? That would be a difficult secret to keep. It seemed to have gone so well, better than any of us could have hoped.

But when the excitement has diminished and life returns to normal, will they still want to associate with us, or was this just a fascinating one-time meeting? Will I ever be able to share this with my parents? Question after question swirled in my head as I lay in bed next to Rita, both of us trying to process everything that took place this day.

One pronouncement from Kenny kept coming back over and over as I finally drifted off to sleep in the predawn hours. While standing in the lobby, with guests wandering in and out half asleep and firefighters moving back and forth from the kitchen fire, Kenny looked at all of us with a slight grin, "This is a message from our mother. She knows we are here. She knows."

14

THROUGH THE FRONT DOOR
ATLANTIC
2002

Pauline knew we had met in Davenport, but it was not by way of a "message" to us conveyed through a hotel fire. Linda and Ken planned to surprise Pauline on Mother's Day. Linda thought Kenny should visit his mother since he drove all the way from Dallas. Pauline would be thrilled Kenny had driven from Dallas to spend Mother's Day with her. They arrived back in Atlantic by early afternoon. When they walked in, Pauline was surprised. But the bigger surprise was for Linda and Kenny.

"You've been to see Bob, haven't you?" she asked accusingly. There was a look of indignation in her eyes, also disappointment. They acknowledged they had met me.

There has always been a mystery over exactly how Pauline knew that Linda and Kenny had met me. Perhaps it was just intuition, the fact that both Linda and Kenny showed up together that morning and near the time Pauline told Linda the secret of my adoption. Knowing her daughter, she may have thought that once she knew she had a new brother, she would do everything in her power to meet him.

Linda had to tell her mother her own secret that she had taken our phone number from her refrigerator and called me. She was the one who initiated the contact. Years later, Kenny told me there were tears and anger over what Pauline saw as a betrayal by her daughter.

Pauline was angry that day but also curious. She asked for details about the trip and wondered aloud about what I was like. At least for Linda and Kenny, everything was out in the open. Would she now agree to meet me? Not a chance. She resented that I had exposed her most private and precious secret by entering her life. The fact that it was really she who outed her own secret must have caused her great consternation. But she did ask questions, perhaps an encouraging sign the door might have opened a crack.

Over the next week, Linda and I spoke practically every day. There was no question she wanted a relationship with her new brother, and I felt the same about her. We explored our similarities (both of us are Diet Coke-aholics), and our differences, primarily religion and politics. Although Pauline was Jewish, neither of her children were raised in the Jewish faith. Linda did not practice any religion, and Kenny was a Messianic Jew (my characterization). Linda's husband was an observant Catholic, but Linda had not adopted his faith. Both of them were highly respectful of each other's religion. That they now had a Jewish brother must have been nearly as shocking as finding out they had a new sibling. In the matter of politics, we were also profoundly different, Linda and Kenny both leaning to the conservative, and I, more to the left. I made a firm commitment to myself that I would always respect our differences.

Religion and politics are usually topics to avoid when talking with friends or relatives. Linda wanted to learn about my Jewish background. That interest would culminate in her attending a High Holiday service in 2002, in which I served as cantor. Politics, on the other hand, was more sensitive. In the coming years, Linda and I would engage in difficult political debate, a couple of times leading to genuine arguments.

A similarity among our families was a collective involvement with law enforcement. I had served as a deputy county attorney in Omaha. My oldest daughter, Angela, was serving as an Ohio state parole officer in 2003.[1] Kenny was a law enforcement officer in Dallas, and Linda's husband, Bill, was the chief deputy and soon to be the sheriff of Cass County, Iowa.

Linda and I spoke often during the next couple of weeks—every evening in fact. We discussed coming to Atlantic to visit. Bill and Linda wanted us to come, but they did not want Pauline to find out we were there. They assured us Pauline would not show up at their door, so we planned an overnight stay in Atlantic a couple of weeks later.

When we arrived, our feelings were unlike the first time we had visited the town. We were no longer on a clandestine mission. This time we entered through the proverbial front door. This time we were welcomed as family.

Entering Linda and Bill's house was like taking a step back in time. Walking into the enclosed porch, I first noticed a large Coca-Cola chest fully loaded with cans of Coke and Diet Coke. We were armed with Diet Cokes throughout the weekend. From the porch, I moved directly into the main rooms of the house. There was a sitting room, a dining room, a kitchen and a sunroom. The bedrooms were upstairs. The house exhibited some skillful shopping through flea markets. The rooms were filled with kitsch, knickknacks, old dolls, figurines, old saltshakers (some not politically correct), several Fourth of July-style ornaments, and a lot of red, white, and blue, all reminiscent of what one might encounter at souvenir shops along old Route 66.

The house exuded an honest, sincere, and peaceful atmosphere. The cooking and baking smells added to the ambience. But it was all unique and genuine. We both loved it. Linda insisted we sleep in the second-floor master bedroom. We all shared the home's one downstairs bathroom.

Early the next morning, we woke to the lip-smacking aromas of freshly baked cinnamon buns, bacon and eggs (I passed on the bacon), toast and oatmeal. It was an incredible feast. I walked down the narrow stairway on that sunny morning realizing we were family after all. The unanswered questions still remained. Who is my birth father? Do I have siblings on my paternal side? Most importantly, would I ever meet my birth mother, this mysterious lady who lived only a block away? I wondered how Linda could be so sure she wouldn't just show up at the door. She never did.

Finally, I asked myself how I will ever reconcile all of this with my parents, who would never know I was just 75 miles away, in an Iowa town they probably never heard of, having breakfast with my "new" family? All of these unresolved concerns were swept away as we sat together as a family at the breakfast table.

*****

1   Angela gave up her job as a parole officer when she became pregnant with her first child. "Time to give up the gun," she told us. I was not disappointed. She later worked for the State of Ohio in a program working with people trying to break their smoking addictions as well as educating young people about the dangers of tobacco use. Angela went on to work for Nationwide Children's Hospital in Columbus in the Community Wellness Department. She currently serves as Health Equity Director, Ohio Medicaid Plan, for Blue Cross Blue Shield, Anthem.

15

NEW FAMILY & FRUSTRATION
ATLANTIC | CHICAGO | ELYRIA, OHIO
2002

I felt deep gratification as Rita and I began to build a genuine family connection with Linda and Bill. Common lineage is a strong tie, and it seemed we were attempting to make up for lost time. On our next trip to Atlantic, we met Linda and Bill's kids, my new nephew and nieces—Matt, Carla, and Denise—and their three grandchildren. My sister was already a grandma. During the summer, Linda and Bill came to Chicago and spent a weekend with us. We went around the city together, visiting many of Chicago's iconic landmarks.

A bizarre moment occurred during dinner at Dick's Last Resort Restaurant in downtown Chicago. Dick's is a special restaurant and a Chicago institution. The servers at Dick's have a schtick that has made the restaurant famous. They insult the customers on anything from their appearance to their slowness in ordering, etc. It's all done in the spirit of fun and everyone can be heard laughing, although the jesting can cross the line and might be considered offensive to some. Of course, that's what brings in the crowds.

When my turn for ridicule came up at the table, the server left for a few moments and returned with a white paper chef hat that looked more like the old dunce cap used in schools. He placed it high on my head. On it was written, "I was adopted." Everyone was stunned by that moniker. Then spontaneously, the laughing erupted. I'm sure the young server, upon hearing our reaction, must have wondered why we thought the hat was *that* funny.

We took dozens of pictures that weekend, at the restaurant, a family picture at Buckingham Fountain, on the swings in Lincoln Park, and Bill singing karaoke in front of the Oscar Meyer Wienermobile.

That fall, we all flew to Texas to visit Kenny and his wife Dee. We stayed at their home in Carrollton. I didn't feel the same strong connection to Kenny that I felt with Linda. The distance between Chicago and Dallas didn't help. Linda and I were talking nearly every day, and Rita and I were stopping in Atlantic every time we went to Omaha. It also probably didn't help that while we stayed with Kenny and Dee, Rita and I were serenaded about 6:30 a.m. with Christian gospel music, blaring from speakers throughout the house. Although I wasn't offended by this music, it seemed a not-too-subtle reminder of the significant differences between Kenny and me.

Over the years, Kenny would often remind me of his Jewish roots or "Jewish blood" as he referred to it. Years later, Linda told me Kenny apologized to her for that early-morning concert. He never mentioned it to me. I believed from the beginning of my search that whatever I discovered about the family I would accept personally. I have difficulty coming to terms with a theology that teaches that one can be Jewish, accept Jesus Christ, become a member of a church, and still claim to be a practicing Jew, or even Jewish. Ken's religious theology may have made it more difficult for me in strengthening our relationship.

During the trip to Dallas, we did the usual sightseeing. There are family pictures taken on Dealey Plaza, the location of the Kennedy assassination, and other locations around the city. A highlight was a visit to a NASCAR race. I did know that NASCAR was important to Kenny, so I was determined to enjoy our afternoon at the track.

Kenny wore his baseball cap, as opposed to his more familiar Stetson. At the stadium, the concession workers served beer out of buckets. Although I was a fish out of water, I enjoyed the afternoon. This sport meant a lot to Kenny, and it meant something to him that we were sharing a day of NASCAR with him. We both had a great time.

I have an extensive music library consisting of hundreds of books, CDs, and DVDs, all opera and classical music. The shelves are crowded with opera memorabilia. On one shelf, amongst busts of Verdi, Puccini, and Wagner, sits Jeff Gordon's miniature NASCAR.

Just as Kenny had invited us to a NASCAR race, I also wanted to share with Linda the considerable importance of opera in my life. I invited Linda to the Lyric Opera of Chicago, one of the leading opera companies in the country. We attended a performance of the most famous double bill in opera, "Cavalleria Rusticana" and "Pagliacci." I am not sure if she really enjoyed it or was just placating me, but it meant a lot to share one of the loves of my life with my new sister. I hope Kenny felt the same way about taking me to the NASCAR race.

Our Chicago-Atlantic-Omaha trips went on for months. Every trip to Omaha included a visit to Atlantic. And every trip involved deceiving my parents. I did not want them to know what I had done. I feared my search would find their way to them. I didn't know how, but it was a continual worry. Linda did not want Pauline to know about our visits either, so these covert get-togethers continued.

The closeness we felt for the Sages was genuine, and we knew they felt the same about us. The fact we were both keeping secrets served in some perverse way to bring us all closer. The level of frustration was incredibly intense when we were in Atlantic, knowing Pauline was living just one block from us. Many times I considered just walking up the street and knocking on the door, but deferred to Linda, who was concerned such an approach would be a disaster, both for me and her. But Pauline was always the elephant in the room.

Linda and I shared the common fear of her mother finding out about her relationship with me. I shared the same concern regarding my parents as well. Linda felt the same guilt in deceiving her mother about our continuing relationship as I did about hiding my search results from my parents. Linda had a close relationship with her mother and remembered the anger and hurt Pauline had felt when Linda and Kenny met us clandestinely in Davenport.

Many discussions between Linda and me gravitated toward religion and Pauline. Intermarriage was far less accepted in the 1940s and '50s than it is today. At the same time, Pauline had experienced antisemitism from her husband Ken's family ("Christ killer"). As a result, she basically adapted a hand's off attitude towards religion and did not raise her kids in any faith. But now Linda was interested, and we shared many discussions about Judaism in general and the role of Judaism in my life.

Linda was intrigued that her mother had insisted I be placed in a Jewish home. She didn't know much about Judaism, but she had also never joined the Catholic Church, of which Bill was an active member. Years later, one of Linda's daughters, Carla, began studying Judaism and attending Friday night *Shabbat* services in St. Joseph, Missouri, where she lived. Rita and I sent her an introduction to Judaism book.

That summer, Linda and Bill accepted our invitation to attend the High Holy Day services in Elyria, Ohio.

The High Holy Days fell in early September in 2002. I was serving as the High Holiday *shaliach tzibbur* (prayer leader) for a conservative (today reform) synagogue in Elyria. Many congregations in the country are too small to have full-time cantors on their staff, but are large enough to need someone who knows the High Holiday liturgy, which is unique to these special days. That person can be an ordained cantor or a layperson versed in the High Holiday liturgy. I fell into the latter category.

Rosh Hashanah (the Jewish New Year) and *Yom Kippur* (the Day of Atonement) are the holiest days on the Jewish calendar. Rosh Hashanah, unlike January 1, is a time of reflection, not a time for parties, drinking, and revelry. How have we behaved in the past year? What sins have we committed? What can we do to become better in the next year? There are ten days between Rosh Hashanah and Yom Kippur. They are supposed to be intense days of reflection. Those days lead to Yom Kippur, the holiest day on the Jewish calendar.

For many, Yom Kippur day is spent in the synagogue. There is incredible and spiritually inspiring imagery attached to both of these Holy days. God, who has watched over us for the past year, opens his Book of Life on Rosh Hashanah, judges us and writes our fate in the book for the coming year, presumably based upon our behavior over the past year. Between Rosh Hashanah and Yom

Kippur, the book is open, and our fate can still be altered. On Yom Kippur, the book is closed and our fates are sealed. Part of the day is spent reciting lists of sins and asking God's forgiveness, both personally and as a congregation.

Among those sins is this one, variously expressed: "We have sinned against you through denial and deceit" or "we have sinned against you by betraying trust." I knew I had engaged in denial and deceit and had most certainly betrayed my parents' trust. There is also the Fifth Commandment, "Honor your father and your mother." By being deceitful, had I violated that commandment? What about Linda and Kenny deceiving their own mother? I always advocated that I had every right to pursue the answers regarding my birth origins. But at whose expense? My feelings were conflicted as Linda and Bill came to Elyria that Yom Kippur to watch me officiate the services.

Despite my conflicted feelings, it was inspirational to have them in the congregation during Yom Kippur services. There is a prayer for the cantor, chanted during the Rosh Hashanah and Yom Kippur service, called *Hin'ni*, meaning "Here I stand." It is a deeply personal plea, offered with humility, asking God to recognize the cantor's prayers on behalf of the entire congregation.

"Here I stand, impoverished in merit, trembling in the presence of the One who hears the prayers of Israel. Even though I am unfit and unworthy for the task, I come to represent your people Israel and plead on their behalf."[1]

This is one of my favorite moments of the High Holiday liturgy. I proudly offered this prayer on that holiest of days, proud to chant it while my sister and brother-in-law sat in the front of the congregation, yet conflicted when I thought of how my mom and dad would have reacted if they knew my secret. These conflicting emotions, pride and guilt, raced through my mind as I offered that alluring prayer on behalf of the congregation and myself. I will never forget how I felt that day.

––––––––

I was a long-distance runner at that time, having finished two marathons a few years back. Make no mistake—I am no athlete.

Competitive sports were nonexistent for me. I was always the last person chosen on a team, no matter the sport. My father tried to get me to play basketball in a JCC league when I was young. I hated every second of it and spent most of the time on the bench. With long-distance running, I could compete only against myself. I loved those runs while wearing my headphones—always an opera to listen to. I would time my long training runs to coincide with the length of the opera.

At some point during those runs, my left hip began to hurt. After a long run, my hip would ache and throb. The pain would become intense and could last for a couple of days. It would hurt at various other times as well. Every so often, someone would ask me why I was limping. I had no idea I was. I went to the doctor at the Illinois Bone & Joint Institute, got tested and X-rayed. The next day I got the call.

"The doctor would like to meet with you to go over your test results," the receptionist said nonchalantly.

"Great, can we set up a time late next week? I'm pretty busy the next few days," I nervously answered.

"Weeeeell, the doctor would like to see you sooner."

"OK, I could come in early next week?"

"Actually, the doctor would like you to come in tomorrow."

I assumed they were not scheduling me the next day to tell me that the X-rays were normal. I spent the rest of the day thinking about the "C" word, cancer.

Instead, I had a disease called avascular necrosis. No blood was flowing to my left hip, and the bone had essentially died. The disease has three known causes: alcohol, trauma, and heredity. I did not drink, and I had never had a trauma to my hip, so that only left heredity. I would need a full left hip replacement. As it turned out, Pauline had also had a hip replacement years before I met her. My doctor said the cause in my case was idiopathic, which to me translated as "no clue why." The cause of Pauline's hip replacement was also idiopathic. I had the hip replacement in December 2002. I was laid up for six weeks, and my running regimen screeched to a halt. We did not visit Linda and Bill during this time, but I spoke to Linda every few days and several times to Kenny as well.

———————

Linda and I always seemed to have things to talk about. The elephant in the room, of course, was Pauline. By now, she was aware through Linda of at least some of the contact among Linda, Kenny, Rita, and me. She wasn't happy about it, but she seemed at least to be more accepting of our relationship. I also knew that Linda's relationship with her mother was strained at times after Linda made initial contact with me. She paid a price that lasted for years. As 2002 became 2003, Pauline showed no indication that she would ever meet me. I had become complacent and resigned to the reality that I would not meet her.

Since Linda and Bill had come to Elyria for the High Holidays, we decided to also invite them to Chicago for Passover in April 2003. They accepted. I have always loved Passover. The Passover seder is one of the most beautiful and meaningful ceremonies in our religion, and it seems both Jews and non-Jews love to be invited to Passover seders. Rita and I were excited to include Linda and Bill in this ritual. I always conducted the first night seder in our home and was committed to making it a meaningful experience for anyone who attended. I admit I was subject to occasional complaints of "It's too long!" But I tried to make it enriching and enjoyable. I was thrilled Linda and Bill would join us on this occasion.

Then a few weeks before Passover, Linda called. She dropped a bombshell.

"Mom is ready to meet you," Linda said matter-of-factly.

"Are you *serious*?" I asked incredulously.

"Yes," Linda replied.

"Do you want me to come to Atlantic, like tomorrow?" I was already concerned she would change her mind.

"No, we'll come to Chicago."

"My God," I exclaimed. I have been hoping for this for nearly 18 years. "This is fantastic."

I was elated. My heart raced, and I was filled with trepidation. She could cancel at the last minute; it had happened before. But this time, it felt different. Linda and Pauline would travel to Chicago in a couple of weeks, and I would meet my birth mother at long last. They would stay for Passover and attend our seder. I don't know to this day why Pauline abruptly changed her mind. Maybe she needed a year to adjust, maybe it was the allure of attending a Passover seder, what would surely be the first in decades for her. Whatever the reason, Rita and I were ecstatic!

*****

1   *Mahzor Lev Shalem* - Rosh Hashanah and Yom Kippur, The Rabbinical Assembly, 2012, p.140

16

COMING TOGETHER
CHICAGO
APRIL 2003

That Pauline knew her daughter, in an act of independence and defiance, had contacted us on her own initiative against her wishes caused friction between Linda and her mother early on. In her initial anger, Linda lashed out, "Are there any more of them out there we don't know about?" And, "Mom, why didn't you ever tell me about this?" For Pauline, there were feelings of embarrassment and shame. For Linda, feelings of hurt at the deception.

The warmth and intimate relationship between mother and daughter would be tested as each had to come to grips with secrets each had kept from the other. Pauline, who never revealed she had given up a son, had effectively deprived her children of knowing they had a sibling.

When Linda took the phone number off Pauline's refrigerator, she had done what Pauline could only have viewed as an act of betrayal, compounded by initiating contact and beginning a relationship with her new brother, all without her consent. This could strain any mother-daughter relationship.

Yet Pauline had decided it was time for us to meet. I wanted to be able to tell her everything turned out OK, her affair over 50 years ago should not cause shame or guilt. For her, placing me for adoption was the correct decision. I was adopted by incredibly loving parents and raised in a Jewish home, all according to her wishes. I wanted to thank her for giving me my life.

I realized what Rita and I had spoken of in the days following the revelations from Kinsolving had come to pass. The phone call we made had altered people's lives. Nothing could be taken back. There were no do-overs. With Linda, Bill, Kenny, and Dee, it had gone well beyond my expectations. Would it be the same with Pauline? I had "outed" her, after all. She had gambled that Rita would call her son and daughter with or without her consent. She was wrong. The story would have ended there. Pauline's mental torment must have been excruciating.

Years later, I learned that after our call, Linda went to Pauline's house the day before Rita had promised to call Pauline back. When she arrived she found her mother in tears. As soon as she walked in the house her mother blurted out, "I had a baby!" From there, Linda learned the story of my adoption and of her mother's clandestine relationship, of which I had long suspected. Now her children knew she had conceived a child out of wedlock and given the child away at birth. How could this not breed ill feelings toward me, even hostility? How could I ever overcome it?

I also reckoned with my own guilt. How could I emotionally prepare to meet my birth mother when my own mother had no idea of the chain of events I had unleashed? I realized meeting Pauline would be more difficult and emotionally involved than meeting my new siblings. I could not escape the feeling I was betraying my own mother and father by arranging this rendezvous with Pauline. At the same time, I was overwhelmed with emotion over finally meeting her. I wanted her to feel, after meeting me, that everything was OK.

———

April 2003. The day had arrived. Linda and Pauline had flown to Chicago together. They would stay for the first Passover seder. Bill, having been recently elected Cass County sheriff, was working and had to forego the trip. Perhaps it was better this way—just mother and daughter. Linda thought it better. I did not pick them up at the airport. This would allow Pauline time to get settled at the hotel and perhaps emotionally prepare for the moment. I could only imagine the anxiety she must have felt anticipating a reunion she had never wanted to occur.

Linda also knew how incredibly difficult this moment would be for her mother. Pauline's emotions must have been a confusing fog of anticipation, guilt, shame, embarrassment, and curiosity. The plan was that Rita would pick Pauline and Linda up at the airport and drop them off at their hotel. We would give them time to check in and get comfortable. I was anything but comfortable.

Rita picked them up and took them to their hotel, which was next to a large outdoor shopping center in Skokie. She told me how anxious Pauline was about this reunion. We agreed we would arrive at the hotel at 3 p.m., call Linda when we got there, and then our meeting would take place.

Rita and I arrived at the hotel a little early and waited in the small lobby. I was anxious and tense. The room they were sharing was on the first floor, down a long hallway visible from the lobby. I called Linda and told her we were there. Linda said they would meet us in a few minutes in the lobby. At least that is what I thought I heard. Rita sat in one of those unremarkable lobby chairs and I paced the lobby, casting furtive glances down the hall in the direction of their room.

Five minutes went by. "Where are they?" I asked no one in particular.

"Just relax and be patient."

Ten minutes went by. They had not come out. I could feel beads of perspiration on the back of my neck.

"Why are they taking so long? What if she changed her mind? Maybe she can't go through with it?"

Fifteen minutes went by. Something had to be wrong. It was 3:15, and I had heard nothing. Linda had not called. What was going on down there? Finally, Rita said, "Why don't you call Linda and make sure everything is OK."

Could this be another last-minute cancellation, like the cancelled meeting Rabbi Gonsher had told us about several years ago? I anxiously dialed Linda, who was about 150 feet from where I stood.

Linda answered on the first ring. "Linda, everything OK?" I asked, barely able to speak.

"Yes, everything's fine. We are waiting for you."

"I'm in the lobby. I thought you were coming down here."

"We thought you were coming to the room!"

It appeared that we were each waiting for the other. Somehow there had been a misunderstanding.

"I'm so sorry," I said. "I really thought you were coming to the lobby. I can come to your room."

"No, we will meet you in the lobby."

"OK," I said. We are here, and I'm really sorry I messed up." I may have used a stronger verb.

This was certainly going well! After Pauline had finally agreed to meet me, the ultimate irony was that she was probably sitting in her room, looking at her watch and thinking that I had cold feet and wasn't going through with meeting her. Meanwhile, I am standing nearby, wondering if she was ever going to come out of the room or just wait until we left and return home to Atlantic.

I watched for the room door to open. After an insufferable three or four minutes that seemed like 20, I heard a door open and watched Linda and Pauline step into the hall. I had played over and over in my mind how that first greeting might go—a handshake and a light hug. Or would she slap my face? I was about to find out as they walked down the long hallway. I had no idea what was about to happen, so I just stood there, Rita at my side, my heart in my throat.

Pauline and I had our eyes on each other from about 25 feet away. I can't remember what she was wearing because my eyes never left hers. She came closer, and I realized that I was holding my breath. Her chestnut brown eyes were as clear as a summer day, and I could see a gentle smile as she approached. She put out her arms; I did likewise. I felt a rush of elation at this spontaneous hug, warm and sincere.

The past 18 years sped through my mind. The frustrations, the dead ends, the always present guilt I felt in betraying my parents, it was all there in that moment. From the second I was separated from Pauline at St. Catherine's Hospital over half a century ago, I was today reunited with my birth mother. I was 54 years old and she was embracing me for the first time. At long last, I had solved the secret of my birth. The search was over.

17

BUILDING RELATIONSHIPS
2003–2006

Our Passover that spring was memorable. Pauline and Linda agreed to stay and attend seder at our townhouse in Chicago. Rita's parents and Abby attended as well. Pauline was dressed in an all-white pant suit. She might have had her hair permed prior to coming, tight salt and pepper curls, nails cleanly manicured, her round eyes, golden brown, expressive and laser sharp. She seemed to enjoy adding her firm voice to the conversation around the table. I wore a white sweater that evening with a brown stripe across the center. A photo of us sitting on a white couch could have been titled "A Study in White."

The beauty of Passover is not only that it celebrates freedom in all its manifestations, but the seder service itself usually takes place in the home and not the synagogue. The seder is designed for family and friends, and there are about as many variations to how the seder is conducted as there are Jews to celebrate. The seder basically retells the story of the Israelites' exodus from Egypt and their wandering in the desert for 40 years searching for the Promised Land. The story is richly illustrated by the sampling of symbolic foods, group readings, and singing.

I am proud of my ability to have led many family seders over the years. I have attended seders that lasted a half hour while others have lasted long past midnight. This one would be special and memorable. Pauline had not attended a seder in more than 60 years.

Everyone participated, which is the tradition at seders around the world. Pauline reminisced about the Jewish foods she remembered from her youth. I was certain she had not participated in any Jewish family traditions for many decades, and she seemed to wax nostalgic while attending our traditional seder.

As I looked around the table, my conflicted emotions told me this was a truly momentous occasion. The journey to reach this evening was incredibly long and arduous. I was gratified that Pauline seemed to be enjoying herself, speaking of past memories of Jewish foods and her Orthodox upbringing. It was as if her Jewishness had been reawakened.

On the other hand, the absence of my parents was disheartening. What would they have thought of Pauline and Linda sitting at my Passover table? I know they would not have understood and would clearly disapprove. I thought about how I would eventually tell them the truth, but I had no idea how I would do that.

One of the first blessings recited during the seder is over *karpas*. *Karpas* refers to a vegetable, usually parsley, celery, or lettuce dipped into saltwater and eaten.

Praised are you, Adonai our God, King of the universe who creates the fruit of the earth.

The ritual act of eating the vegetable, after reciting the blessing, symbolizes the coming spring, a time of renewal and new beginnings. I found this apropos to the new beginnings in all our lives and the words "New Beginnings" that we had engraved on the boxes we presented to Linda and Kenny. Even more appropriate was the *Shehecheyanu* prayer recited near the beginning of the seder:

Baruch atah, Adonai Eloheinu, Melech haolam, shehecheyanu v'ki'imanu v'higiyanu Laz'man hazeh. (Blessed are you, Lord our God, Sovereign of all who has kept us alive, sustained us, and brought us to this season.)

The seder felt rich in meaning and deeply emotional for everyone present. Meanwhile, my parents were in Omaha for Passover. They did not travel much anymore. I said a personal prayer from my heart that my parents would understand what I had done.

We made sure we had ample time to spend with Linda and Pauline in Chicago. One discussion led to my search process and her reaction to being found. She opened up about being discovered and about her relationship with Rabbi Gonsher. Her comments reinforced what she had told us during those first phone calls a year ago. She reiterated that she had been living in fear of being "outed." She was afraid to go to her mailbox for fear Linda or Bill would retrieve her mail and want to know why she was receiving correspondence from a rabbi in Omaha.

Pauline brought up the incident she had mentioned to Rita during those first phone calls in 2002, when the Rabbi called. Linda immediately asked her why a rabbi was calling her, and Pauline lied and told her he was calling for a fundraising project. Linda accepted the explanation, but it mortified Pauline—too close for comfort. As I listened to her tell this story, I imagined she was beyond upset. She must have felt gut wrenchingly embarrassed for lying to her daughter. She had not only kept her deep secret about my birth, but was now lying to her daughter as well.

Pauline's feelings toward Rabbi Gonsher turned to displeasure and indignation. She agonized over every phone call and every trip to the mailbox. She told us of the face-to-face meeting she had with him years before. During the meeting, she broke down in tears and asked that the contact stop. She had a difficult time processing that he was a rabbi, a position she held in high esteem. I explained to her that Goshner had been acting at my behest, because my adoption had been handled by JFS, of which he was not only a friend but the Executive Director of the agency. I told her how sorry I was the rabbi's contacts had caused her such distress. I tried to assure her he was really a decent person, and I was sure he did not realize what he perceived to be friendly, non-threatening contacts were causing such anguish. I told Pauline I was certain that Gonsher felt these periodic contacts would keep the door open and eventually she would agree to meet with me.

This is what the rabbi had signed on for by agreeing to represent me, and I wanted Pauline to understand that he was acting on my behalf over the years. I also assured her that he did not disclose any names or addresses to us. All identifying information was received instead through an independent detective agency. Further, he was not aware we had hired a detective agency that produced the information which led to her identity. Finally, I let her know I had sent Gonsher a letter informing him I was no longer requesting his services, and it was unlikely she would hear from him again.

I was not sure whether Pauline accepted my explanation for the rabbi's actions. She had built up a great deal of resentment and anger over the years. I felt terrible knowing the pain she had felt with every call or holiday card.

Pauline was very clear that she had never wanted her children to know about what she had done in 1949. Other than her sister Esther, she had never shared the story with anyone. Pauline had always portrayed herself to her children as a faithful and loyal wife. That I had outed her to her family could not be swept under the rug. As the years passed, and our relationship grew, I knew her feelings toward me sometimes wavered. I knew it was because I exposed her secret and that she was forced to share her story and shame, as she sometimes referred to it, with her family. Esther also did not help the situation.

We had not met her, but I think Esther didn't like Rita or me from the beginning. She was deeply suspicious of my motives in seeking out Pauline and the Sages. She made her feelings clear to Pauline many times.

"What does he want? What does he really want? Maybe someone should call his mother and tell her about this." Esther clearly resented what I had done, and there was nothing I could do about it. I would not come face to face with Esther for 15 years, and that would be at Pauline's death bed.

The very idea someone, perhaps Esther, would call my parents and inform them of this situation struck genuine fear in my heart. I knew there was going to come a time when I would have to confront the problem of letting my parents know at least some of what I had done. Finding out this sensitive information in a phone call from Pauline or her sister would be devastating and catastrophic to my relationship with my parents. Fortunately, it never happened. I finally did share some of the story with my parents, and it did not go well. More on that later.

We made numerous trips to Atlantic over the next several years. Now there were no secrets. We would go to Linda's for the weekend, and Pauline would often come over and spend time with us. One summer weekend in 2003, Linda's girls Carla and Denise came with their families. At first, the girls were skeptical of me and perhaps even shared some of Esther's hostility. By late 2003, the initial hostility seemed to have dissipated, and I had become "Uncle Bob." It was strange to hear these words from people who until recently had been strangers, but it was gratifying to have been so readily accepted as a member of their family.

Rita and I brought gifts during one of those family get-togethers. We were staying at Linda's, and her girls had joined us. We awoke to the aroma of breakfast cooking. Most of the family were there: Pauline, Linda and Bill, Carla and Denise, their husbands, and their children. The breakfast table was set in a small kitchen that could only be described as colorful. A red-and-white checkered tablecloth covered the table. Linda's house always had a patriotic flair. There was an American flag bunting hanging from the cabinet to the rear of the kitchen table. On a small table adjacent to where we were sitting was a poster depicting the Twin Towers prior to 9/11, proudly towering over the New York City skyline, with a large, waving American flag superimposed in back of them. It was an impressive display of patriotism, which I in part attributed to Bill's career in law enforcement.

In one photograph taken from that morning, everyone is looking at the gifts we had brought, Pauline overseeing her family with a look of peace and contentment—every bit the family matriarch. A couple of the gifts we had brought included a set of Topps Baseball Cards for Tyler (Carla's son) from the year he was born. To Carla, who enjoyed horror and science fiction, it was a first edition of a Stephen King novel. To Pauline, I gave a prayer book that had been inscribed by the synagogue clergy to me for my bar mitzvah in 1962. Pauline told me she would treasure the *siddur* (prayer book). She kept it for the rest of her life. Linda returned it to me shortly after Pauline's death in 2017. I also gave her a brochure listing an Elderhostel course I was teaching later that summer. She framed the brochure and hung it prominently on a dining room wall. She was proud of my accomplishments, and it made me smile whenever I saw those items displayed in her house.

Memories tend to blur, but over the next couple of years my relationship with Pauline and Linda strengthened. We visited Atlantic often, mostly en route to visit my parents. I still had not told them any of this. Pauline is decent and kind-hearted, and Rita and I were both grateful to have her in our lives. Linda and Bill became an important component of our family, and we spent much time together, including a memorable trip to New Orleans.

We learned much about Pauline, her background and her marriage. I was cautious about bringing up my birth father, but we did raise the subject a few times. During one of our discussions, Pauline finally confirmed that Ken Karnes Sr. was not my birth father. By now, as previously stated, I had long suspected this was the case, so I was not surprised to have my suspicion confirmed. She told Rita and me about the confrontation that took place between her husband and her lover, my birth father (described in Chapter 1), her decision to end the relationship, and her subsequent decision to place me for adoption. It was difficult for her to tell her children about her affair but it was done and she had come to terms with it.

Pauline was adamant she would not disclose the name of my birth father, ever. She was uncomfortable with and avoided almost any discussion on the subject. For whatever reason, this was one secret she was not going to disclose. Perhaps it was the only secret remaining in her control, and she was determined to maintain that control.

I think she did not want us to search him out like we did her. I told her I was satisfied with the information we had and did not feel the need to continue searching. In that I was sincere. I didn't feel the same drive to locate my birth father as I did in searching for my birth mother. I accepted that the search would end. Unless Pauline changed her mind at some point, I would never know his identity. She did tell Rita, privately, that I was a "spitting image" of him.

One may wonder after all the years of searching, why I was now willing to abandon the search without the name of my birth father. The reason is fairly straightforward. I had learned the story of my adoption. I knew how I had come into the world and why I was put up for adoption. I knew why I was placed in a Jewish home. I knew at least half of my medical history. I knew who my birth mother was. She was a remarkable woman with whom I now had a close relationship. I met my biological sister, whom I had come to love. Ken, living in Dallas, made the possibility of visits more difficult, but our relationship was solid as well.

Pauline rarely discussed her relationship with my birth father. She did tell us the mystery man had left Omaha/Council Bluffs many years ago, and she was not sure he ever knew she was pregnant. She made it clear to us that the affair was not a simple one-night stand. My birth was the result of an ongoing relationship. She met him at a local soda fountain just a couple blocks from where she was living with her sister and parents. She described her lover as very handsome and being head over heels in love with her. I was content with this information.

There is an interesting black-and-white photograph of Pauline at about this time taken in a drug store or soda fountain. She is standing at or near what appears to be a lunch counter with no one else in the frame. It appears she is standing on the serving side of the counter, as trays and salt and pepper shakers are clearly visible on shelves she leaned on. She looked directly into the camera wearing what appears to be a white blouse and neat, middle-creased pants. Her hands are laced together in front of her just over the belt. This is clearly a posed picture with an open, friendly smile, lipsticked lips parted showing a perfectly straight row of teeth. The most intriguing feature is her cap. It seems that it might be slightly too big for her, which gives me the impression it might not be hers. The cap seems to accentuate her features in a slightly suggestive manner. On the cap if one looks hard, the name "McConnells" is visible.

McConnells was the name of a drug store that opened in South Omaha circa 1920. It is obviously part of the uniform of a soda jerk or other store employee. Pauline had told us she met her sweetheart at a local soda fountain where he was working. I like to envision Pauline posing at the counter of the drugstore where he might have been working, wearing his McConnells cap. He is standing directly in front of her taking the picture, hence the suggestively crooked cap and smile, the hands folded and posed across her petite figure. Of course, there is no way to verify this, but it so fits the scene.

The photograph captures perfectly her youthful exuberance with a hint of sexiness at the time she most likely had her affair with her paramour. It is obvious from the photo how the young man was attracted to her, and she looks both carefree and untroubled. This is my favorite picture of her.

As I got to know Pauline, she spoke of her childhood, marriage, children, religious upbringing, and many other subjects. However, she remained steadfast in her refusal to name the person with whom she had her affair. She pointed with pride to the fact that the relationship was not fleeting, and her feelings for him were reciprocated. Sometimes when she did speak of him, it seemed as if she were relating a pleasant dream, a youthful memory of a love past but not forgotten, memories that had lingered for more than 50 years.

She also tearfully related the story of the tragic death of her young son Ricky Arthur.

18

PAULINE
2003-2007

Pauline devoted much energy to holding her marriage together. She wanted nothing more than to enjoy a happy and successful marriage and for Ken and her to raise their young son, Ricky Arthur, together. A year after the tumultuous breakup with my birth father, coupled with giving up her son for adoption, Pauline decided the time was right to visit her husband, who was still serving his tour of duty with the U.S. Marine Corps in California.

In 1951, Pauline did not drive a car. Her best travel option was passenger train. The California Zephyr ran between Chicago and Oakland, California, with dozens of stops along the way, including Omaha. In early 1951, when Pauline would most likely have taken this train, it was relatively new, having had its first run in March 1949. At that time, it had been called the most talked about train in America. The train passed through some of the most spectacular scenery in America on its route during the daylight. Pauline looked forward to the journey with great anticipation. The trip took several days, as she traveled closer to the husband she was committed to, her young toddler in tow.

While in California, she stayed with relatives on her husband's side of the family. Pauline recollected that it was January when Ricky Arthur contracted meningitis. She never discussed the treatment Ricky received while in California. It was in 1944 that penicillin was first reported as an effective treatment for meningitis, But for reasons unknown, it was too late for her young son.

In February, Ricky Arthur died after suffering for a relatively short period. He was just two-and-a half-years old. Pauline provided us little detail about what happened after the death. She accompanied the body back to Omaha where the young child would be buried.

Ricky Arthur's small body was stored on the train back to Omaha. Pauline told us it took seven days to get home. She did not tell us whether her husband was with her on the train.

It is difficult to imagine what Pauline must have been thinking on that trip home. If she had traveled to California in high spirits, the return trip must have been excruciating. That she gave up a child for adoption, followed a year later by the sudden death of her son, was in her tortured mind some sort of divine retribution, a punishment for giving her son away. The train ride must have seemed to go on forever, an endless agony knowing her dead son was on the train with her. Pauline's guilt clung to her like sweaty clothes on a stiflingly sultry day. This feeling of self-condemnation remained with her for decades. Although she shared the tragic story with her children, she rarely spoke of the subject.

Ricky Arthur was interred at St. Mary Magdalene Cemetery in Council Bluffs. His gravesite, which Rita and I visited in 2018, was only a small headstone with a simple inscription etched on a speckled gray stone block. In capital letters: RICHARD ARTHUR. Directly under it, KARNES in larger and deeper engraved letters. Under that was "1948" on the left side and a cross in the middle and "1951" on the right. When Rita and I visited, the headstone was tilted and slightly off its pedestal. Rest in peace, brother.

Pauline was no stranger to difficult times, having grown up in a strictly controlled and struggling household. She also was an enigma. She could be forthcoming and willing to speak about her childhood, marriage, children, and more. She could also be elusive and restrained, depending upon her mood. As the years went on, we learned bits and pieces of Pauline's background, intertwined with memories of her Jewish childhood.

Pauline was the daughter of Shulem (1870-1936) and Evelyn Faltz Newman (1903-1952). Shulem died at age 65 when Pauline was only eight years old. His wife followed him in death at age 48. There was a 33 year age gap between Shulem and Evelyn. Shulem's marriage to Evelyn was a second marriage for Shulem. Pauline and Esther, her younger sister, were then raised by their mother and her maternal grandparents, Pearl and Louis Faltz.

The *Omaha World-Herald* ran an undated poignant story about Lou Faltz. It was a typical story of immigration from the early 20th century.

"Louis Faltz, shoe salesman in a large department store in Omaha, was all smiles today when he appeared at the Federal building with a telegram received from authorities at Ellis Island, telling of the arrival of his wife and three daughters there, from whom he had been separated for eight years."

The telegram was an inquiry into Faltz's financial status, if he had enough money to pay to travel from New York to Omaha and what sort of home he could provide for his family.

The story tells how his bank book showed deposits of more than $1,000 and title to a furnished home. Faltz was now awaiting his family.

"I have spent $2,500 just in getting my wife and children out of Poland," Faltz said, "and I shall be overjoyed to see them again."

Pauline's family was related to the Newman family of Omaha. Shulem Newman's name was located on the extensive Newman family tree along with his brothers and first wife, Ida Somberg. Pauline's mother Evelyn is curiously and inexplicably left off the family tree.

Certain members of the family went on to become the founders and owners of the Hinky Dinky grocery chain, which owned many grocery stores in Omaha and the Midwest. Shulem owned a small grocery store in South Omaha. At some point, according to Pauline, he sold it possibly to the "Hinky Dinky" Newmans. He also owned several parcels of property in the Omaha area, but they were eventually lost due to unpaid property taxes.

Shulem Newman never had any stake or interest in the successful Hinky Dinky grocery chain. No one in the family knows why. In speaking with an elderly member of the Newman family, I was told neither he nor any other member of the Newman family had any knowledge of the Shulem Newman family. The relationship between the Shulem Newman family and the other Newman family remains cloudy.

Shulem and Evelyn raised their daughters Pauline and Esther in the Orthodox tradition. Pauline described her childhood as very strict. Evelyn and Shulem believed in the maxim "spare the rod and spoil the child." Corporal punishment was sometimes used to discipline the young girls.

Pauline recalled early memories after her father died of she and her sister being picked up in a limousine (as described by Pauline) and taken to one of the Newman family homes for "feasts" during various Jewish holidays. Shulem and Evelyn kept a strictly Kosher home. No one could bring any "outside" food into the home. She remembered that even the soap had to be Kosher. Many of Pauline's memories were centered around foods traditionally associated with certain Jewish Holidays. Pauline's memories of her mother and grandmother were warm. She remembered little of her father since he died when she was so young.

After Shulem's death, the grocery store was sold, and the family fell on hard times. Pauline said they often did not have enough to eat. Her mother worked for a time at the Dr. Sher Home (the Jewish Old People's Home) in Omaha and described how her mother would sneak food out of the facility to ensure there was food on the family table. The Sher home was a Kosher facility, which would mean that Evelyn could only bring Kosher food into the house. During Pauline's teenage years, she had no father or father figure in her life, while her mother was struggling to put Kosher food on the table. I can speculate that the absence of a father figure in Pauline's formative years might have influenced her behavior during her adolescence and early adulthood.

While researching this book, several years after Pauline's death, Rita discovered two articles in the *Omaha World-Herald* regarding Pauline's early years. One was from December 22, 1940.

"Pauline Newman, 12, suffered cuts about the face and loss of four teeth Saturday evening when struck by an automobile as she was running across Farnam street at Twenty-fifth avenue. She was hospitalized."

Linda told us that Pauline had veneers in the front of her mouth but had not known the reason.

Three years later, at age 15, the *World-Herald* reported on July 2, 1944, that Pauline Newman and another young girl were picked up and booked in connection with a theft of two hundred dollars from a private home. There was no record of the disposition of the case. Her family's dire financial condition certainly contributed to this situation. Pauline spoke occasionally about her childhood, but it was easy to see that it had been tough and demanding.

Despite the orthodox religious background, Pauline elected to not raise her children in the Jewish religion. When she married Lawrence Kenneth Karnes, her mother and grandmother, not surprisingly, did not support Pauline marrying a Catholic. She painfully described how badly she was treated in the Jewish community when she became pregnant. She felt that her family offered her no help or assistance, which would not have been untypical during that era. In addition, antisemitism from Ken's Catholic family exacerbated the situation. As discussed in an earlier chapter, Pauline related that one family member on her husband's side would ask her "Why did you kill Christ?" or call her "Christ killer." These antisemitic slurs caused the young bride great mental anguish. Having felt shunned by both the Jewish and Catholic communities, the couple decided to not raise their children in a religious environment. Yet her Judaism never left her, as evidenced by her decision upon my relinquishment that I be placed in a Jewish home. Hence the enigma.

When Rita and I went to Israel to attend my daughter Alicia's wedding in 2009, Pauline requested that we bring back "holy dirt" from the Holy land. She wanted to sprinkle the dust on the graves of her mother and grandmother. We obediently collected dirt in Jerusalem and mailed it to her in a small package from our home when we returned from Israel. The next thing we knew, she was angry at us because we had mailed the dirt to her instead of hand delivering it. "You don't send holy dirt in the mail!" she snarled at us. We were surprised that this would make her angry, but we found it endearing, nonetheless. This story demonstrates her unspoken ties to being Jewish despite the lack of observance for such a long time. This is one of my favorite stories about Pauline. Pauline told me she would always treasure the prayer book I had given her from my Bar Mitzvah. I knew why she did.

Pauline was a great Nebraska football fan. On one of our trips to Atlantic, she gave me a collector's wine decanter bottle in the likeness of Johnny Rodgers, the 1972 Nebraska Heisman Trophy winner. The decanter rests on a shelf with other treasured Nebraska football memorabilia in my home. She also began presenting us with the official annual White House ornaments each Christmas. When these gifts were given to me, she would proudly point out that the same gifts were given to both Linda and Kenny. The fact we did not celebrate Christmas made no difference. The ornaments were beautiful, and they came from the heart.

We learned Pauline was employed for many years at the Mastercraft Furniture Company in Omaha. She was personally familiar with the Katzman family, the owners. Once or twice, she was invited to lunch at their home. This was astonishing because the Katzmans lived directly across the street from where my family lived and where I grew up. The Katzman boys, Michael and Larry, were close childhood friends throughout elementary school and beyond. Pauline may very well have visited the Katzman home while I was living directly across the street. Perhaps we had even met each other. Who knows?

Pauline tightly embraced her ties to Judaism. She was proud of her Jewish heritage and would fondly reminisce about holidays celebrated as a child. We would often bring bagels, pickles, *challah*, and other traditional Jewish foods to Atlantic when we visited. Pauline loved the goodies and would tell us how it reminded her of foods she had eaten in her youth when her family observed the Jewish holidays. She was proud I had been raised in a Jewish home and that Judaism played a significant role in my life. Yet she had decided to not raise her children in the Jewish faith. It may have

143

been because she had married outside the faith. Or it may have been because of the perceived ill treatment she received from the Omaha Jewish community, coupled with the antisemitic sentiment from her husband's non-Jewish family.

She never explained why being raised Jewish was important for the child she gave up, but not to the two children she raised. I believe that Pauline had tremendous love and respect for the Jewish faith, which was passed on from her parents and grandparents. She adhered to her faith her entire life, even though she might have lost faith in organized religion.

Linda, who still does identify herself as Jewish, also celebrates Christmas with her family, and will, out of respect, occasionally attend a church service with her husband. Bill is a devout Catholic, who attends church regularly, but has never imposed his faith on Linda. Bill is an outstanding husband and father whom I respect and admire.

Kenny's Messianic Judaism is quite different and stands apart from all recognized branches of Judaism. Many adherents of Messianic Judaism are ethnically Jewish and will argue, as would Kenny, that one can be Jewish and still accept Jesus Christ as their savior. The Supreme Court of Israel has rejected claims of messianic Jews related to citizenship requests under the Law of Return, which allows any Jew in the *diaspora* (lands outside of Israel) to come to Israel and claim citizenship. They have ruled that Messianic Judaism is a form of Christianity. Their adherents try to straddle the line between Christianity and Judaism.

Messianic Judaism causes me unease; my core belief system does not allow for this. I believe you can be Christian or Jewish. You cannot be both. That Kenny and I are brothers binds us together. Kenny, Dee, and I have had several lively discussions about religion, afterlife and more. We do not discuss whether one can be Jewish, accept Christianity, and still remain Jewish.

When it comes to politics, Linda and I have strong differences of opinion. Our conversations often veer into the realm of politics. One time, while Linda and Bill were visiting us in our winter condo in

Florida, Linda and I got into an uncomfortable discussion about government and government benefits. It rapidly progressed from discussion to argument. By the end of the conversation, Linda was angry at me and considered moving to a hotel (they were staying with us). We soon made up and the argument was forgotten, but the encounter stuck with me. Maybe the adage about friends not discussing religion or politics should apply to adoptees and their birth families as well. Linda and I have had political discussions since that argument, but they have always been respectful and cordial. I actually think we both enjoy the back-and-forth banter.

Interestingly, Pauline and I shared most political viewpoints, which I found ironic given her children's opinions. We were both lifelong Democrats. We discussed everything from politics, the Obama administration, economic and foreign policy, and many other subjects, finding ourselves almost always in lock-step agreement.

When we visited Pauline in Atlantic, we always checked with her before going to her home. She hosted a group of neighborhood ladies who came over mornings for coffee and cards. She wasn't sure how to introduce me, so I never met them. I did not let her reluctance affect our relationship even though I hoped she would find a way to release the guilt and shame she felt about the affair. She did not want to be judged by her peers and found wanting.

As our relationship strengthened and deepened over the years, she began to, more often than not, introduce me as her son. This was uncomfortable. No matter how strong our relationship had become—and make no mistake, I was grateful every day for our relationship—yet I could never escape the daily feelings of guilt that I was betraying my parents. I could not bring myself to call Pauline "mom" no matter what the circumstances. This would eventually cause a rift between us.

By 2006-07, I was still feeling tremendous guilt. Because of the fear of my parents finding out about Pauline and the Sages, I never discussed my double family life with anyone outside of Rita and our children. I never followed up with my sister Jane who along with Dorand, her late husband, had helped us early on during my search.

Not keeping her in the picture was a regretful mistake and resulted in awkwardness when she finally met Linda for the first-time.

They met at a birthday lunch/party for Rita a few years after we had met Linda and Bill. Linda approached Jane and introduced herself. I was standing by. Linda told Jane she had heard a lot about her. Jane's reply was that she knew very little about Linda. After a couple minutes of uncomfortable conversation, the encounter ended. I felt terrible about the first-time meeting, but realized it was my own fault. I should have kept Jane in the loop but had not done so. I was sorry and owed Jane an apology, which I eventually delivered.

After much soul searching, I finally decided I should tell my parents something regarding my search and its results. I would only share information in small doses, then gauge whether they wanted me to go further, like tiptoeing into the shallow end of a pool to acclimate to the water. In the summer of 2006, I finally did talk with my parents. It did not go well. It is a difficult and painful story.

WHEN THIS COPY CARRIES THE RAISED SEAL OF THE NEBRASKA STATE DEPARTMENT OF HEALTH, IT CERTIFIES THE BELOW TO BE A TRUE COPY OF AN ORIGINAL RECORD ON FILE WITH THE STATE DEPARTMENT OF HEALTH, BUREAU OF VITAL STATISTICS, WHICH IS THE LEGAL DEPOSITORY FOR VITAL RECORDS.

DATE OF ISSUANCE

Freda Theis

DIRECTOR,
BUREAU OF VITAL STATISTICS

Dec 31, 1981

LINCOLN, NEBRASKA

STATE OF NEBRASKA
DEPARTMENT OF HEALTH
Bureau of Vital Statistics

Bk. 4 - Page 534

CERTIFICATE OF BIRTH

State File No. 3 - 8996

Full name of child   Robert Joel Yaffe

Sex Male   Color or Race   White   Date of Birth   December 4, 1949

Born in the United States of America   Omaha, Nebraska

Full name of father   Sol Yaffe

Date of birth   May 4, 1911   Color or race   White

Citizenship   U.S.A.   Birthplace   Omaha, Nebraska

Residence   3106 Dodge St. Omaha   Usual occupation   Printer

Full name of mother   Dorothy Ann Yaffe

Date of birth   February 25, 1918   Color or race   White

Citizenship   U.S.A.   Birthplace   Omaha, Nebraska

Residence   3106 Dodge St. Omaha, Nebraska

This certificate is issued under the provisions of Sections 71-526 and 71-627 Revised Statutes of Nebraska, 1943.

Dated the   25th   day of   September   19 50

(SEAL)   *Robert R. Troyer*

County Judge.

Filed the   28th   day of   September   19 50

My two birth certificates. One with my adoptive parents, Dorothy and Sol Yaffe.
(See page 148)

147

PHS-794(V3)
REV. 4-49
FEDERAL SECURITY AGENCY
PUBLIC HEALTH SERVICE

STATE OF NEBRASKA
DEPARTMENT OF HEALTH
Bureau of Vital Statistics
CERTIFICATE OF LIVE BIRTH

49-029708

BIRTH NO. 126

1. PLACE OF BIRTH
a. COUNTY Douglas
b. CITY OR TOWN Omaha
c. FULL NAME OF (If NOT in hospital or institution, give street address or location) HOSPITAL OR INSTITUTION St. Catherine Hospital

2. USUAL RESIDENCE OF MOTHER (Where does mother live?)
a. STATE Nebr.
b. COUNTY Douglas
c. CITY OR TOWN Omaha
d. STREET ADDRESS (If rural, give location) 814 North 16 Street

3. CHILD'S NAME (Type or print)
a. (First)
b. (Middle)
c. (Last)

4. SEX M
5a. THIS BIRTH Single ☒ Twin ☐ Triplet ☐
5b. If TWIN OR TRIPLET (This child born) 1st ☐ 2nd ☐ 3rd ☐
6. DATE OF BIRTH (Month) (Day) (Year) 12-4-49

FATHER OF CHILD

7. FULL NAME
a. (First)
b. (Middle)
c. (Last)

8. COLOR OR RACE

9. AGE (At time of this birth) Yrs.
10. BIRTHPLACE (City, town or county) (State or foreign country)
11a. USUAL OCCUPATION
11b. KIND OF BUSINESS OR INDUSTRY

MOTHER OF CHILD

12. FULL MAIDEN NAME a. (First) Pauline
b. (Middle)
c. (Last) Stahl
13. COLOR OR RACE W

14. AGE (At time of this birth) 21 Yrs.
14. BIRTHPLACE (City, town or county) (State or foreign country) Omaha, Nebr.
16. Children Previously Born to This Mother (Do NOT include this child)
a. How many OTHER children are now living? 1
b. How many OTHER children were born alive but are now dead? 0
c. How many children were stillborn (born dead after 20 weeks pregnancy)? 0

17. INFORMANT'S SIGNATURE OR NAME—Relationship
Mrs Pauline Stahl-Karnes (mother)

I hereby certify that this child was born alive on the date stated above at 3:40 P.m.
18a. SIGNATURE Mrs. Swoboda & Smith
18b. ADDRESS 482 480 2 x St Omaha Neb
19a. M. D ☒ Midwife ☐ Other (Specify)

20. DATE REC'D BY LOCAL REG. 12-9-49
21. REGISTRAR'S

18. MOTHER'S MAILING ADDRESS
same as #2

ADOPTED

K-652

0691090

The other with my birth mother, Pauline Stahl-Karnes. Pauline told us she went by
Stahl so her maiden name, Newman, would not be recognized. Note the fathers
name on the original birth certificate was left blank.

Pauline Karnes would have felt intimidated by the imposing cross at the entrance to the former St. Catherine's Hospital in Omaha, Nebraska, where she gave birth to me in 1949.

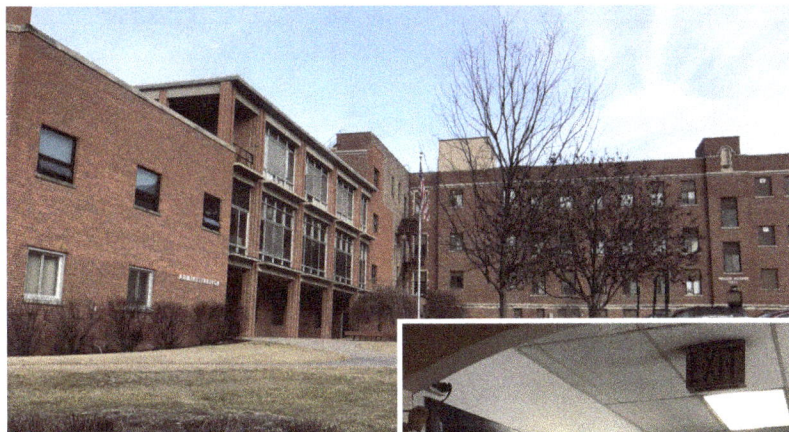

Grace University, no longer open, is the site of the former St. Catherine's Hospital in South Omaha.

The viewing window to the music room at Grace University was the maternity ward in 1949 when I was born. Parents would view their newborns through the window.

RELINQUISHMENT

KNOW ALL MEN BY THESE PRESENTS, that we, the undersigned,
LAWRENCE KARNES and PAULINE KARNES, husband and wife, of the City
of Omaha, Douglas County, Nebraska and parents of
KARNES, a minor male child, who was born at said City of Omaha,
Douglas County, Nebraska, on the 4th day of December, 1949, do
hereby voluntarily relinquish all of our right to the custody of
and power and control over our said minor child to Federation for
Jewish Service, a corporation duly organized under the laws of the
State of Nebraska and having its office at said City of Omaha, and
we, and each of us, do hereby authorize and empower said Federation
for Jewish Service to procure the adoption of said minor child by
some suitable person or persons.

DATED at Omaha, Nebraska this 22nd day of December, 1949.

In the Presence Of:

Jacqueline Tucker   _Laurence Karnes_

Jacqueline Tucker   _Pauline Karnes_

STATE OF NEBRASKA)
)SS.
COUNTY OF DOUGLAS)

On this 22nd day of December, 1949, before me, the undersigned
a Notary Public duly commissioned in and for said county, personally
came LAWRENCE KARNES and PAULINE KARNES, husband and wife, to me
known to be the identical persons described in and who executed the
foregoing Relinquishment, and they acknowledged the same to be their
voluntary act and deed.
Witness my hand and notarial seal this 23 day of December,
1949.

Jacqueline Tucker
              Notary Public

My Commission expires: 9-23-50

In this relinquishment order, Pauline and Ken Karnes officially gave up all parental rights and authorized the Federation for Jewish Service to procure my adoption.

150

IN THE COUNTY COURT OF DOUGLAS COUNTY, NEBRASKA

IN THE MATTER OF THE ADOPTION OF)   BOOK 4   NO. 534
ROBERT JOEL YAFFE   )   CONSENT TO ADOPTION.
)

       Comes now FEDERATION FOR JEWISH SERVICE, a duly
licensed agency and respectfully shows the court:

       1. That said Federation for Jewish Service is a duly
licensed agency by the Board of Controls of the State of
Nebraska with its principal office at the city of Omaha, in
Douglas County, of said state.

       2. That the above named minor child is of the age of
nine months having been born on the 4th day of December, 1949.

       3. That on the 22nd day of December, 1949 the parents of
said child were the natural guardians thereof and then had the
exclusive care, custody and control of said minor child, and
did by written instrument duly signed and acknowledged, surrender
said child and the control and custody thereof to the aforementioned
Federation for Jewish Service, and did thereby relinquish all
right and claim to the child.

       4. That said Federation for Jewish Service hereby
consents to the adoption of said minor child by Sol Yaffe and
Dorothy Ann Yaffe, husband and wife, and voluntarily relinquishes
all right to the custody of and power and control over said minor
child and all claim and interest in and to the services and wages
of said minor child, and to the end that such child shall be fully
adopted by said Sol Yaffe and Dorothy Ann Yaffe, residents of the
city of Omaha, in Douglas County, Nebraska

       Dated at Omaha, Nebraska, this 20th day of September, 1950

                 FEDERATION FOR JEWISH SERVICE

                 By_____
                     Executive Director.

In this consent to adoption order, the Federation of Jewish Service agrees to my adoption by Dorothy and Sol Yaffe.

STATE OF NEBRASKA   )
) ss.
COUNTY OF DOUGLAS   )

       BE IT KNOWN that on this 20th day of September,
1950, before the undersigned, a notary public duly appointed,
qualified and acting in and for Douglas County, Nebraska,
personally appeared PAUL VERET, the executive director of
said Federation for Jewish Service who is personally known
to me to be the executive director and the identical person
whose name is affixed to the above Consent, and acknowledged
that said Consent was signed by him as the executive director
of said Federation for Jewish Service and that the same is
his free and voluntary act, and the voluntary act of said
Federation for Jewish Service, for the uses and purposes there-
in stated.

       WITNESS my hand and Notarial Seal the date aforesaid.

                       Marjorie G Larson
                       Notary Public.

151

Mr. and Mrs. Sol Yaffe

Outside

Announce the adoption

of

Robert Joel

February 15, 1950

Inside

The fancy birth announcement from my very proud parents announced my
adoption to the world on February 15, 1950.

My earliest photo with mom on my adoption day.

My first birthday with Mom and Dad.

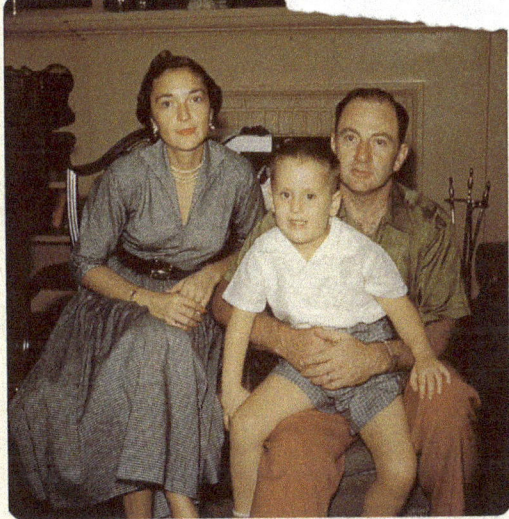

I am three years old in this photo with my parents.

This favorite photo of Pauline is described in the book. With her lovely cap and beautiful smile, this photo was taken in the late 40's most likely at the time of her affair with Sam Clark.

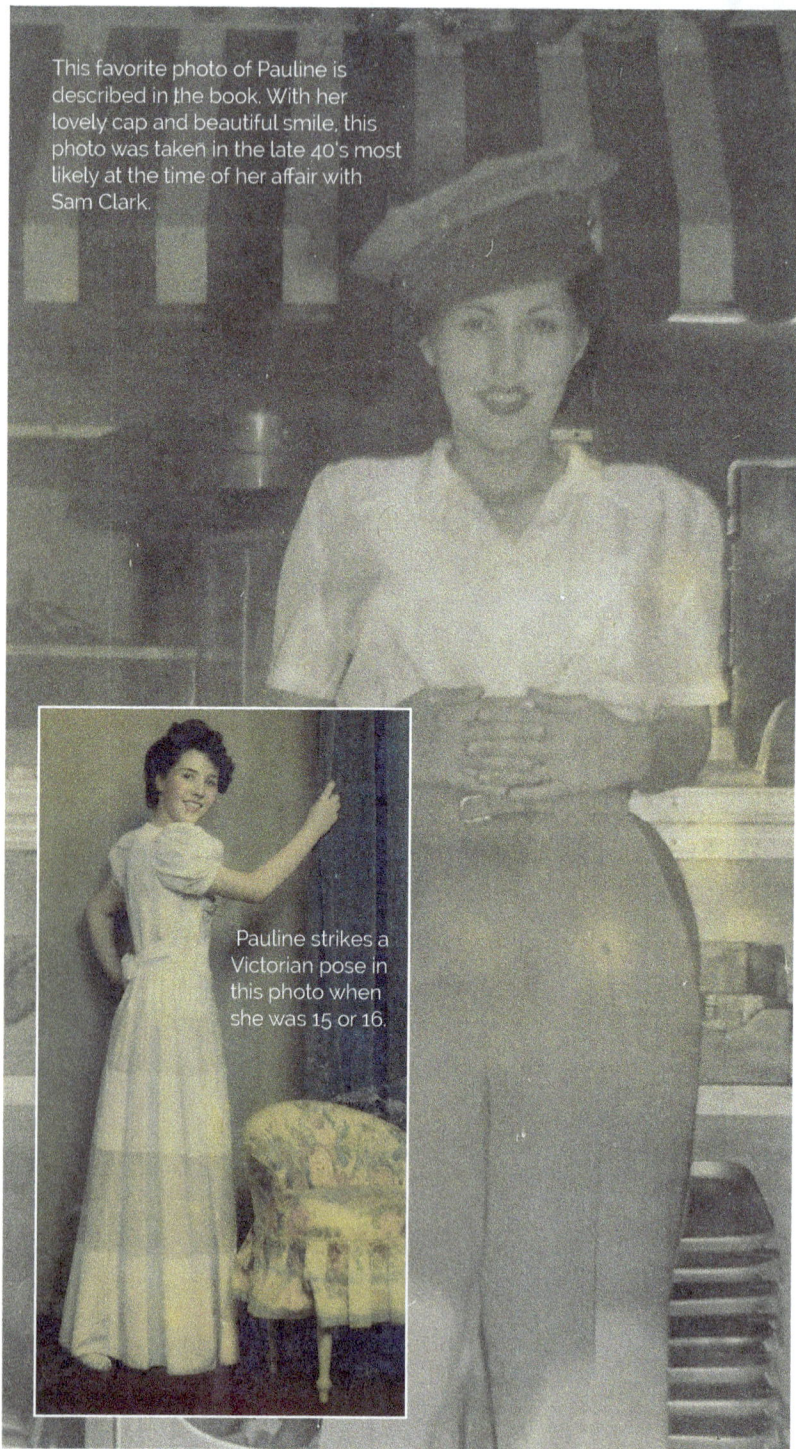

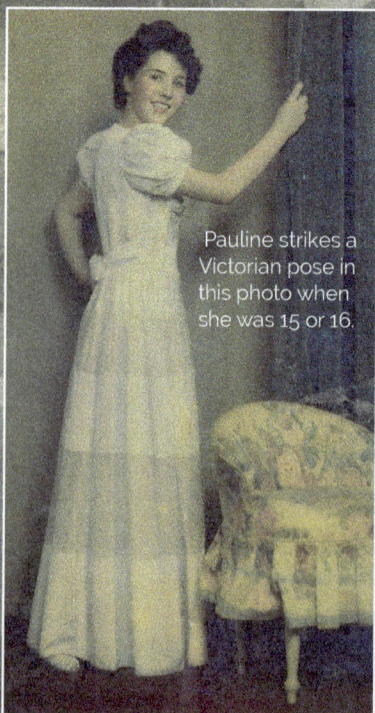

Pauline strikes a Victorian pose in this photo when she was 15 or 16.

With Ken Karnes on the left and Linda Sage. I was elated to meet them at our first meeting in 2002 in Davenport, Iowa.

Group photo on Mother's Day weekend in Davenport: In the back row, it was Kenny Karnes, Bill Sage and me (left to right). In the front row (left to right), it was Kenny's wife, Dee Karnes, my sister Linda, and my wife Rita.

The hat I was presented appropriately sat on my head at Dick's restaurant in Chicago.

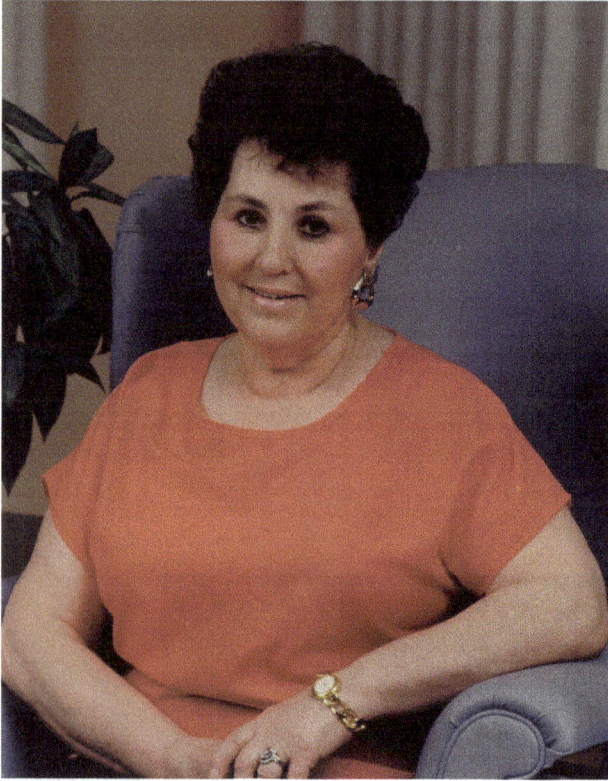

My birth mother, Pauline Karnes, is pictured.

Pauline and I are together on the night of our Passover Seder.

CATHOLIC
CHARITIES

December 29, 2016

Dear Pauline,

I am a counselor with Catholic Charities in Omaha, Nebraska. I am attempting to locate Pauline................, born in August of 1928. I am doing so at the request of a gentleman, born in April of 1946 in Omaha, Nebraska. I have some important information that I would like to share with you. Would you please contact me at your convenience? My number is ██████████ If you would happen to get my voicemail, please leave a message and I will return your call at a time that works well for you and to the number that you provide. Thank you very much.

Sincerely,

Sue Malloy
Program Director
Family Services

Linda and Bill found this letter from Catholic Charities in Pauline's mailbox the day after her funeral. This led to discovering Pauline's second secret.

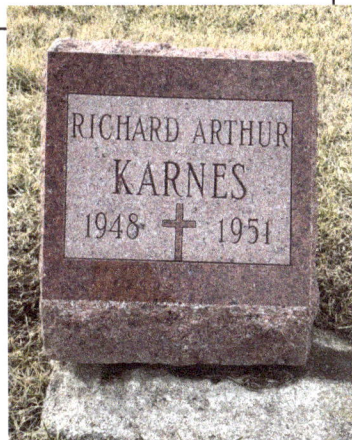

RICHARD ARTHUR
KARNES
1948 ✝ 1951

Because of the tragic death of Ricky Arthur, I would never know my brother.

157

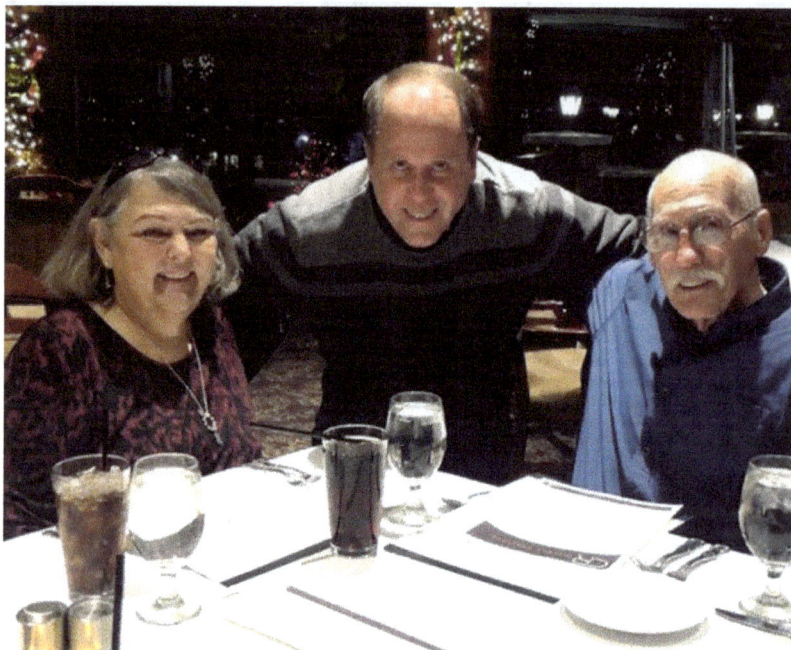

Rita and I first met Daniel Katskee over dinner.

Daniel Katskee and his wife
Peggy, is pictured.

This photo of Joseph Clark Sr. blew my mind. I knew instantly that he was my brother.

Joe and I first met outside of the famed Stanley Hotel in Estes Park, Colorado.

Another photo of the three amigos.

Patra and Tyrone Clark, August 2018. Our first day together in Estes Park, Co.

Tyrone, me and Joe (left to right) posed for this photo in Estes Park.

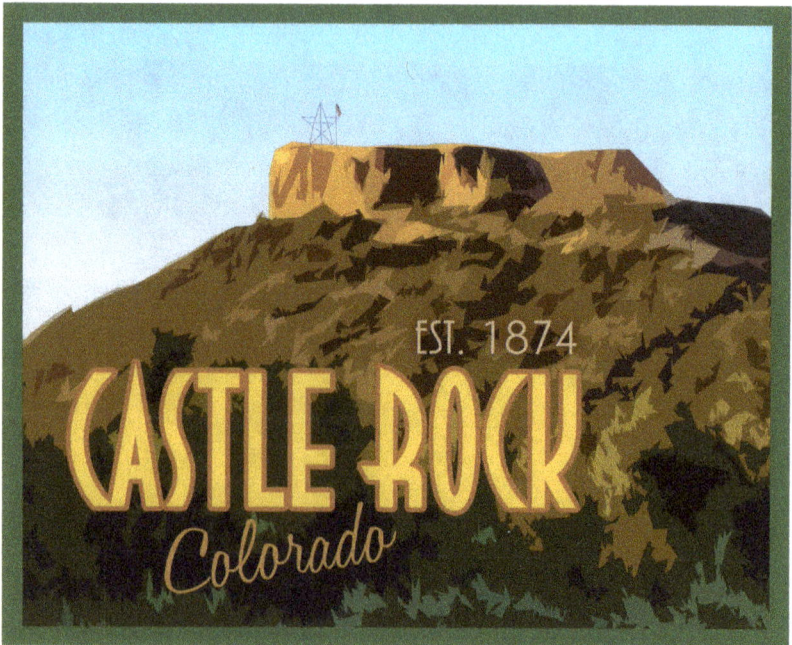

A artist's vision of Castle Rock, by Stacia Mann.

A smiling Sam posed in his work truck.

My birth father Sam Clark years later.

Sam always seems to be smiling, pictured at the time of his affair with Pauline Karnes.

Room 325-5
Name Boy Harris
Date of Birth 12/4/49 Time 3 40 PM
Birth Weight 8 Pounds 4 1/4 Ounces
Length 20 1/2
Doctor

ST CATHERINE'S HOSPITAL
OMAHA. NEB.

PET MILK

Compliments of The Pet Milk Company

3988B

Pauline 8-12-28
Sam Clark 26
Affld Missouri
5-11-180
High School
good heath - mechanical
Jolly, did not drink
Dark,

This card was placed in my bassinet at St. Catherine's Hospital. My name is on the front, and Sam's name is on the back, written in Pauline's own hand. The answers to my questions were hiding in plain sight.

Mom and Dad, Dorothy and Sol Yaffe.

I am pictured with my parents.

My sister Jane and I posed for this picture.

My daughter Angela, whose DNA matched Joe Clark Jr, with my grandson Edin Abenaim, who was with us when the bassinet card at JFS was turned over revealing the identity of my birth father.

Celebrating Rita's big birthday.

19

WHY ASK?
LAKE DELTON, WISCONSIN
2006

My parents would not have wanted me to write this book.

On a radiant July Sunday morning, I drove from Chicago to Lake Delton, Wisconsin, about a two-and-a-half-hour drive. Lake Delton is home to the famous Wisconsin Dells, a resort center and family getaway in the southern part of the state where I would be teaching a weeklong course on opera. The class was under the auspices of Elderhostel of America (today called Road Scholar). I had been an Elderhostel instructor for about 10 years, teaching opera classes for one week every summer. I was gratified that my courses always sold out and humbled by the number of returning students who came from across the country. Most attendees at these programs ranged from the curious and interested, to serious students of opera, to novices and retired musicians. The programs were for seniors older than 55 and the attendees were always active, engaged, and eager to learn and explore opera.

Wisconsin Dells is filled with kitschy and fun theme parks and entertainment centers, souvenir shops, and more. I was headed to the Perlstein Resort Center, the location of the Elderhostel program. Perlstein was a rustic vacationland/tourist trap nestled within a forest, overlooking Lake Delton. This truly beautiful and alluring place offered both solitude and easy access to the Dells.

My mood was bright and lively as I traveled north that morning. About halfway there, my father called. My initial thought was he was calling to check on me. However, it became quickly apparent he was not calling to check up on my trip. My mood changed abruptly, like a dark cloud passing across a full moon on a clear evening sky.

About a week before the Elderhostel trip, I spoke with my parents while on a weekend visit to Omaha. I had decided it was finally time to tell them about Pauline, Linda, and Kenny. It was time to tell them I had conducted a search for my biological family, and the search had achieved positive results. I had been living with my self-condemnation and remorse for too many years. How much information I was going to share would be determined by their reactions.

I didn't think they would be angry, and I hoped they would not be disappointed or hurt. I never wanted to dissatisfy my parents. I also couldn't get it out of my head that eventually someone was going to say something that would get back to them and they would be devastated. Better they should hear it from me.

My adoption had never been a secret in my family. I had wonderful parents who had provided for me, seen to my education, and did everything they could to ensure I had every opportunity to become a successful adult.

Shelly Kapnek Rosenberg, an adoptive parent and special needs consultant, states that some adoptees have endured difficulties and pain in living with and coming to terms with their adoptions. She cites several of these difficulties as identified by Deborah N. Silverstein, MSW, and Sharon Kaplan Roszia, co-author of *The Open Adoption Experience,* including issues of "loss and separation, rejection, guilt and shame, grief, identity, intimacy, and mastery/power."[1] These issues have presented challenges to thousands of adopted children. None of these challenges ever seemed to apply to me. I never had to confront any of these obstacles during my formative years or as an adult. This sense of stability and confidence is a testament to my parents who were always open with me regarding my adoption.

I had previously explained to my parents that I might someday seek information about my biological family for the reasons I have laid out. I was always sensitive to their feelings and explained that my curiosity really did not have anything to do with them. I was forever grateful to have them as my parents and for their love and support. Yet the answers to questions regarding my origins always remained elusive and out of reach until the spring of 2002 when Pauline, Linda, and Kenny became a part of my life.

Until I located my biological family, Rita and I both agreed, that in deference to the anticipated negative feelings and reactions of my parents, the search should never be discussed with them. Until 2002, there was never any reason to be forthcoming because the search was not only laboriously prolonged, but also had resulted in no solid information. There had been nothing to tell them.

Yet I put off telling my parents for another four years, and I could never escape my persistent feeling of dishonesty. I had been deceiving them since 1985, when I began the search. During trips to and from Omaha, my father would routinely call us while we were on the road, inquiring as to where we were. Inevitably, I would lie.

"Oh, we're almost home, about 15 miles to go," I would say. In reality, we would have just left Atlantic, 75 miles east of Omaha and over 300 miles from Chicago.

I had my share of conflicts with my parents, particularly with my mother while growing up. However, I never lied to them. They could always depend on my honesty, no matter what. The deceptions which began after making contact with my new family weighed heavily upon me every time we visited. It wasn't even so much lying about our location when we were in Atlantic; it was the information I now possessed that they knew nothing about. Every time I was in Atlantic, I felt I was betraying them. When I was in Omaha, I often felt mentally imprisoned, as if I was engaged in a private conspiracy of silence. At other times, I felt a sense of justification. My parents were well intentioned, but one self-justified truism never left me—I had the right to know the secrets of my birth origins. After all, who gave them the right to determine for me that my biological roots are not important? The secrets I searched for were the secrets of my existence.

Rita and I spent months discussing whether I should make a full and open disclosure to them. I could not escape the almost daily fear they would find out secondhand. That we had made contact with the family raised the possibility that a comment from any one of them to a friend or neighbor could somehow find its way back to my parents. The results would have been catastrophic. All of this weighed heavily on my conscience.

It was the week before my 2006 Elderhostel class when I decided my parents needed to know I had discovered my birth family. I had carried the secret long enough. I also recognized the need to be selective in what and how I told them. I would not lie to them, but I would not tell them everything. I would not even tell them Rita and I had met them much less that we had been carrying on a relationship with them over four years. I would offer them the opportunity to learn more information, but only if they wanted to. I hoped they would want to know more and ask for details. I thought I was handling this in the most sensitive manner possible. I could not have been more wrong.

The conversation took place as we stood in the narrow kitchen of their Omaha condominium. Rita and I decided she wouldn't be there. This was my responsibility, and I needed my parents to know that ultimately everything I had done had been my decision, uninfluenced by anyone else.

"Guys, there is something I want to discuss with you. It shouldn't be a big deal, but it is something I think you should know about," I said.

"OK," my mother replied. That was it. Dad said nothing at all. I clearly had their attention.

"Remember when I mentioned I had been interested in finding out who my natural parents were?" I asked, somewhat sheepishly.

"Yes," my mother replied. Silence. This was not going to get any easier.

"Well, I wanted you to know that I have found out information about my biological mother and her family."

They were waiting for me to continue my statement, as if my sentence had been broken off midstream.

"Well, I just wanted you to know that I did find out who they are, and I have spoken with them on a couple of occasions."

Silence as thick as a lead wall.

"Do they live here?" asked my mother, after an uncomfortably long silence.

"Not in Omaha but in a town in Iowa, fairly close to Omaha." I did not mention the name of the town or that it was only 75 miles east of Omaha. More silence. Long pause.

"It's not like I have a permanent or ongoing relationship with them, I just wanted to know who they were, to satisfy the curiosity I have harbored for years, maybe answer some questions about my medical history. That's it, nothing more."

I had moved from not telling my parents about my search to lying about it. I had never lied to my parents so blatantly. I didn't know where this conversation was going, but it wasn't going well.

"Have you met these people?" asked my mother. This was getting more difficult by the second.

"Rita and I met them, but that was pretty much it," was my answer. I desperately tried to give only minimal information and to avoid lying if possible. I remembered an old adage, "A lie is like a snowball; the longer it is rolled, the larger it is."

I paused, took a breath, then proceeded cautiously. "I just wanted to be upfront with you. If you want me to go further, I can share information with you, the names, the town where they live, and anything else you might want to know. Do you want me to keep going?"

"Not really," my mother replied. "We never knew, nor did we want any information at the time of your adoption. I have never known anything about them throughout your life, and I don't want to know anything now."

"Since they don't live too far from Omaha, I just did not want to run the risk that you might hear something from someone else. I

169

wanted you to know I had made contact and I wanted you to hear it from me. I also want you to know this had nothing to do with you guys. I wanted to know my birth origins, to be able to answer some basic questions, like medical information, the circumstances under which I was born and why I was put up for adoption, and so on."

My dad asked, "Are they good people? Nice people?"

"Oh, absolutely," I answered quickly.

My palms were sweating, and my heart was racing. My parents were clearly uncomfortable and I needed to bring closure to the conversation. I also wanted to offer them a way out.

"I want you both to know that I didn't want you to think I was in any way ungrateful or that there is or ever was something missing in my life. Nor was I looking for a new mom and dad. You raised me, and gave me everything I could ever have wanted. I only wanted to fill in the blanks, know my origins, try to find out my medical history, learn if I had any blood relatives, find out why I was given up and how I came to be adopted by you. If you wish, I won't discuss this again with either of you."

Mom said that was fine with her. She firmly reiterated that she had no desire to learn the details then and had no desire to learn of them now. Dad didn't say anything; he just looked on.

"You do understand why I did this, and you understand this does not have anything to do with my relationship or love for either of you? It was only my curiosity and desire to answer these questions that led me to do this search. Those were my only motivations." I was starting to ramble.

My father replied, "Sure, we understand." The one thing I knew was that they did not understand.

That was it. No questions about any of the new family I met, no names, how many times we had met, how many siblings or anything else. Not even any medical information I may have discovered. They really did not want to know anything.

I thought having this conversation was the right decision. I did not tell them Rita and I had established ongoing personal relationships with them. The conversation had not gone as I had hoped, but probably, all things considered, as well as I could have or at least should have expected. I was disappointed they had not asked even a single question, but I had to accept that they did not want to know any more information in 2006 than they did in 1949.

A week later, I took the call from my father on my way to Wisconsin.

"Hi, Dad," I cheerfully answered.

"You on your way to Elderhostel?" he asked.

"Yes, looking forward to it as always." A few of the usual questions followed, what am I teaching, how many participants, when are you back home, etc.

At first, I thought this was just a routine conversation. My dad usually wore his emotions on his sleeve. He loved making conversation. He was very proud of his family. He would call me nearly every day and would always ask questions about work, what course I was teaching, the weather, or just anything. On this day, it was clear he had an agenda, something specific he wanted to discuss.

"Your mother and I have been talking, and there's something I want to ask you." I knew this could not be good.

"OK, what is it?" I asked.

"Last week, you told your mom and I that you had located your biological family." I hadn't expected this conversation again.

"Yes." I paused, unsure of what to expect.

"You also said that you had made contact with them."

"Yes, I made contact on the maternal side, not the paternal." I was being careful not to use mother and father terminology, "mother's side, father's side." I did not want to sound like I was personalizing the situation or was in any way referring to these people as Mom and Dad. I was trying to keep this as dry and impersonal as I could. The conversation would be a repeat of last week's conversation. I was no longer focused on the lovely day or the upcoming Elderhostel.

"We were just wondering why you decided to tell us this?" It was more of a statement than a question. He was clearly upset.

"Because I never wanted to do this behind your backs. I felt it was time I shared the information with you, if you were interested. After all, you have always told me you knew next to nothing about the circumstances of my birth. I felt it was wrong that I now had information and had not shared it with you. I just thought you might want to know some of the details," I responded.

"We just wondered why you would want to bother other people, another family, to intrude in their lives in that way?" Again, more of an accusation than a question.

"Well, Dad, I can tell you they are nice people, and they do not see this as an intrusion," Of course I knew, at least as far as Pauline was concerned, it had been a monumental and traumatic intrusion, to say the least.

The conversation had become disconcerting and uncomfortable. All my fears of telling my parents were being realized. I was practically driving on autopilot as I approached Milwaukee.

"Well, I did get to meet them. As I said, they were very nice people. It's not like we are going to be seeing them on a regular basis (untrue). We just wanted to meet them, to introduce ourselves, to see if there is someone in the world who looks like me. I wanted to learn what I could about my medical history and the circumstances of my birth."

It was the best answer I could come up with. I was struggling.

"Why did you feel the need to do this," he asked. "Why did you have to ask?"

"As I said, I wanted to know my medical history. This is information you would never have been able to provide me with," I offered. I kept returning to my medical history, or lack thereof. This seemed to be the safest explanation I thought my father would understand.

After all, who does not want to know their medical history and be able to fill out a medical history form at the doctor's office?

Then came the hammer blow.

"Well, your mom was very hurt and upset. Was there something missing in your life? Did we not provide enough for you? Were we not good enough for you?"

There it was. Words I had never wanted to hear. Spoken as plainly and succinctly as they could be. I could hear the pain I had caused. This was the most difficult conversation I had ever had with my father. I had so wanted to avoid the lack of understanding and the hurt feelings of my parents. How do I explain to them that my search really had nothing to do with them? Although I knew this discussion would eventually take place, I was still not prepared for or had expected that this discussion with my father would take this direction. My mother had never been a very emotional person. That this conversation had so upset her wounded me to my very core.

I tried to assure him that they had indeed given me everything I could ever have wanted.

"Dad, this is exactly what I did not want to happen. Everything I am I owe to you and Mom. Please understand, I was not looking for a new mom and dad. They will never fill the role of the parents you have been to me. I only have one set of parents, and that will never change. I only wanted answers to understand the circumstances of my birth and subsequent adoption.

"I wanted to know my medical history and learn the circumstances of how I came to be adopted. I told you because I did not want to do this behind your backs. I felt you had a right to know. I did not want you to feel this way, and I feel terrible that you do."

My voice quivered. I feared that I had permanently damaged my relationship with my parents.

I reiterated that I was not seeking a permanent relationship with these people, and what I had told them was all there was to know. I finally promised I would not bring up the subject again, especially with Mom. That was the end of the conversation. We talked about other subjects, none of which I remember. It didn't matter. The damage was done, and I had inflicted it.

I kept my promise that I would never bring the subject up again. My parents and I never spoke of my adoption again. My father died in 2008, and my mother passed away in 2015. Despite what I thought were the right reasons at the time, I now realize discussing my adoption search with them was a mistake.

Finding out everything about my birth parents was just learning about me, enabling me to finally answer the question, "Who am I?" My parents could not understand this, and I could not understand why. What I did know was that I could not repair the hurt. I would have to live with the consequences. I often wondered whether they ever thought about our conversation again. Years later, my sister Jane told me that Mom told her about that kitchen conversation, and they had both been deeply hurt by it. Neither of my parents ever mentioned my adoption to me again, and there were no discernable changes in our relationship.

Rita thought my parents had successfully put the entire matter out of their minds. "I don't believe they ever gave it another thought," she would tell me on more than one occasion. I'm not so sure, but I tried to find solace in the hope they had put the conversation out of their minds.

To my parents, an adopted child is no different than a biological child. Just as my adoptive parents never knew my biological origins, they thought I also had no need to know those origins. They felt contacting my biological family had to mean something was missing in my relationship with them. What they could not understand was that I had the right to know my biological origins. They were my origins after all. I was the one who could never fill out a medical form, not them. The fact I desired this information did not mean there was some psychological distance between my parents and me. Unfortunately, there were no words in which I could successfully make them understand my feelings and the dilemma I felt over the years. I wish I had handled it differently.

*****

1   Shelley Kapnek Rosenberg, *Adoption and the The Jewish Family*, Jewish Publication Society, quoting Deborah N. Silverstein, MSW, and Sharon Kaplan Roszia, 1998, p.29

20

———

A CHANCE ENCOUNTER
OMAHA
2007

The fortuitous encounter was brought about through a series of unrelated events.

In Omaha, June means one thing only: the College World Series (CWS). The NCAA Division I National Baseball Championship tournament has been held in Omaha since 1950. The tournament was held at the old Rosenblatt stadium in South Omaha until 2010, when it moved to the newly built TD Ameritrade Park in downtown Omaha. The old stadium was completed in 1948 and became the host for the annual eight-team, double-elimination tournament from 1950-2010, when the stadium was replaced. Named after a former mayor of Omaha, Rosenblatt Stadium was for a time the largest minor league stadium in the country.[1]

The old stadium was just blocks away from the former St. Catherine's Hospital, where I was born, and across the street from the Henry Doorly Zoo, one of the top-rated zoos in the world.

The CWS helped weave the fabric of my youth. I spent every June at that old ballpark with friends watching hundreds of college teams vying for the championship. In my memory, the games will always be associated with euphoric times, the end of elementary school and the start of summer vacation. Yes, there was summer camp, family driving trips, the smell of lilacs and peonies (my favorite fragrances)—but first, CWS marked the official start of summer.

My father's business, N.S. Yaffe Printing Company (the "N" was for my paternal grandfather Nathan and no one knows what the "S" stood for, if anything), printed the game programs. He and his brother Irv had owned box seats over the third base dugout since the series' first year in Omaha.

Each year, I would sneak the 15-cent program into the first game so no one would question how I had a program before I got into the stadium! My oldest friend Gary Colick and I would arrive early in the morning and spend the entire day at the ballpark. We would watch as many as four games a day, eat at the nearby Zesto (an outdoor food and ice cream stand) and visit friends. It was a time of simple innocence, childhood pleasures, and great fun.

In June 2007, Rita and I stayed at my parent's condo in Omaha. We planned on attending a couple of CWS games. Gary, who lives in Phoenix, had flown into town with his son and planned to attend a game with us. This trip marked a rare occasion when Rita and I flew from Chicago to Omaha instead of driving. We invited Linda and Bill to join us for the Saturday afternoon game as well. It would be the first time we had ever introduced Linda and Bill to any of our friends. The plan was to meet Gary and his son at the stadium to attend the game followed by dinner. One of my parents' two cars was in the repair shop. They were not planning to leave the house that Saturday, so they had no problem with us taking their second car to the game and dinner. The weather created a perfect day for a baseball game. All was good.

Rita, Linda, Bill, and I sat together behind third base. I was using my parents' season tickets, as I had hundreds of times before. Gary and his son were a few rows away. He was enthralled to meet my biological sister, and it was indeed an extraordinary experience to introduce Linda to my oldest friend.

After the game, we all arrived at an Italian restaurant. Rita, ahead of the rest of us, headed through the restaurant doors. She stopped and exclaimed "Fuck!"

"Bob, come here, come here!" she implored. "YOUR PARENTS ARE HERE!" The words didn't register. Not possible, I thought. Their car was in the garage for repairs, and we had their other car. The restaurant was miles from their condo. They were staying home. What was Rita talking about? She had to be mistaken. I looked at her, questioningly. Her eyes were streaked with tears.

I looked across the restaurant. My parents were about 15 feet in front of us with another couple.

Linda sheepishly asked me, "Are your parents here?" Indeed, they were. My first thought was to back out of the restaurant before they could see us. But it was too late. When I looked from Linda to the table where my parents sat, they were both staring at us. Rita actually started to laugh, hysterically and nervously, laughing and crying at the same time. Had all our efforts to ensure my parents never found out just come to a screeching halt?

We couldn't get away, and my parents were looking directly at us, surprise on their faces. Gary and his son were looking on, unwitting participants in this unfolding drama.

We quickly asked the hostess for a table on the other side of a wall from where my parents were sitting. At least they would not be able to see us from there. Linda and Bill made a beeline for the table while Rita, Gary, and I headed to my parents' table. Once rational thought returned, I knew once again I would have to lie, make up some story about who Linda and Bill were. I certainly could not just bring Linda over to their table and say, "Mom, Dad, this is Linda, my biological sister." Of course, my parents would not have known who Linda and Bill were in any event, but rational thought had deserted me.

After greeting them, they spoke briefly to Gary whom they had not seen in some time. My mother had been friends with Gary's mother for many years before her death. I told them how surprised I was to see them here since they had said they were staying home and had no car.

Mom explained that while we were at the game, the friends they were with at the restaurant called them and invited them out to dinner. Because they didn't have a car, their friends offered to pick them up, and here they are. Out of the hundreds of restaurants in Omaha, we had chosen the same one!

My emotions swirled, and I had an immediate if not irrational fear that our secret was about to be exposed. It had only been a year since they had made it crystal clear to me they did not want any information about my biological family and were resentful I had even pursued it. Now here I was with my birth sister, just inches from my parents. I felt like a spouse about to be exposed as a cheater. I knew the hurt my parents would feel if they knew who was with me in the restaurant.

After this exchange, we joined Linda and Bill at our table on the other side of the wall. Rita was still in shock. Linda was also visibly upset and nervous. She never expected she would ever come face to face with my parents. Bill was a calming influence, especially to Linda. Gary and his son Zachary absorbed the situation. I desperately wanted this to be over soon. It was not.

As we waited for our order, Rita suddenly covered her mouth. I could hear what she said. "Incoming." She repeated it several times, and I looked toward the front of the restaurant. My dad was making his way to our table. He was standing next to me before I had a chance to think about what I would say.

In his always friendly tone, he asked, "So who are your friends here? I don't think we have met."

"Dad, this is Linda and Bill Sage. They are friends from Atlantic, Iowa. They went with us to the game this afternoon," I intoned as innocently as I could.

My dad, "Hello, nice to meet you." To me, "So how do you know the Sages?" This was not getting easier.

"Bill is the Sheriff of Cass County, Iowa. We crossed paths back when I was in the County Attorney's Office and have been friends since. We invited them to the game and to dinner along with Gary and Zachary."

I knew this answer was lame. I was never a good liar. It must have seemed odd to my dad that I had never mentioned these people. I had also been out of the County Attorney's Office for 20 years! I thought my explanation was foolish, but it was all I could come up with. Dad seemed OK with it and after small talk headed back to his table. My parents finished their meal and left with their friends without stopping by. I left the restaurant feeling utterly deflated. I had once again lied to my parents, and this time the Sages were part of the deception. None of us felt good leaving the restaurant.

When Rita and I arrived at my parents' house later that evening, I was a bit more relaxed. I felt we had dodged a bullet. When rational thought returned, I knew there was no way they could have ever guessed the true identities of Linda and Bill. As we got ready for bed, there was a knock at our door.

"Bob, are you up?" my dad asked.

"Yes, what's going on?" I replied.

"Your mom and I would like to speak with you in the bedroom. Do you have a minute?"

"Sure, I'll be right there." My heart was in my throat. They had to know I lied to them and the other shoe was about to drop. If they asked, I would have to tell them the truth. I couldn't make up another lie. I was in turmoil.

I went into their bedroom and waited.

Mom stood next to a large antique flat desk at one side of the room. Dad stood next to the large king-size bed. Over the bed was a charcoal drawing of my father when he was three years old. He wore what looks like a dress and a shawl, as was the custom in 1914. His bangs covered his tiny forehead. The portrait is one of our family's treasured possessions, having been drawn by William Schwartz, an artist of some prominence whose works are displayed to this day in some New York galleries. Schwartz had been a friend of my grandfather in Russia before they both emigrated to America.

It looked like mom had just finished writing a check. She held it and walked over to me. I realized I had been holding my breath and began to slowly exhale. She handed me the check and my dad said, "We just wanted you to have a little extra money to cover your expenses. This will cover your trip to Omaha and will help out with things." She handed me a check for $500.

This moment is seared in my memory. Never was the guilt I felt over this entire search more intense and overpowering than at that moment. I was flooded with both love and guilt. They were giving me money after I had engaged in a total deception just a couple of hours earlier. They did not suspect they had met my flesh and blood, the subject of whom had caused them pain a year ago. I felt disconsolate and utterly disheartened as I sheepishly left the bedroom, check in hand.

As I lay in bed, I felt dishonest and demoralized. At the same time, I was gratified that the Sages had become such important people in our lives. The Sages are good, warm, accepting people and I could not condemn myself for devoting more than 20 years of my life to finding them. Once again, conflicted emotions. My relationship with my parents would endure, but I would have to accept that I have withheld this most significant aspect of my life from them. Why did I feel so badly about all of this? The guilt I felt over the years by withholding information about my search had reached a new plateau.

Knowing my parents' backstory will better illustrate the people they were and explain the guilt I felt for deceiving them all those years.

In most ways, my parents had not changed since my adoption. Dorothy and Sol, as described in the caseworker files, are the parents I came to respect and love. My father rarely spoke about himself. But he did give a video interview to the Jewish Historical Society of Omaha in 2004 when he was 93. I discovered the interview existed only a couple of years ago and secured a recording. I learned a great deal about his character from that 30-minute discussion.

My dad's parents came over from Russia in the early years of the 20th century. They were part of the European wave of immigrants seeking a better life in this country. His father was engaged when he arrived and married soon after leaving Ellis Island. My grandfather Nathan started a printing business in Omaha in 1906 with $50. My dad was a high school athlete, lettering in track, football and basketball. His first two years were at Omaha's famed Central High School, where he was the quarterback on the football team. He transferred to Omaha Tech High after his second year at Central because they offered instruction in the printing business, which he felt would be useful to him in his father's business.

My dad was the Omaha city handball champion and won two matches in the national tournament in Chicago, missing the quarterfinals by one match. He played golf until he couldn't see the hole any longer ("someone had to stand in front of the hole so I could see it") but expressed pride in his ability to shoot his age until he finally had to stop playing in his late 70s.

He loved working his entire life at the family business, Yaffe Printing Company. He planned to attend college after one year at the company but instead stayed for 56 years.

He met my mom at the old JCC in Omaha. "Very smart girl, pretty too," my father said with a smile. My dad and mom were married in 1942. Dad had finished Army boot camp and was on his way to Virginia for officer candidate school. While back in Omaha, he married my mom. He wore his uniform to the wedding. During the video interview, he described his marriage in two words, "always great."

Dad served four years and was released after World War II, retiring as a captain. He was assigned to the Army quartermaster corps during the war and was in command of 200 troops, most of them black. He landed on Omaha Beach shortly after the Normandy invasion, but he could "still hear the bombs flying over our heads."

Once when he was on a bivouac with his troops in some remote town in the middle of Texas, they stopped at a local restaurant and were told that the black soldiers were not allowed to eat there. Dad said to the owner, "To hell with this! These soldiers are fighting for your country. They need to eat." The restaurant owner wouldn't let them in.

After the incident, he wrote a letter "through army channels" complaining of the outrageous racist behavior of the restaurant owner. He soon was called to the headquarters where he was thrust into a room with colonels and a general.

"These guys are fighting for their country. The least we can do is send a wagon so they can have food like everyone else."

The army complied, wagons were sent, and the troops under his command were able to eat good food, not just the army rations they would have been stuck with otherwise.

This story succinctly demonstrates my father's character. I don't believe he had a prejudiced bone in his body. I proudly wore his captain bars when I served in the Army JAG Corps. No one I knew ever had a negative thing to say about him.

My parents were good people who devoted their lives to Jane and me. Despite that I knew my search for my biological origins was for me the right thing to do, I was dismayed that I may have hurt them and felt guilty about the deception over those years.

When we returned to Chicago, the entire restaurant incident weighed so heavily on my mind that I decided to speak to the rabbi of the synagogue where I worked as executive director. (I had recently taken a new position in Chicago as Executive Director of a large conservative synagogue). I told him of the dilemma, the conflict and the guilt I was feeling. He spoke of *"Shalom ba-Bayit,"* Hebrew for peace in the home. He also invoked the Fifth Commandment, "Honor Your Father and Mother." He said there are certain occasions when it may be acceptable to lie, including keeping peace in the home. There was no compelling reason to tell my parents something I knew as a certainty would cause pain to them both.

There is a debate described in the Talmud over the question, "What words should people call out as they dance in front of a bride?" The Talmud is the central text of Rabbinic Judaism and the primary source of Jewish law and theology. One school argued that one should always declare, "What a beautiful and gracious bride." The other school argues that one should speak the truth, no matter what. That school cites Exodus 23:7, "Keep far from a false charge." It appears the most favored answer is, "What a beautiful and gracious bride." Every bride wants to be assured she looks beautiful on her wedding day, and it would inflict unnecessary pain to tell her otherwise.

Noted lecturer and bestselling author Rabbi Joseph Telushkin once wrote: "Where one's goal is to avoid inflicting gratuitous emotional pain on another, Jewish law becomes remarkably tolerant of half-truths and 'white lies.'"[2] He cites two examples.

"Genesis 18 records the visit of three angels to Abraham and Sarah, at a time when Abraham was ninety-nine years old and his wife, eighty-nine. The angels tell Abraham that within the year Sarah will give birth. Listening nearby, Sarah laughs to herself, saying: 'Now that I am withered, am I to have enjoyment, with my husband so old?'"

In the next verse, God asks Abraham: "Why did Sarah laugh, saying, 'Shall I bear a child, old as I am?'" (Genesis 18:12-13). Telushkin points out that in God's response to Sarah He leaves out Sarah's reference to Abraham being "so old," presumably out of concern that such a comment might hurt Abraham. Based upon this passage, the Talmud concludes: "Great is peace, seeing that for its sake even God modified the truth."[3]

Telushkin also cites a well-known *midrash* (rabbinic commentary on a biblical text) in which Aaron, Moses' older brother and the High Priest, chose to make peace between two feuding parties and to do so lied to achieve it.

"When two men had quarreled, Aaron would go and sit with one of them and say, 'My son, see what your friend is doing! He beats his breast and tears his clothes and moans, 'Woe is me!'" "How can I lift my eyes and look my companion in the face? I am ashamed before him, since it is I who treated him foully." Aaron would sit with him until he had removed all anger from his heart. Aaron then sat with the other man and told him essentially the same thing he told the first man. "Later when the two met, they would embrace and kiss each other."[4]

Telushkin concludes, "The Rabbis endorse Aaron's behavior, not because Jewish law approves of lying per se—it does not—*but because it recognizes that in cases where peace and truth conflict, peace should sometimes take precedence."* (emphasis added)[5]

Telushkin succinctly summarizes these examples. "Thus, from Judaism's perspective, truth is a very important value but not an absolute one."[6]

Did all of this make me feel better? Maybe a little. It helped to know I had Jewish law and tradition on my side. I would live with it. I could think of no circumstance in which telling my parents the truth as to Linda's identity had even the remotest possibility of a positive result. I could not tell them who they actually met in the restaurant, especially after the discussion in their kitchen a year before. Nevertheless, conscience is a powerful force, and mine bothered me still. The encounter in the restaurant haunts me to this day.

One thing I knew for sure. I had found my maternal birth family. Perhaps someday I would locate my paternal family as well. But I knew I could never call anyone but Dorothy and Sol my mom and dad. This issue of title would become a disruptive issue in my relationship with Pauline.

*****

1   In 2012, Rosenblatt Stadium was torn down and the new TD Ameritrade Park was opened in 2011, becoming the new home to the CWS.

2   Joseph Telushkin, *Words That Hurt, Words That Heal*, (New York: William Morrow and Company, Inc. 1996), p. 138

3   Ibid., p. 138, citing Babylonian Talmud, *Yevamot*, 65b, p.138

4   Ibid., pp. 138-139

5   Ibid., p. 139

6   Ibid., p. 140

21

MOTHER'S DAY DILEMMA
2008–2016

It was sometime after Mother's Day 2008 when Linda casually mentioned Pauline was unhappy with me.

"Why?" I asked.

"Because you did not send her a Mother's Day card," she replied.

"But why was she expecting one from me?" This was not the most well thought out question I could have asked.

"Because she is your mother, and after six years, it would be a nice gesture to her," Linda explained.

Linda was correct. It would have been a nice gesture—more than a nice gesture. I could have acknowledged Pauline was my mother, which, of course, she was. But I couldn't bring myself to send a Hallmark card. Since finding Pauline, I had always called her "Pauline."

The situation was complicated. Pauline's feelings about me had evolved over the years from refusal to meet me to eventual acceptance that led to genuine affection and perhaps more. Now she wanted me to accept her as my mother. She wanted me to call her "Mother," as she began occasionally referring to me as "Son." She told us she was grateful Rita and I had come into her life. She wanted us to be there for Linda and Kenny. Pauline was a highly sensitive woman who felt she had been mistreated by the religious community, but somehow, I had come back and perhaps in some way had afforded her closure and maybe helped to complete her life. She knew her decision to have me placed in a Jewish home was correct. Now the forgotten son had returned, her kids were understanding and everything would be copacetic.

When it came to Linda and Kenny, I had no dilemma about calling them brother and sister. I did it from the beginning. I have never referred to them as half brother or half sister. I never felt this was disloyal to my sister Jane. After all, one can have numerous siblings. But whatever Pauline expected of me, I could never call her Mom. I would refer to her as Pauline or my birth mother. I had made many uncomfortable adjustments over the years regarding my parents. Yet I was enjoying a meaningful relationship with Linda, Kenny, and Pauline.

Even though I had come to love Pauline over the years, I could not love her in the same way I loved my mom and dad. Dorothy and Sol Yaffe had raised me, nourished me and devoted much of their lives to me. Pauline had become an important person in my life. She was the woman who gave me life after all, but she could not be my mom. Sending dual Mother's Day cards was a step over the precipice—I couldn't do it.

Author, therapist, and adoption counselor Holly van Gulden wrote:

"A successful inner reunion allows the adoptee to integrate both the heritage family and the adoptive family and not to reject either one. The adoptee doesn't have to act on the heritage. 'It's not who I am, it's who I would have been,' one adoptee explains."[1]

For me, understanding my past profoundly enhanced my love and respect for my parents.

At some point, Pauline stopped talking to me. There was no defining moment or incident. It just happened. We were still visiting Linda and Bill in Atlantic, but communication with Pauline was filtered through Linda. My relationship with Linda did not seem to be affected. It may even have been strengthened. This drifting apart continued for two or three years. Rita would often encourage me to call Pauline, but I somehow couldn't do it. Pauline knew when we would come into town; she would hear it through Linda. I should have called her and tried to discuss my feelings and attempt to better understand hers. I sincerely regret I did not.

My father died in March 2008. It was a difficult time. It seemed my parents had been blessed with good genes. Dad was 97 years old and had lived a good life. He was totally devoted to my mother and to Jane and me. He was the most genial and kindest person I have ever known. He had not a bad thing to say about anyone, ever, and that's not an exaggeration. I cannot recall him ever raising his voice to me, and he most assuredly had many appropriate opportunities to do so. At the end of the 30-minute video interview he gave to the Jewish Historical Society of Omaha, Dad looked directly at the camera, and said, "I love you; I'll always love you, and if you ever need anything, I'll be right there."

I regret he never approved of me searching for my biological family, and I was profoundly hurt the one time I tried to explain it during that terrible meeting in their kitchen. This was a self-inflicted pain that I live with to this day.

My dad was a unique man. I think often of his story about standing up for his troops in the face of racial prejudice and my pride when I proudly wore his captain bars on my uniform while serving in the Army JAG Corps. Only a few months prior to my father's passing, Rita lost her father. Both of us losing parents in one year made for a distressing but reflective time. May both of their memories be for blessings.

Gradually, my relationship with Pauline returned to the pre-Mother's Day period when we first met. Again, there was no specific moment; things just evolved. We began talking again, and we visited her regularly on our visits to Atlantic. I never sent her a Mother's Day card, but I did send flowers, made sure to call her and gradually saw the relationship restored.

———

And life goes on. During the next several years, I served as executive director of two Chicago synagogues, one conservative and one reform. Rita continued to work for The Packaging House, the company she worked for 15 years before retiring.

During one visit to Atlantic, Pauline presented us with a set of cookware. She had recently purchased three sets to give to each of her children, me included. The white cookware had oblong green leaves with yellow and red dots throughout the design. She wanted to be very clear she had given the exact same sets to Linda and Kenny, explaining how important it was to her that each of us have the same cookware, as if these items somehow served to symbolically bind us together. It was a tender and heartfelt gesture, and we use the cookware to this day.

Our relationship continued to grow stronger. I believe that over the years Pauline became more comfortable with our relationship. Linda and I formed a close bond. We called each other often. Rita, too, established close relations with the family. She spoke to Pauline quite often, usually more than I did. When we were together with Linda and Bill, Rita and Linda could have been mistaken for sisters.

From the day we first spoke to Pauline until the day of her death, the identity of my birth father was off limits. She would sometimes speak *of* him, but without disclosing his identity. For reasons of her own, she told us she would take his identity to her grave. I wasn't sure if this was out of respect for her husband's memory or from a fear that we might search him out and disrupt his family, much as she perceived we had disrupted hers. Whatever the reason, I knew not to bring up the subject and never did.

On the other hand, Pauline was more than willing to reminisce about her Jewish upbringing. She would still mention the "Jewish" foods she remembered from her youth. Rita and I would usually bring *challah* or matzo ball soup from a deli in Chicago. She was genuinely happy when we did, and we brought Jewish food often. When Pauline was feeling reflective, she asked me to promise I would say a Jewish prayer at her funeral. Her desire was to be buried, in her words, "as Jewishly as possible." I was deeply moved, and I made the commitment to her that day. It was a promise I would keep.

My mother, Dorothy, passed away in November 2015. She, like my dad, was 97. Mom was very different from my dad. She was stern and could be tough, but she was as committed to Jane and me as was my dad. After suffering what was considered a debilitative heart attack in the early '60s, she returned to college at Omaha

University (now the University of Nebraska at Omaha) and received her master's degree in speech pathology. It was quite unusual for women to go back to school then and enter the workforce. She ran the speech pathology clinic at Omaha's Methodist Hospital, and while there, she founded the Omaha Stroke Club, whose mission was to help stroke victims regain their speech.

After my mom's death, I was approached by a woman at Beth El Synagogue who told me about her deceased father, who, many years ago, had had a debilitating stroke. She told me she remembered my mother coming to their house numerous times, working with her father to regain his speech. She told me, with a hint of emotion, how my mother had changed her father's life. The story overwhelmed me. I never knew how my mother had brightened the lives of people, and I am sorry I was never able to tell her how proud it made me feel to know that she helped others. Since her death, I have heard similar stories from others.

My mother taught about the importance of education and to strive for the best. I was truly blessed to have these wonderful people as parents. Pauline, in giving me up for adoption, wanted the very best for me. I'm grateful that during her lifetime she was able to learn she had succeeded beyond her expectations.

Pauline's health began to decline in 2015. She was diabetic and Linda and Kenny agreed it was becoming more and more difficult for her to live independently. In 2015, she suffered a stroke that crippled her left leg. She left her home and became a resident of Atlantic Specialty Care. From the beginning, she thought she would be there for a short stay and then return home. The rest of us knew she would not be leaving.

*****

1   Shelley Kapnek Rosenberg, *Adoption and the Jewish Family*, The Jewish Publication Society, 1998, quoting Holly Van Gulden p.79

22

GOD'S WAITING ROOM ATLANTIC
2017

Florida is often referred to as God's Waiting Room. The huge number of elderly people and corresponding nursing homes makes this an unfortunate reality for this state. The Atlantic Specialty Care nursing home in Iowa gives full credence to this sardonic joke. Pauline spent the last year and a half of her life there from mid-2015 until her death in January 2017.

God's waiting rooms seem to come in many shapes and sizes. Unfortunately, I have visited family members and friends in a variety of them. In Toledo, a friend dying of brain cancer had a lovely room with a beautiful view of trees and vegetation. The Rose Blumkin Jewish Home in Omaha has a lobby that resembles a small town, complete with storefronts reminiscent of a Hollywood movie set, detailed facades with signage named after businesses that once lined the downtown streets of Omaha.

The entire lobby is picture perfect. Every Friday, it is transformed into a New York-style deli that is open to the community. This popular lunch spot serves as a popular pre-*Shabbat* gathering place for the Jewish community. Until you visit the residents' section, you would never know you were in a nursing home.

Both my parents spent their last days at the Blumkin Home. To this day, it is hard to separate feelings of sadness and approaching death from the lively and cheerful atmosphere on a Friday at lunchtime with community members gathering for companionship and a deli lunch. I remember when my father was there near the end of his life. Dementia had set in, and he was no longer able to live at home with my mother. Rita and I would frequently visit him in his Blumkin Home private room. I don't believe he ever truly understood where he was living. In the early evening, when it came time to leave, Dad would ask where we were all going for dinner.

"Dad, it's time for us to leave."

"I'm hungry, where are we going for dinner?"

"Well, you have to stay, this is where you are living now," I would answer.

"I don't understand why I can't go with you," he would reply.

These painful and heartbreaking conversations came from this man who had lived an exemplary life of compassion, kindness, love, and understanding. We would leave him sitting on the edge of his bed, night after night. Dad had a particular phone habit I found annoying. I would call him just to check up on him. The conversation would go like this:

"Hi Dad, how are you doing?"

"Great! Hey, your Uncle ---or Aunt--- or friend (whoever happened to be there) is over here. You haven't talked to him/her in a while, say hello!"

"Dad, wait a second." He had already left the phone before I could take a breath. I really didn't want to talk to anyone else but my father.

In the background, "Bob's on the phone, he'd love to talk to you."

"Dad, DAD!!"

"Hi Bob, good to talk to you."

Well, that was my dad.

This habit took a heartbreaking twist during his last days in the home. I called him at least once every day while he was at the Blumkin Home. One evening, as we were about to say goodnight, he asked if I wanted to talk to my mother.

I said, "Dad, is she still there with you? I thought she would have gone home earlier." It would have been unusual for Mom to have been with him at the Blumkin Home that late in the evening.

He would always want me to speak with Mom whenever I spoke to him. Before we ended a call, he would inevitably say, "Here … let me put on your mother."

"No, she's here, probably in the kitchen, let me call her," he said, in the same tone of voice he had used thousands of times before.

"Dorothy, DOROTHY!" Dad was calling her to the phone. The realization struck me like a hammer striking a rock. He did not know where he was, but his impaired mind allowed him to believe he was at home in the den of his condo, watching TV or sleeping on his chair, and Mom was doing something in the kitchen. In fact, she had gone home hours earlier. Listening to this 97-year-old man calling for his wife in the kitchen of their condo, while he is lying in bed in a nursing home, was gut wrenching.

By the time my father was admitted to the Blumkin Home, we knew the end was near. He lingered for about six weeks. Whenever I am at the Blumkin Home on Friday, with my wife or friends having matzah ball soup and a turkey sandwich in front of the colorful marquee storefronts, I inevitably glance from the colorful lobby, down the resident hallways, and the memories come flooding back.[1]

I had an elderly aunt, of blessed memory, who lived in a nursing home in St. Louis, Missouri. You would think you were in a lavish, plush hotel after the doorman opens the entrance door. The lobby is furnished with expensive couches, chairs, and tables. Opulent chandeliers hang from the ceilings over tables with floral arrangements, and there is even a fully stocked bar in the lobby. The tables are arranged and the meals are served like an upscale restaurant. One evening when Rita and I were in St. Louis, we joined her for dinner. We ordered from a menu offering gourmet entrees while listening to strolling musicians.

No one said God's waiting rooms were created equal.

Rita and I visited Pauline often while she lived at the care center. The outside of the nursing home probably looks like many other nursing homes—a one-level, clean, well-landscaped brick structure. The uniform windows of the resident rooms facing the street and parking lot offer a neutral but pleasant enough view of the outside.

A large kennel in front of the home directly across the street from the facility housed two of the largest dogs I have ever seen. For some inexplicable reason, they reminded me of Cerberus, the monstrous three headed dog from Greek mythology, that guards the gates of the underworld. Outside, weather permitting, I usually found residents watching and waiting for their next doctor's appointment, family member, or just someone willing to listen to whatever portion of their life story they might want to chat about. Loneliness is a constant companion of many of these residents.

After entering the facility through security doors, a small lounge area to the left has an old couch, a couple of basic chairs, and a small TV with attached DVD player. Often, we would visit Pauline in this lounge. Sometimes, someone else would come into the lounge or hover around outside the entrance, listening and sometimes joining in our conversations.

The heart of the facility features a large, circular desk area that lets nurses and caregivers look out over the entire domain. The dining space takes up more than half of the entire room with a TV/DVD and places to sit for residents, many with wheelchairs and walkers.

Many of the residents, Pauline included, have staked out their personal niche, a strategic vantage point where they can view the daily goings-on. Pauline picked a location to the left of the semicircular "control desk." It offered a vantage point covering the circumference of the room. A prime spot indeed! You quickly begin to recognize people by their locations. Almost any day, the same people will be in the same spots, regardless of the time of day. It was like a macabre game of musical chairs, each day a glance around the room to see who is in their spot and who is not. In the dining area, the residents often linger over cups of coffee with newspapers folded on the tables.

From this central area, various hallways branch out like protracted branches extending from the trunk of a large oak tree. These hallways encompass the resident rooms. From Pauline's "spot," she could be wheeled to her dining table, maybe 25 feet away, in a matter of seconds.

There are odors associated with nursing homes—a combination of cooked food, disinfectant, and sometimes a faint aroma of urine. The TV/DVD area always seems to be occupied. Even there, residents are placed in the same spots. An old movie, or a daytime talk show, is likely showing. Most stare glassy eyed toward the set, while only a few appear to be watching. There is no real artwork to speak of, just an entryway with meeting rooms off to the side, leading to the large, open communal area.

I felt I knew some of the residents even though I had never spoken to them. Some we gave names to. There was "Cowboy," a six-foot-tall dude who always walks around the place wearing a black felt cowboy hat. He acted like he oversaw things, although I am not sure what he was responsible for.

Another resident seemed to hang around the main entrance, chain smoking an astounding number of cigarettes. He would barely stamp out one before the next one was in his mouth. He would often get picked up when we were there and sometimes brought back before we left. We learned it was a girlfriend who was coming to get him. We never really learned why he lived at the facility. He seemed oddly out of place.

I found the Atlantic Specialty Care Center to be both sterile and depressing. We tried to talk Pauline into going to a different facility. There was one nearby, but she would have none of it.

"Why can't we move you somewhere else?"

"Because I don't want to go anywhere else."

"There are even places in Omaha that could give you really good care."

"But I don't want to go to Omaha. I'm happy right here." Stay there she did.

Variations of this conversation would be repeated by Linda, Bill, Rita, and me, but with always the same result. We eventually stopped bringing it up.

Pauline refused most of her scheduled therapy sessions despite her advanced diabetes and painful knees. Because therapy was painful, she simply refused to do the exercises. She was told that if she did not do the therapy and exercises, she would likely never walk again. It didn't seem to matter. She just wanted to be left alone.

For some months, she talked about returning home as if she planned to get up and leave the facility. She eventually seemed resigned that she would not be going home. I believe she just gave up, yet she seemed to be at peace. She spent most of her last months confined to a wheelchair. She had to be mechanically lifted in and out of her bed and placed in the chair.

She was moved to a couple of different rooms during her time there. One roommate had a rather distressing habit of waking up in the middle of the night screaming and shouting. Linda was able to get her mother moved to another room.

One memory of that facility involved handwarmers. Pauline was always cold. It did not matter if it was 85 degrees outside. Linda would take her outside, and Pauline would wear her sweater with a blanket wrapped around her legs. Linda began bringing her hand warmers, those little packets you break open and place in your gloves during a cold November football game. One day a staff member assigned to Pauline told Linda she could not bring them anymore. Pauline would use them, forget about them, and be left with burns on her skin. At first Linda was angry, but she came to realize these seemingly harmless hand warmers could actually hurt her mother. Linda brought more blankets.

In January 2017, we got the call. It was Bill. "If you want to see her again, you had better come soon. The end is near."

Rita and I hurried to Atlantic and the facility. We came upon a scene that had become all too familiar in our lives. It was clear Pauline was spending her last hours on Earth. She was sleeping, but had been unresponsive for hours. It was the sleep of the dying, her face ashen and expressionless, her tortured breathing shallow and short. We were not able to speak to her, but we did say our goodbyes, collectively and in our hearts. I prayed that in the end she was content I had entered her life, and that she realized she made the right decision in 1949.

We stayed in the room with her for several hours with Linda and Kenny. Pauline's sister, Esther, was there as well as Esther's daughter and husband. It was surreal meeting the lady after 15 years who had questioned my motives from the start and never seemed to want to meet me. Her daughter and son-in-law drove her to the Atlantic facility from Council Bluffs. We spoke briefly with awkward but cordial small talk. We left late in the afternoon for a somber and reflective trip back to Omaha. Pauline never regained consciousness that afternoon, and we left knowing it would be only a matter of hours until she passed.

As Rita and I left, we overheard Esther's daughter and husband outside Pauline's room asking Linda, "Who in the hell are those people who have been in the room with us the last three hours? We have no idea why they are here or who they are."

Linda replied, "You are kidding! Esther never told you. That man is Pauline's son, a son she gave up for adoption 67 years ago!" After 15 years, Esther had not confided to her own daughter that her sister had placed a child for adoption and that they had a new relative. We had spoken briefly to Esther when we arrived but were not introduced to her daughter and husband. During the three hours in Pauline's room, I didn't feel it was appropriate to introduce myself as Pauline's son, so they just sat there wondering why there were strangers in the room.

It was less than an hour after we arrived home that Bill called to inform us of Pauline's passing. We later learned there was much discussion that night as Esther's family spread the news that Pauline had had another son. In spite of the sorrow I felt over Pauline's passing, I was able to smile at that!

For Pauline, her time in God's Waiting Room was over. "*Zikhrono livrakha*," (of blessed memory). May her memory always be for a Blessing."

*****

1   Unfortunately, the Friday deli is no more, having been discontinued during the COVID pandemic. Hopefully, it will be restored.

23

IN LOVING MEMORY
JANUARY 8, 2017

In the end, I knew little—only small facts, a few anecdotes, a mere glimpse of the 88-year life of Pauline Newman Karnes. She said she would take the identity of my birth father to her grave, and she did. Perhaps this was done out of respect to her husband Ken. I could speculate, but I would never know. Yet my life would not exist but for the specific circumstances of an act of wild abandonment and passion between them.

The relationship between Pauline and me had grown over the years. At times, it was painful for her. Our relationship had ups and downs, twisting and turning like a narrow, winding mountain road. But by the last years of her life, we had both grown into a relationship with which we felt comfortable. She felt an affinity, an undeniable blood connection with me that conflicted with the knowledge that I had been the worst intrusion in her life. At least it started that way. I believe in the end, she loved me and I her.

I had previously told Linda that Pauline had asked me to offer Jewish prayers on her behalf at her funeral. Armed with this knowledge, Linda asked me to come to the funeral home and help plan Pauline's funeral ceremony.

Funeral homes are depressing under any circumstances, and the funeral home in Council Bluffs where Pauline was being prepared for interment was no different. When Rita and I arrived, Linda and Bill were there with their two daughters, Carla and Denise. We were escorted down a short hallway into a small conference room. The receptionist was smiling and funereal at the same time. They must be trained to look and act and talk that way. We met the staff person assigned to planning the graveside-only funeral.

Pauline would be laid to rest at Ridgewood Cemetery in Council Bluffs with no clergy presiding. Kenny and Bill would speak at a small memorial gathering in the funeral home's chapel. The service would not be religious. The interment would consist of a few words spoken by family members, and then I would recite a prayer.

A small dilemma arose when the discussion turned to the memorial pamphlet to be handed to family and mourners. I saw the uncomfortable issue coming. The funeral director asked how the family wanted to list the surviving family members. There was an awkward silence. Linda provided her name and Bill's along with Kenny and Dee. They agreed there was no need to list the names of each grandchild or great-grandchild. Esther would also be named. I was the elephant in the room. My hope was I would be quietly passed by. It just somehow seemed inappropriate for me to be listed. Just as there was awkwardness when we were with Pauline at her deathbed, I felt that people attending the funeral service would read my name, wonder who I was, and would react with shock when they found out. I did not want any of the attention at the funeral diverted to me, but rather directed to Pauline which was as it should be.

Even though Pauline had acknowledged and accepted me as her son, I had never seen this acknowledgement in writing. Something about my name being printed along with Kenny and Linda felt wrong, but I was confident the moment would pass, and they would discuss another topic. It didn't.

Denise asked, "What about Bob?" There was silence in the room. Linda finally responded that the pamphlet should only list Kenny and herself as it might be uncomfortable for some, especially Esther. Other family members who would be attending the graveside service might not know who I am. Esther had never told her daughter, who only discovered my identity at Pauline's deathbed days before. I interjected, "Please, it is OK not to list me as a survivor. I do not feel it should be an issue."

I felt uncomfortable and even a bit embarrassed. I wanted this to go away. I did not want to become the focus of this meeting, but Denise wouldn't let it go.

"Well, I think Bob should be listed," Denise persisted. "He has been a member of the family for many years and was close with Grandmother. He is part of our family and should be listed."

I interjected again. "Please, let's just move on. I do not need to be listed as a survivor. I will treasure my relationship with Pauline over the years, and whether or not my name is listed will not impact the relationship I had with her. Also, this conversation should not focus on me but on Pauline. I think Linda is correct and we should just move on."

Finally, this awkward moment was over and they did move on. I would not be listed as a survivor. The pamphlet read:

Pauline is survived by her daughter; Linda Sage (Bill), son Lawrence Kenneth Karnes (Dee), her loving grandchildren, great-grandchildren, and a great-great grandchild and sister, Esther De George.

I had previously helped Linda and Bill pick out the casket. They asked for my help. In the Jewish tradition, we chose a simple wood casket. Linda wanted to respect Pauline's Jewish heritage as much as she could while planning the funeral in the way Pauline would have wanted.

It was a cold, wintry but sunny afternoon when we arrived at Ridgewood Cemetery for the funeral service. The few people present were all immediate family. The pallbearers brought the unadorned casket to the burial site. I fulfilled Pauline's request for me to intone Jewish prayers. In spite of everything, she had maintained her Judaism to the end. Perhaps it was meant to be that the son she gave up would offer traditional Jewish prayers at her funeral service. It was overwhelming and emotional.

I presided over a very brief service. I began with Psalm 23:

Adonai is my shepherd, I shall not want. God gives me repose in green meadows and guides me over calm waters.

At the end, I offered the *Eil Malei Rahamin*, the plaintive Jewish prayer recited with a mournful chant at Jewish funeral services. I had chanted the same prayer at the funerals of my mom and dad.

Exalted, compassionate God, grant perfect peace in Your sheltering Presence, among the holy and pure who shine with the splendor of the firmament, to the soul of our dear Pauline Karnes who has gone to her eternal home.... May her memory always inspire us to attain dignity and holiness in life. May she rest in peace. Amen.

So it was that I conducted a Jewish funeral service in a Catholic cemetery. I left with a cogent sense of closure. It had been a long journey from the beginning of the search in 1985 to standing graveside and praying over the life of my birth mother. Today, my mind is littered with the questions I never asked Pauline. I don't know whether I would have received answers, especially those relating to the nature of my birth father. It seemed those were answers I would never have.

I was privileged to know Pauline for more than 15 years. She was an exceptional woman with a good soul. As painful as it must have been, I am forever grateful she accepted Rita and me into her life. She lived through difficult times; a strict unbending childhood, growing up poor, giving up a child for adoption, losing another son shortly thereafter and negotiating an often-troubled marriage in its early years. Yet she managed to raise two children and keep her marriage intact. She lived to enjoy grandchildren and a great-grandchild, to meet the son she never knew, and to learn that her wishes for him were carried out when she gave him away. I will carry Pauline's memory for the rest of my life.

Much of Pauline's life was shrouded in secrecy. She rarely spoke much of her childhood, education, or marriage to anyone, not even Linda or Kenny. She rarely discussed the affair she had in 1949 or the child she gave up for adoption. Only Esther knew her deepest secret. Yet there was another secret Pauline took to her grave. This was a bombshell, a secret that was about to explode into all of our lives like a tsunami crashing onto a beach. And it happened the day after the funeral.

24

PAULINE'S SECRET
OMAHA
2017

Throughout 2016, Linda and Bill often visited Pauline's home, sorting through documents, memorabilia, bills, and everything that accumulates in the home of someone who has lived alone for years. During one visit shortly before Pauline's death, they found the bar mitzvah *siddur* (prayer book) I had given her 15 years earlier.

I thought it a subtle or perhaps not-so-subtle way to thank her for her insistence I be placed with a Jewish family. When Linda and Bill found the siddur, they found a note tucked inside the book written on a piece of plain paper in Pauline's handwriting. She had written, "I FORGIVE YOU."

Linda felt Pauline was speaking directly to her. In Linda's mind, Pauline was forgiving her for initiating contact with me, which led to our reunion and everything thereafter. She had always thought Linda had betrayed her, especially after Rita had told Pauline we would never call either her or Kenny without her permission. Perhaps the note was meant to be conveyed to me, Pauline having foreseen that the book would be returned to me someday, presumably after her death. In the end, I found the note oddly comforting, regardless to whom it was directed. Pauline had clearly made her peace with all of us. I was accepted by her and her family, and Linda was forgiven for making the call that started everything. Although I did not think either Linda or I had done anything requiring forgiveness, I was gratified Linda received solace from the note.

Pauline must have known, maybe subconsciously, that when she entered the Atlantic Specialty Care Center, she would never return home. Linda and I had both made life-changing decisions by making momentous phone calls binding us together for the rest of our lives. Pauline was an enigma. Many of the decisions and actions in her life were unpredictable, puzzling, and inexplicable. This note was no exception.

Shortly after Pauline entered the care center, Linda and Bill had Pauline's mail forwarded to their home so they could pay her bills and answer any mail requiring a response. This went on for 18 months. Pauline had not received home mail delivery for nearly two years.

Linda and Bill went back to her home the day after the funeral to make sure all personal items were out of the house and to ensure there were no important papers they might have missed before they sold the house.

As they left the house, Bill impulsively decided to check the mailbox, just in case some random piece of mail fell through the cracks and had not been forwarded. He could never have imagined what he was about to find.

There was a single, lonely envelope in the box, addressed to Pauline Karnes. By the date on the postage, it had only been there a couple of days. The return address on the envelope was from Catholic Charities in Omaha. Linda joined Bill at the mailbox. Both were curious about the contents of the only piece of mail that had not been properly forwarded. That it had been mailed only a couple of days before Pauline's funeral cast an ominous sense of anticipation about the contents of this envelope.

Standing outside Pauline's home, Bill and Linda read the letter together.

> *Catholic Charities*
> *December 29, 2016*
>
> *Dear Pauline,*
>
> *I am a counselor with Catholic Charities in Omaha, Nebraska. I am attempting to locate Pauline Karnes, born in August of 1928. I am doing so at the request of a gentleman, born in April of 1946, in Omaha, Nebraska.*

I have some important information that I would like to share with you. Would you please contact me at your convenience? My number is 402-###-####. If you would happen to get my voicemail, please leave a message and I will return your call at a time that works well for you and to the number you provide. Thank you very much.

Sincerely,

Sue Malloy
Program Director
Family Services

The letter was dated December 29, 2016, but it did not land in Pauline's mailbox until a day or two before the funeral, and was not opened until the day after the funeral.

The first reaction from Linda was, "Why are we getting this letter now? We have known about Bob for years?" They went home, and Bill called the number on the letter.

"Sue, I want you to know that we received this letter earlier today," Bill explained. "My wife's mother passed away earlier this week, her funeral was yesterday, and we just retrieved the letter from her mailbox, which was supposed to have been forwarded but wasn't."

After expressing her condolences, Ms. Malloy explained that the gentleman referred to in the letter had reason to think Pauline was his mother.

Bill quickly interjected, "But we have known about Bob Yaffe for many years. Not sure why we would get this letter now." The birth date in the letter, April 1946, did not match my birth date, December 1949, a detail missed in the emotion of the moment.

"But this person is not Bob Yaffe. It is someone else," Sue interjected. Linda stood close to hear the conversation.

Stunned silence. "This can't be right. There can't be someone else," Bill answered, stupefied. "But there is, and they would need your consent to agree to give him your names and vice versa." Cold reality set in. Was it possible Pauline had given up another child?

After all the years and all that had happened, Pauline still had one more secret she had taken to her grave. There was someone else!

Later that afternoon, Linda called. My jaw dropped when I received the stunning information. "I can't believe this," was all I could say. I, like Linda, also felt betrayed. "Is it possible that after 15 years, Pauline would never have told any of us about another child she had given away?" It was true. None of us saw this coming.

Linda asked if I would contact Sue Malloy at Catholic Services. Linda was dealing with the intensely emotional turmoil of having just buried her mother. Her grieving period had barely begun. How could she handle yet another secret her mother never told her?

Perhaps there was another explanation and this was an unfortunate and untimely error. The irony did not escape me that after the many years of searching for my biological family, I was now on the other side of an adoption search. I was the one tasked with discovering who this man was claiming Pauline Karnes was his birth mother. It was almost too much to absorb.

I called Ms. Malloy the next morning. She told me the letter was not a mistake. She apologized for the letter's unfortunate timing. She explained that the person seeking the identity of his biological family had begun the process through Jewish Family Services. JFS does not have the staff to conduct adoption searches. Those searches are contracted to Catholic Services. Their agency handles all Jewish adoption searches.

"So how do I identify this individual?" I asked.

"You need to provide our agency a release, and I will obtain a release from the interested party. When both consent forms are returned, I can give you his name and contact information, in which you are free to contact him or not."

"Is there anything you can tell me about him now? Does he live in Omaha?"

"Yes."

"Is he Jewish?"

"Yes."

"Is he from an Omaha Jewish family whose name I might recognize?"

"That would be very possible."

To say that my curiosity was piqued is a grand understatement, like winning $10 million in the lottery and responding, "I'm kind of excited." I was numb with excitement and anticipation. The next day, I returned my consent form to Catholic Services. Sue called me back that same afternoon. She received the consent form from the other party. She would now share with me the name and contact information of my new brother.

25

DANIEL
OMAHA
2017

"His name is Daniel Katskee," Sue Molloy announced over the phone. "He has been given your name as well."

I was stunned. I was familiar with the name Katskee—a well-known and respected name in the Omaha Jewish community. I am acquainted with one of the Katskees, Jerry, whom I grew up with. We were in the same class at Creighton University Law School, and both of us worked in the Douglas County Attorney's Office. He was in the civil division while I worked on the criminal side. Another Katskee, Milton, was a professor at the law school, although I never had a class with him. But who was Daniel Katskee? I searched my memory, but I could not recall meeting him.

This phone call was easier than the initial calls to Pauline, Linda, and Kenny. Yet I still felt the same apprehension and uneasiness I felt those many years ago. It was extraordinary that I was now the party being searched out, and I was representing the family I had searched for years ago.

I called Daniel almost immediately after receiving his contact information. A gruff voice answered on the first ring. For the third time in my life, I was speaking to a new sibling. Daniel and I exchanged introductions. I learned he was three years older than me, born in 1946. He was married and raising two teenage granddaughters he and his wife, Peggy, had formally adopted.

Daniel had learned through Catholic Charities that his biological mother was Pauline Karnes. Interestingly, he was originally told she had recently died in Des Moines. He was told Pauline had no children. The assigned caseworker called him back later and told him the woman from Des Moines was not his biological mother.

There had been a mistake, and there was another Pauline Karnes who lived in Atlantic, Iowa, who was his birth mother. Daniel was stunned to learn this and instructed Sue Molloy to send a letter to Pauline Karnes in Atlantic to inform her that he believed her to be his biological mother and seeking her consent for him to contact her. The letter was sent on January 4, 2017. Pauline died January 8. This was the letter Linda and Bill retrieved from Pauline's mailbox the day after her funeral.

Daniel was not aware he had three siblings, so I told him about Linda, Kenny, and me. I also told him Pauline had just died several days before our making contact. It must have shaken him to the core to be terribly misinformed about his birth mother passing away in Des Moines, only to receive the correct information and learn his real birth mother died just days earlier. It was mind-boggling to think about what might have happened had Pauline been alive to open the letter from Catholic Services. Would she have responded differently than she had in 2002? It would have been déjà vu all over again for her. We would never know.

I told Linda about the call and Daniel's identity. She wanted Rita and me to meet Daniel first but wanted to be called after we had met. She wanted to remain detached and did not express interest in meeting Daniel, at least not yet. I was anything but detached. I was both curious and eager to meet my newest brother!

We met at a nearby Olive Garden restaurant. The Katskees stood up when Rita and I entered, and I met my new brother, Daniel, 32 years into my adoption search. As soon as we made eye contact, we searched each other's faces, probing for similar characteristics that might identify us as brothers. Daniel was tall, very thin, and balding with sparse silver-white hair. His small brown eyes were penetrating and expressive, like my own features. Peggy was friendly and seemed both excited and overwhelmed by what was happening.

I learned that Daniel had suffered debilitating illnesses, including cancer of the stomach, the loss of a lung, and diabetes. He said he nearly died in the hospital when his weight dropped to just over 120 pounds. He told me later that his doctor said he could expect to live another five years. At the time we met, he was within those five years.

Daniel knew from an early age he had been adopted. His stated purpose for his adoption search was to obtain medical information he could pass down to his children and relatives. He was clear he was not looking for a new family, only for medical history. One of his daughters has diabetes and other ailments, and he wanted her to have answers as well. Searching for medical information was one reason I conducted my search. In Daniel's case, however, it was the primary motivating factor.

Although Daniel and I had not known each other, his two twin sisters were classmates of mine throughout Hebrew School, and I remembered them. According to Daniel, our fathers knew each other, and Daniel and I had mutual friends who lived in the neighborhood my family grew up in. I also learned about my several new nieces and nephews.

Daniel served several years in the U.S. Marine Corps, including a tour at Camp Pendleton, California. He exuded a tough exterior, spoke of fighting in high school to demonstrate his strength and command. He played football and was on Omaha's Central High School track team. We were very different when it came to athletic prowess. The only athletics I participated in high school was watching from the stands, and my only fights were debates.

Daniel spent his military tour roughing it with the Marines at Camp Pendleton, mine with the Army JAG at Fort Lee, Virginia—most of it in courtrooms. Daniel describes himself as hard, disciplined, and fair. He is a stereotype of the retired Marine. I once referred to him as an ex-Marine. Daniel emphatically let me know that there is no such thing as an ex Marine.

"Once a Marine, always a Marine," he proudly declared. He often wore a Marine Corps jacket and a Marine Corps flag flies proudly in his front yard. A friend of mine who knew Daniel growing up said he always liked him, but Daniel was the neighborhood kid the other children were not allowed to play with. Despite the tough exterior,

I found him instantly likeable, as did Rita. He was 72 years old, and, along with Peggy, raising two granddaughters.

Daniel and his wife Peggy each had been previously married. Peggy's son was unable to care for his daughters so Daniel and Peggy adopted their granddaughters when they were just three and two years old, respectively.

Despite our significant differences, I felt drawn to this crusty Marine. His story of adopting and raising his granddaughters aroused my interest and respect.

The big question was if Daniel and I were full or half-brothers. Did we share the same father and mother? It seemed unlikely the man Pauline had known in 1949, who had begged her to run away with him, could have impregnated her three years earlier, resulting in Pauline giving up a child in 1946, then another child in 1949, from the same man. Then who was Daniel's father?

He didn't know. I immediately called Linda and Bill on the way home from dinner and described what had taken place. She wanted to learn about her new brother, but was shocked about how this had come about, trying to reconcile feelings about her mother who she now knew had kept two secrets from her. She was not ready to meet Daniel.

My heart ached for Linda. I was simply stunned by the whole turn of events. There had been many twists and turns, but I never saw this coming. Pauline had kept this secret from all of us. Linda must have felt betrayed again. Who really knew Pauline Karnes?

Daniel and I went to lunch several times over the next few weeks. He shared two letters with me, one from JFS signed by Mrs. Grace D. Saferstein, Case Worker, Jewish Welfare Bureau (JFS), dated July 12, 1946. Another letter dated 70 years later on November 30, 2016, from Sue Malloy of Catholic Services, is a summary of the 1946 document as well as additional information from the JWB files. This is a summary of the information Daniel received from Sue's 2016 letter:

Dear Dan,

I have received your adoptive parent's record for social and background information. All information that was provided to Jewish Family Services is from your birth mother. There is no legal document containing your birth father's name or signature.

You were born at 11:25 am on April 11, 1946 in Omaha, Nebraska at St. Catherine's Hospital.... You remained at St. Catherine's until June 1, 1946, while your birth mother was trying to make a decision about your future. She signed her consent to the adoption on May 27, 1946. You spent time in a temporary foster home through Jewish Family Services until joining your parents, Sheff and Ruth Katskee on October 5, 1946. Your adoption was finalized in the County Court of Lincoln County, Nebraska on March 25, 1947.

Your birth mother was seventeen years old when you were born. Information in the record indicates that she was born in Omaha, Nebraska. She is of Jewish ancestry. She had completed high school through her sophomore year and had quit school at the age of sixteen. She was considered an average student.

Your birth mother stated that your birth father was twenty-six years of age at the time you were born. She also stated that he was serving in a penal institution for a robbery charge at the time of your birth. The record contains no information about his ancestry, except that he was non-Jewish.

There is no current medical or social information contained in the records. We would need to obtain that information by locating and contacting your birth family.

Sue Malloy

Mrs. Saferstein's letter from 1946 contained additional facts:

> *Mother-unmarried, about 17 and a half when the baby was born. Mother, Jewish. Two years of high school education. Did average quality work there. Quit school at sixteen because she wanted to. Now intends to go back to school to complete high school course.... Pleasing personality, friendly, honest, particularly responsible but inclined to be rather happy go lucky. Physically in good health....*

The letter briefly discusses the father who was in prison at the time of Daniel's birth.

> *... he has been institutionalized in a reformatory previously.... I don't know about his education but from letters he has written, I gather that it has been limited and that he is not bright. It seems that others in his family have criminal records. I have no knowledge of medical significance about his family.*

It seemed highly unlikely Daniel's birth father could have been my birth father. Pauline had a relationship in 1946 with a man serving time in prison who was 26 years old while Pauline would have been 17. At the time of conception, Pauline was probably 16 years old. The age of consent in the State of Nebraska was 16 years at the time. How did she become involved with this man, with such a sordid history, at such an early age? I will never know the answer to this or any other question relating to this pregnancy and birth.

In addition to the identity of my birth father, this is another secret Pauline took to her grave. If Daniel's birth father was 26 years old at the time and Daniel was born in 1946, that would mean he was born in 1920, making him 100 years old in 2020. He is unlikely to be alive, and the JFS memo indicates they have no written record of his identity. In all likelihood, his identity is likely to remain unknown. Daniel will most likely never learn the identity of his birth father.

I was particularly disturbed by the information about Daniel's birth father. I knew how betrayed Linda felt by her mother never telling her about her affair, my birth and subsequent adoption. I now experienced the same sense of betrayal. How could Pauline have kept this a secret from all of us? That Daniel's father was an unsavory character made it all the worse. Maybe I didn't know Pauline as well as I thought. What in her childhood and upbringing led her down this path? I was disappointed and incensed that I would never be able to discuss this with her. I'm sure Linda was going through worse. I knew this was why she was not anxious to meet Daniel.

Daniel described our first meetings as "kind of scary, strange." He perceived me as family without really being family. I felt the same. Daniel and I decided we should have our DNA compared just to be sure. In July, Daniel and I had our mouths swabbed for DNA tests. The results confirmed what we already knew—we were half-brothers. As to whether we were full siblings, the probabilities were less than 1 percent. Regarding our being half-siblings the DNA report stated:

"With regard to the question of whether they are half siblings or unrelated, they are 48,884 times more likely to be half siblings with a probability of 99.99%."

Though we shared the same DNA, our differences are noteworthy. For the most part, nurture seems to have dominated over nature. Daniel is an in-your-face kind of guy. He speaks his mind openly and sometimes without a filter. He worked for many years in a managerial position for R & V Scales Service, a scale manufacturer best known for servicing Toledo Scales. He is brusque, speaks in a husky, growly voice, and has no problem stating his opinions, a trait he and I share. Daniel is conservative, so once again I find myself in political opposition to my newest sibling just as I was with both Linda and Kenny.

During the following year, Daniel and I met up frequently. Our families dined out together. The more time I spent with Daniel, the more I respected him. Although he had insisted he searched out his biological family for medical reasons—and I don't doubt that at least initially—he now seemed deeply pleased, even elated over discovering his new family.

Linda finally met him as well. We all met in Atlantic for lunch. Daniel and Peggy brought their granddaughters as well. Linda had kept a certain aloofness from Daniel that he noticed. There have been scattered phone calls, but she did not seem to want to establish the relationship with him that I have. I think her reasons are complicated, and I'm not sure they directly relate to Daniel. This has been hard on her, and sometimes we have half-joked about whether there might be even more siblings out there. After years of adjusting to a new brother and feeling deceived by her mother for much of her adult life, another brother from another father may have been too overwhelming. Kenny and Daniel are friends on Facebook, but that's about it.

Over the past two years, Daniel has spent many hours delving into the Newman family history. He has spent hours at several Omaha cemeteries seeking out the graves of Newman family ancestors. I have accompanied him on a couple of these excursions, and his passion and exuberance is contagious.

————

The Katskees are coping. They live a stressful life, which is heightened by one of the granddaughters occasionally running away. These situations are agonizingly difficult, waiting for her to be located and then returned. Things are stable for a while, and then everything repeats itself, like a recurring nightmare. The Juvenile Court has also been involved on several occasions.

When I met the girls, they were residents of Boys Town—the famous Father Flanagan's Boys Town in Omaha. The same Boys Town made famous in the film starring Spencer Tracy and Mickey Rooney. Boys Town is dedicated to the care, treatment, and education of at-risk children. It was hoped the girls could benefit by the structured living environment that Boys Town has been famous for decades.

Daniel's twice invited me to family meetings with him, Peggy, and Boys Town staff assigned to the treatment and supervision of the girls. Daniel and Peggy did not agree with the care and treatment the girls received during their residency. I learned that Boys Town offers a holistic program enforced with measured discipline for infractions. I was there to offer advice and, along with Peggy, to keep Daniel's short temper in check. Peggy and Daniel had come to believe that the girls could better thrive in a different environment than that offered at Boys Town. Although I was very late to the game, I agreed with them. The girls left Boys Town after the 2017-18 school year, lived at home with their grandparents, and enrolled in public school. I was honored to have been asked to be a part of those meetings, and I hoped that I helped in some way, although my contributions were meager.

———

Daniel and Peggy are truly exceptional people. It is difficult enough to raise teenagers in the best of circumstances. Daniel and Peggy have managed to raise two challenging teenage girls.

Daniel knows about his birth father only from old records from JFS that do not paint a pretty picture. The final straw is that all of this happened when Pauline was 17 years old. What does this say about Pauline? She was very young and likely taken advantage of given the difference in age. What does this say about Linda's relationship with her mother? Pauline never told her about either of the children she had given up for adoption. In the past three years, there have only been two or three times when Daniel, Linda, and myself have been together.

For Rita and me, Daniel has been a welcome addition. I have come to admire and respect him. He finally met some of our Omaha family at my 70th birthday party in December 2019. Daniel is tough on himself, tougher than need be, but underneath that rugged Marine exterior is a genuinely caring person. Family is the central tenet of his belief system. He is committed to his wife, daughters, son, and granddaughters, and he regularly visits his adoptive parents' graves, adorning them with Stars of David (Daniel's adoptive parents were both Jewish) and American flags (which the cemetery staff often remove, which generates his annoyance and rouses his temper).

———

It seemed my story could end here after serendipity brought us together. I had known and come to love Pauline like a close friend, a deep personal relationship unique to that person. Pauline was an extraordinary human being, and I was fortunate to have found her. I had grown very close to Linda over the years. Now there was Daniel and his family. Pauline would undoubtedly have been shocked that Daniel and I had come together, both of us representing what must have been a stormy and tumultuous time.

Daniel and I shared one thing in common—neither of us knew the identities of our birth fathers. That was surely how Pauline would have wanted it. But things were about to change for one of us.

26

ANCESTRY
COLUMBUS
APRIL 2018

It seems these days everyone is curious about their origins. Companies such as Ancestry.com and 23andMe now make DNA testing as simple as spitting into a tube, placing the vial in the mail, and then sitting back to wait for the results. The results may confirm what you already know about yourself or perhaps reveal long-buried family secrets, new relations, ethnic origins previously unknown, or discover some gene in your medical past just waiting for the right time to announce its presence. The results can be exhilarating or disheartening. Opening Ancestry email can be like getting the results of a college final or an annual physical.

My daughter Angela took the test for the most mundane of reasons. She was looking for a gift to buy her husband, Asher, whose birthday happens to fall on April Fool's Day. She came across a notice on "The Bexley Buzz," the Bexley, Ohio, neighborhood info/mostly gossip rag that features a sales section. Angela spotted a two-for-one offer from a neighbor. She and Asher could both take the test for half price. Two tests for a hundred bucks.

She thought it would be interesting for her husband, an Israeli by birth with Moroccan ancestry, to learn his results. Angela and Asher had Israeli friends of Moroccan ancestry who had sent their samples to Ancestry.com. It turned out some of their Israeli friends had a larger percentage of Italian ancestry than Israeli, which, of course, opened the door for good-hearted teasing. Angela was not adopted and, of course, knows who her mother and father are. No surprises expected. But a surprise there was, one that would reveal a tightly kept secret.

Upon hearing about Angela's birthday present for Asher, Rita ordered three Ancestry kits, two for us and one for her mom as a Mother's Day gift. Angela and Asher received their results in late April. Our kits were submitted the first week in May.

Asher's results were pretty much as expected: Moroccan-Jewish descent with percentages from other Middle Eastern countries, including some Italian. Angela's results reported 64% European Jewish. No surprise there. The next highest percentage listing came as a bit of a surprise, 13% Ireland/Scotland/Wales. Where did that come from? Some hidden gene that had been buried for generations, like a treasure discovered deep in the earth during an archaeological dig. We knew enough about Pauline and her family to know there was no Irish ancestry in her family.

One name on Angela's match list was Daniel Katskee. Angela and Daniel were listed as close relatives with the highest level of probability. Angela had never met Daniel, yet the two of them were linked together by DNA, that material present in living organisms, which carries our genetic information. That Angela was a direct match to Daniel Katskee spoke directly to the accuracy of the Ancestry.com results.

But there was someone else listed on Angela's results. Directly above Daniel Katskee was the name "Joseph Clark Jr." He was listed as a first cousin, with the highest probability of accuracy. The obvious question was, "Who is Joseph Clark Jr.?"

That evening, Angela called Rita and me at home. By now, Angela was used to surprises and revelations from my continually evolving family story.

"Do you know who Joseph Clark Jr. is?" Angela asked.

I repeated Joseph Clark's name a couple of times, the name rolling off my tongue as if I were repeating a word in a foreign language course.

"I don't know the name at all. I have never known anyone named Clark, and I have never heard this name referred to by Pauline, Kenny, Linda, or Daniel."

Then it hit me like a bolt of lightning. My heart began pounding. "Could this be a link to the paternal side of my family?" I thought out loud. This could be the answer to the secret Pauline would never talk about, the secret she took to her grave. Was I on the verge of learning the identity of my birth father?

Angela agreed to email Joseph Clark Jr. to see if he was interested in communicating with her. I asked Angela to see if she could find out where he lives. I wanted to determine whether he had a connection to Nebraska.

About that time, I remembered our previous meeting at the offices of Jewish Family Services. Since we had learned the identity of my birth mother, Teresa has been willing to allow us access to most of my adoption file at JFS. That is how I was able to obtain copies of the original case file notes documenting my parent's 1949-50 home study described in Chapter 3. There was also a small card Teresa had shown us that was most likely placed on my bassinet at St. Catherine's Hospital after my birth. The front of the card has "Baby Boy Karnes" imprinted on it. We already had this information so it was not a revelation. She also told us there was a name written on the back that she could not disclose on the chance it was the name of my biological father. She didn't know whether it was or wasn't, but she was not comfortable letting us see it. Now that conversation came back to me like a blast of frigid air on a hot, humid day.

Teresa: "I can't release this to you because of privacy laws, and there's no release on file."

I responded: "How can there be a release, if we don't know who to get the release from?"

"We don't know for sure that this is the name of your birth father, but I will tell you that it's a very common name," she added, almost teasingly. We made a couple of wild guesses, like Bill Smith, or John Jones. We left JFS that day with a lot of information, but not the name on the back of the card I had since forgotten about. Now my thoughts returned to that day, a common name. Joseph Clark. Common enough.

27

CONNECTION
OMAHA | COLUMBUS | ARVADA & CASTLE ROCK, COLORADO
APRIL–MAY 2018

It took a couple of days before Angela received an email from Joseph Clark Jr. replying from Highlands Ranch, Colorado, a suburb of about 100,000 residents about 12 miles south of Denver. Colorado borders Nebraska, so the Clark family was within a day's drive. There was also the common family name. Finally, the DNA matches added intrigue.

"Angela, this is exciting and compelling. Will you contact him and ask if he would be willing to speak to you directly?" I asked. We could have a conference call, the four of us, Angela, Rita and I, and Joseph Clark Jr. Let's do it."

Angela emailed Joe again, and he immediately agreed to a conference call on May 12, 2018. I felt the same nervousness I had in 2002 when I spoke to Linda for the first time. But this time, the tense, edgy anxiety felt even more intense. Pauline never told me the name of my birth father, partly to protect him, and I think to protect herself from what she perceived as further embarrassment and shame. It would have been incredibly difficult and painful for her to confront this man again, a name and face she had put out of her mind for half a century. Was I about to discover his identity?

For the conference call, Rita and I were at home in Omaha, Angela in Columbus, and Joe Jr. in Colorado, three different time zones. After awkward introductions, I could tell that Joseph Clark sounded quite young, too young to be my birth father. He explained that he was actually Joseph Clark Jr. That explains why he was listed on Angela's Ancestry report as a first cousin. His wife Kimberly was on the phone as well. Yes, that would be Kimberly Clark, as in the American multinational personal care corporation. She told us there was unfortunately no relation, just Kimberly marrying a guy with the last name Clark.

"Is there a Joe Clark Sr.?" I asked with bated breath.

"Yes, that would be my father, Joe Clark Sr. He lives in Arvada (a northern suburb of Denver)."

"Could this be a brother?" I wondered.

"My father also has a brother, Tyrone, who is my uncle. He lives south of Denver in Castle Rock," Joe replied.

Did this mean I had two new brothers? My heart raced. This was all happening so fast. But so far, the only connection beyond the DNA match was the Clarks happened to live in a neighboring state, and they have a common name. Joe Jr. told us the Clark brothers also have a sister, Shirley, born to Tyrone and Joe Sr.'s mother, but from a first marriage. This meant she would not be related to me in any event.

A pause. It was time to lay the cards on the table. "Well, I have reason to believe we are related, closely related. I think you are my nephew," I said. "I'm Angela's dad, and she matched your DNA. Our report says you are her first cousin."

Another pause. "This is really incredible." Joe sounded excited.

It was time to ask a crucial question. Does your family have any connection to the state of Nebraska?" I told them we were from Omaha.

"Not really, "Kimberly interjected.

"But Grandpa might have," Joe jumped in, sounding a little breathless and excited. "I think he came across the Midwest many years ago before he ended up settling in Denver."

My God, my mind was now really racing. This could mean Joe Jr.'s grandfather is my biological father. Now there was a direct Nebraska connection. The evidence was tenuous but mounting. "Do you think he might have lived in Omaha at some point?"

"Not really sure of that," Joe replied.

"My God," Kimberly breathlessly interjected. She sounded like a revelation had been revealed. "Grandpa was always very secretive about his life back then. We knew he was keeping some secret. We didn't know what it was. He would never talk about it. Do you think it's possible ...?"

She stopped abruptly mid-sentence. For several seconds, no one spoke. I knew what she must be thinking. "Yes, I do," I quickly answered her unfinished question. "Joe, I believe your grandfather could be my birth father," I blurted out.

A stunned silence. The words just hung in the air, like a mountain climber dangling from a precipice. There was one question remaining. I held my breath waiting for the answer.

"Is your grandfather still alive?" Would I, as I neared the end of over 30 years of searching, now meet the man who gave me life, the man who begged Pauline to run away with him on that fateful day in 1949?"

"No, I'm sorry, but he died many years ago, actually back in 1994," Joe Jr. answered. My disappointment was palpable. If this truly was my paternal family, I would hopefully meet my new brothers, but I would never meet my birth father.

"He died in 1994, 24 years ago," Joe added. He was dead almost the entire time I was conducting my search. Pauline had been protecting a ghost of her past. I was sure she did not know he had died so many years ago. The information she could have provided, the story of their relationship, their feelings for each other, what he was like, all those many questions which she chose not to discuss with me, boggled my mind.

Through these swirling thoughts and emotions, I knew I was jumping the gun. There was no confirmation Joe Clark Jr.'s grandfather was my birth father. But the evidence was mounting.

"I'm so sorry to hear that," I said to Joe. "Deeply sorry," I offered, for a myriad of reasons.

"What was his name?" I said, realizing I had not asked.

"Sam, Sam Clark," Joe said. My mind again raced back to that meeting at JFS almost a year and a half ago. The name on the back of the card is a common name, Teresa had told us. Before we hung up, we agreed to exchange family photos. Of course, I wanted to see if there was a family resemblance to any of them. I also wanted to see a picture of Sam Clark, the most likely candidate to be my birth father. I didn't have expectations. I didn't look anything like Pauline and really had no resemblance to Linda or Kenny. For that matter, I could never find any resemblance between Linda and Kenny, or either of them to Pauline. I did see a resemblance between me and Daniel Katskee, but only slightly in the eyes. I was not expecting to find a physical resemblance to the Clarks either.

The next morning, I began to receive photos from the Clarks. The first picture was of my "brother," Joe Clark Sr., looking directly toward the camera. There is no real background, just a wall with a corner of a mirror visible to one side. Joe is wearing a baseball-style cap. His head is leaning to the right, and his lip is curled upward on the left side in a half smile, as if he isn't 100% sure he wanted the picture to be taken. I did a double take. I was looking at my own reflection. His face is my face.

It is almost impossible to document my thoughts. I looked away, then back at the photo. I was stunned and felt a shudder traveling down my body. I couldn't take my eyes off the photo. After 68 years, for the first time in my life, I was staring at a face I recognized, yet I was looking at a total stranger. It was like finding your doppelgänger, except we were related. This image did not quite register. I knew at that moment I was looking into the face of my brother, my flesh and blood. For the next several weeks I shared that picture with just about everyone I knew. The reactions were always the same, "Oh, my God!" and "Holy shit! He looks just like you."

The next day, I received more pictures from Joe Jr.'s wife. Kimberly was as enthusiastic and exuberant as anyone we had spoken to. The black-and-white photos of Sam Clark must have been taken near the time of my birth. One is a serious headshot. In the other, Sam is standing with his arms crossed. The picture shows a young man, wearing an unbuttoned light-colored jacket. His hair is short on the sides but slicked up on top—a wavy swooping pompadour that was popular in the '50s. He is thin as wallpaper and very handsome, just as Pauline had described him. He sports a wide, brimming smile. He looks happy and content. He could be Danny Zuko in Grease or James Dean in *Rebel Without a Cause*.

The text Kimberly sent me that evening was the first direct connection to my new brother whose name I learned was Tyrone. "We just talked with Tyrone, and he is blown away that he has an older brother and he's very curious about you and looking forward to meeting you. He wants us to give you his phone number so you two can catch up."

An interesting turn of phrase, "so you can catch up." "So, what have you been up to for the last 60 years?" I might ask, like Rip Van Winkle awakening from his 20-year sleep.

I called Tyrone early the next morning, but there was no answer, and his voicemail was full. I texted Kimberly. Apparently, we had caught him while in the middle of yard work. Kimberly replied, "His yard is pretty huge." My mind was running with this tidbit of information. "I gave him your number," Kimberly informed me. "He is in shock and disbelief."

I received the call later that afternoon.

My 33-year search had reached its denouement. Tyrone seemed to be as surprised and bewildered as me. He had discussed our revelations with his half-sister Shirley. I learned that Shirley acts as the Clark family genealogist and had more extensive knowledge of Sam's early history than anyone else in the family. Tyrone was going to call Shirley back later that evening. We discussed the physical resemblance between us. The rest of the conversation was simply introducing ourselves to each other and expressing the incredulity we felt over the course of events.

I learned that Tyrone is a successful business owner in the insurance industry. His wife, Patra, is of Greek descent, and they have a six-year-old son, Raphael. Tyrone also has a son and daughter from a previous marriage. I told him about my background. There was no discussion about a face-to-face meeting. Not yet.

I also left a voicemail for my other brother, Joe Sr. In the meantime, Kimberly had sent more pictures, including Joe Jr. with his mother Cindy (Joe Sr.'s wife). There was also a picture of Joe Sr., and Tyrone's mother, Corrine. The black-and-white photo depicts an attractive, dark-eyed young girl, probably in her late teens or early twenties, with what appears to be shoulder-length hair with a flower to the side. Her resemblance to early photos of Pauline was striking.

Tyrone carefully brought up the subject of seeking confirmation through an independent DNA analysis. I wasn't sure it was necessary, as Angela's DNA had clearly matched Joe Jr.'s. The circumstantial evidence seemed convincing as well. Rita agreed with Tyrone that an independent confirmation was a good idea. The family resemblance seemed too strong to be some sort of a coincidence. The consensus was that we should do an independent DNA analysis. Fine with me.

The day after talking with Tyrone, I finally reached Joe Sr. I felt the same exhilaration as when I spoke to Tyrone. Even in phone conversations, Tyrone and Joe were quite different from each other. Whereas Tyrone was talkative, Joe seemed more circumspect and even a bit shy. Joe had worked for Tyrone for several years but retired early after suffering a life-threatening auto accident while driving for him. I am nine years older than Tyrone and six years older than Joe Sr.

Joe also noted his father, Sam, had been very secretive about his early years. He began in Springfield, Missouri, and traveled across Nebraska, finally settling in Denver. Apparently, he drifted from town to town, taking on sundry jobs. We surmised he must have passed through Omaha at some point in the late '40s and met Pauline there. She had told us he was working at a local drug store when she met him in Omaha. Sam eventually moved on until settling in Denver. He successfully leased and managed a parking lot in downtown Denver as well as additional lots. He eventually became a successful businessman.

Tyrone related a story Sam had told him years before his death. While traveling across the Midwest in his youth, Sam had an incident with a man chasing him with a shotgun. He would not offer details as to why he was being chased or what led to the situation. I thought the story Pauline told us about her husband Ken chasing her "friend" from the porch of their home with a shotgun was too similar to be a coincidence. In my mind, the story was one more confirmation Sam Clark was my birth father.

In addition, both Tyrone and Joe remembered stories of traveling to Fremont, Nebraska, when they were very young. Their half-sister Shirley had family there. Joe remembered that on one of those trips, their mother Corrine was upset and crying on the way. He didn't know why. Fremont is only about 20 miles northwest of Omaha.

All of these conversations took place over a couple of days. Kimberly, Joe Jr.'s wife, and I texted quite late one evening. One of her last texts around midnight said, **"You and the Clarks have a lot to talk about. Also, Your family resemblance is undeniable. Everyone thinks so."** Kimberly seemed convinced Sam Clark was my birth father.

A couple of days later, Rita and I left for a previously planned summer road trip with friends from Chicago to Tennessee to visit the major sites—Beale Street, the Grand Ole Opry, The Jack Daniel's Distillery, Chattanooga, Gatlinburg, and more. All the while, thoughts of Tyrone, Joe Sr., and Sam Clark were on my mind every minute of every day. On the return trip, we picked up my grandson Edin, who was spending the summer with us in Omaha.

I was absolutely convinced Sam Clark was my birth father. As I was about to discover, the final proof had been hidden in plain sight all along.

28

SEEKING CONFIRMATION
OMAHA | CASTLE ROCK | ARVADA
MAY–JUNE 2018

When Tyrone heard about a long-lost brother attempting to contact him, he initially thought it was a scam. His wife Patra's first reaction was, "Does he have a job?"

All the evidence before us—the DNA match between Angela and Joe Jr., Sam Clark's Nebraska connection, the common name, the strong family resemblance between Joe Sr. and me, the story of their father being chased with a shotgun, corroborated by the similar story told to us by Pauline, presented evidence as was clear, convincing, and indisputable.

Nevertheless, Tyrone had suggested we might consider getting an additional DNA test from an independent laboratory, just to confirm the Ancestry.com results. Rita agreed. Tyrone and I had begun talking about meeting each other, but I had a sense Tyrone wanted to be sure all this was legit. I agreed to arrange for the tests.

I decided to use the same lab that had confirmed the DNA connection to Daniel Katskee a year earlier. It would be somewhat more complicated this time since I lived in a different city from the Clarks, so it was back to Modern Medicine, which is connected with several labs across the country. One Modern Medicine location is close to Castle Rock, Colorado. Tyrone enthusiastically told me the lab was very close to his office.

The process, as explained at Modern Medicine, was that Tyrone, Joe Sr., and I would have our mouths swabbed at their respective labs. The labs in Omaha would coordinate with the lab in Colorado. The individual samples would then be sent to Any Lab Test Now for processing. That lab's DNA Diagnostics Center would send the results to each of us. In addition, all three of us would need to provide our samples at roughly the same time. It seemed complicated, but we all agreed to follow the instructions.

Edin, our 12-year-old grandson, was spending the summer in Omaha with us, which would include attending the College World Series and then a family trip to South Dakota. He was excited to be with us while we were discovering the Clarks and very much wanted to go to the lab with me to provide my DNA sample.

"I'm back again," I cheerfully announced to the young lady at the Modern Medicine office. I reminded her that last year I had matched my DNA to my brother, Daniel Katskee. I told her I wanted to compare my sample to others I thought were my brothers— a different father than Daniel but from same mother. The receptionist, remembering Daniel and me from last year, told me this was one of the most unusual stories she had ever heard. Once again, they swabbed my mouth and told me we would have results within two weeks. Edin wanted to record the event for posterity, so there are unflattering pictures of me with my mouth wide open while the technician swabs the inside of my cheek.

Following the DNA test, we took Edin on a week-long road trip to Mt. Rushmore and the South Dakota Badlands. During that time, I kept waiting for the DNA results.

When we returned to Omaha, nothing. I called Modern Medicine. No results. Three weeks went by; a fourth week passed. I waited and waited. Nothing. Finally, I got an answer. There was a problem with one of the samples. For some reason, Joe Sr.'s sample was insufficient to conduct all of the required tests.

"Why?" I asked.

"I don't know the reason," was the reply, "but this is the first time I have ever seen anything like this."

"Can't we just get the results that are available?"

"I will have to call the lab and check."

"Please do that!" I was ready to burst like a champagne cork.

Apparently, the company had been told to wait for a new sample from Joe Sr. before proceeding. No one knew where this instruction came from. After speaking to the Any Lab Test Now analyst, they agreed to release the results without the full sample from Joe Sr. Since Any Lab Test Now is a client of Modern Medicine, they could only release the results directly to them. Modern Medicine staff followed through. Finally, on June 22, about five weeks after we provided our samples, I was called with the results.

Regarding Tyrone M. Clark: "Based on testing results obtained from analyses of the DNA sample listed, the probability of half-siblingship is 99.98%. The likelihood that they share a common biological parent is 5,779 to 1."

Regarding Joseph D. Clark: "Based on testing results obtained from analysis of the DNA sample listed, the probability of half-siblingship is 65.8%. The likelihood that they share a common biological parent is 2-1."

The difference between Joe and Tyrone's sample was because Joe Sr.'s sample was incomplete. A few days later, I received the written reports in the mail. The test from Modern Medicine validated the results from Ancestry.com.

Tyrone and Joe Sr. are my brothers! It was almost too much to comprehend. I was exhilarated and couldn't wait to share the results with them.

When I spoke to Tyrone, I could sense his exhilaration and elation. I now had all the answers I had been searching for. My maternal and paternal history was complete. Angela and Joe Jr., two individuals who had no idea the other existed who both did DNA testing for unrelated reasons, received amazing results that would bring two families together and change their lives. It had taken me 33 years, but I had solved the mystery of my birth. I knew the answers, both on my maternal and paternal side. This emotionally satisfying moment defies description. The next step would be the reunion, or "catching up," as Kimberly Clark described it. For the third time, I would come face to face with newly discovered siblings.

I came to regret I lacked the foresight to test my own DNA earlier. I had done so only after my daughter had done hers. Had I only taken the test a couple of years earlier, I would most likely have discovered the Clarks while Pauline was still alive. Armed with the identity of my paternal father, Pauline might have opened up about him, shared stories, and anecdotes. I will never know.

My own DNA was also not without a surprise or two. It turned out that I am only 46% European Jewish. 46%! I am not even half Jewish, at least by DNA. I should not have been surprised, having always known that my paternal father was not Jewish, but it was still sobering to see that number on the test report. I am also 14% Ireland/Scotland/Wales and 13% Scandinavian. The Clarks are partially Irish. I now know where the "Irish" in my DNA came from. My DNA was a match for Joseph Clark Jr.

———

Rita and I had planned to return to JFS to review my pertinent adoption records. The final confirmation of my birth father's identity might be hidden in plain sight in my adoption files. There was still that card with the handwritten name on the back in my file that Teresa, our JFS caseworker, would not let us see. We had only been allowed to view the front side. Teresa had given us most of my adoption files, but not that card. We remembered guessing common names, which was the only hint she gave us at the time. Armed with the name "Sam Clark," Rita and I decided we would try again to obtain the card or at least ask Teresa to confirm if Sam Clark's name was written on it.

During our appointment, we did not tell Teresa our true mission, only that we wanted to again review my adoption files. I thought it fitting that Edin accompanied Rita and me to the appointment. It was, after all, his mother whose DNA search led us to discover the Clark family. We had the name Sam Clark, and we hoped to convince Teresa to confirm whether it was Sam Clark's name on the back of that card. Our strategy was to ask Teresa for the other documents in my adoption file and slowly work our way to "the card." I felt that in spite of all the other evidence, I desperately wanted Teresa to share with us the name on the back of that card. If it was Sam Clark, this would provide the final confirmation. But what if there was a different name on the back? What then? How would that square with everything else we had learned, especially the DNA results?

After exchanging pleasantries, she allowed us to review and make copies of some documents in my file. We cautiously broached the subject of the card. I explained to her that through my daughter Angela's Ancestry.com DNA search, we were all but certain we had identified and located my biological family on the paternal side. We made it a point to tell her my suspected birth father had died in 1994. We wanted her to know the man who we were sure was my biological father could never be contacted so there would be no issue with a release. We thought this would make it easier for her to let us see the name on the card. Teresa congratulated us on our luck and good fortune.

"Now that I am sure I have located my birth father's family, the evidence including two DNA matches, physical resemblance and the Nebraska connections, I have a question." I sounded like a lawyer, but also more than a bit nervous.

"If I can answer anything I will. You've pretty much seen everything in your adoption file."

Not quite everything. It was now or never. Everything came down to this moment. Would she allow us to see the name on the card? If not, it would be torturous to walk out of the office never knowing. If it was Sam Clark's name, it would positively confirm he was my biological father. Or would there be another name, a name that would forever cast a cloud over whether Sam Clark was my birth father, despite the DNA and all the evidence pointing to him as such. If the name was not Sam Clark, what could this mean? Who could the mystery man be if not my birth father? I took a slow, deep breath and asked the question I had come to find the answer to.

"Well, there is one thing," I said, my voice trembling. "Last year, when we found Daniel Katskee, you gave us several documents from my files. You showed us a card, a card that was on my bassinet at St. Catherine's Hospital during the time of my birth. It had basic birth information—date of birth, time, weight. It also identified me as

Baby Boy Karnes, which, of course, we now know was the last name of my biological mother."

I paused. Teresa looked stoically ahead, waiting for me to continue. Perhaps she had forgotten there was information on the back of the card.

It was time to play our hand. I glanced at Rita, took a deep breath. Edin seemed transfixed by the scene playing out in front of him.

I jumped in. "It was the little card that was on my bassinet. You told us you believed the back of the card might include the name of my biological father. You told us you were not comfortable telling us the name without us securing a release. Of course, we would not have known from whom to obtain a release. Last year, you told us it was a common name, and you gave us the opportunity to guess it if we could. Well, we are very sure we know the name on the back of the card, and that name is the name of my paternal father. Would you at least be willing to confirm the name if we give it to you?"

Teresa hesitated a few seconds, which seemed like minutes. The three of us waited, all eyes on her. "I don't see why not." I let out an audible sigh of relief. I glanced toward Rita.

Teresa rifled through my file until she found the three-by-five-inch bassinet card that recorded my birth statistics, including the mother's hospital room number. At the top right of the card is a crude drawing of a baby that seems to be floating on a blanket. It looks like the baby is about to float off the card. At the bottom right of the card there are three little prancing lambs. The bottom reads, "St. Catherine's Hospital, Omaha, Neb." Directly below it, "Compliments of the Pet Milk Company" with a picture to the left of a can of Pet Evaporated Milk. The middle of the card has the statistical information:

> Room - 325
> Name - Boy Karnes
> Date of Birth - 12/4/49
> Birth Weight - 8 pounds 4 and a quarter ounces
> Length - 20 and a half
> Doctor -Not filled in

"The name of my biological father is Sam Clark. Hopefully, that is the name on the back of the card," I said, more as a question than a statement.

The three of us watched Teresa intently. I understood how an Oscar nominee must feel while waiting for the presenter to tear open the envelope.

She turned the card over, looked at the back. She dramatically placed the card on the table, the back now facing us. A broad smile. "Jackpot," she exclaimed. "Sam Clark is what is written on the back."

I was speechless. Rita was overcome with emotion, tears rolling down her cheeks. The confirmation we were looking for. Sam Clark was unquestionably my birth father. Edin was observing all of it, knowing he was witnessing an intense scene of extraordinary emotion. I felt a shiver run down my spine. This was the smoking gun. It was like inserting the final piece of a 5,000-piece puzzle. My search had truly reached its resolution. Tyrone Martin Clark and Joe Clark Sr. are my brothers. Finality. Sam Clark was my birth father.

Case closed.

The name Sam Clark stood out on the card like the Empire State Building against the New York skyline. This is what was written on the back of the card:

> *Pauline 8/12/28*
> *Sam Clark 26*
> *Springfield, Missouri*
> *High School*
> *Good health - mechanical*
> *Jolly, did not drink- dark*

Later that summer, I showed Linda a copy of the card. She turned it over, read it, looked at Rita and me, and said in a trembling voice, "That's my mother's handwriting."

"Are you sure?" I asked, knowing the answer to my question.

"One hundred percent. I know her handwriting. That's definitely her handwriting."

I felt a wave of emotion—it was as if Pauline was speaking to us from the grave. Those words, written by her in 1949, were words that would, in 2018, alter lives forever. The words might as well have been carved in stone, like the Ten Commandments. This was her handwritten personal description of Sam: "good health, jolly." For reasons known only to her, it was important to add "did not drink." So little information, yet so much revealed. The back of this card was the only place on Earth Pauline had revealed her secret. She would never speak his name again, not to her husband, not to her children, not to me, not to anyone.

It is almost impossible to wrap my mind around the fact that the secrets of my adoption were revealed on both sides of a card buried in the files of Jewish Family Services, the maternal name on one side, the paternal name on the other. It was all right there! It boggles my mind to this day.

My thoughts turned to Rabbi Gonsher, who for 17 years would have had access to the card buried deep in the JFS files. Had he ever noticed the card? If he did, did he ever turn it over? Had he done so, he might have asked Pauline about the name on the card. It might have led to locating the Clarks and possibly meeting my birth father. Sam Clark had died just nine years into my search.

When Teresa turned over that card, my 33-year search for my biological parents came to an end. End of story? Of course not.

On to Colorado to meet the Clarks!

29

THE STANLEY HOTEL
ESTES PARK, COLORADO
AUGUST 2018

We met Tyrone's wife Patra before we traveled to Colorado. She had visited her niece Maria, who was attending Creighton University in Omaha. Patra's sister Gina, who was visiting from Greece with her two children, accompanied her on the trip as well as Raphael (Raphie), Tyrone and Patra's six-year-old son. Maria's sister Vasha was attending law school in Wichita, Kansas, and Patra and her sister were going from Omaha to Wichita to visit her. Tyrone asked Patra to meet us in Omaha. He remained in Colorado due to business commitments.

We all met at a restaurant for breakfast and were greeted with warm hugs from everyone. Patra was warm and charming and seemed as excited to meet us as we were to meet my new sister-in-law. She is young (41), pretty, vivacious, and speaks with a heavy Greek accent. When we entered the restaurant, I noticed Raphie staring at me. He circled around me, very obviously looking me over. I glanced at him and we made eye contact. His first words to me were, "You look like my dad!"

"Your trip could be a life-altering event." Those prescient words from Bella, my 99-year-old mother-in-law, permeated our thoughts as we headed for Colorado on a bright, sunny August day. (Rita's mom Bella was a bright and feisty lady and had followed the twists and turns of my adoption search for many years. She passed away in 2021 at the age of 102). Tyrone, Patra, Joe Sr., Shirley, Rita, and I planned to meet in Estes Park to become acquainted with each other before bringing on the rest of the Clark family. That would happen on Sunday night, when Tyrone and Patra would host a party for the rest of the immediate family, including Tyrone's three children, Joe Sr.'s four adult children, their wives and children, and several other family members.

We would spend the two days in Estes Park, then drive south to Castle Rock. While there, we would also meet Joe Sr.'s wife Cindy, whose health prevented her from traveling to Estes Park. As mentioned earlier, Shirley was Tyrone and Joe's half-sister from their mother Corrine's previous marriage. Sam Clark was Corrine's second marriage. Patra had made reservations for us to spend two nights at the famed and "spirited" Stanley Hotel in Estes Park. The hotel is considered one of the most haunted hotels in the United States, boasting decades of documented, paranormal experiences of guests and staff.

The Stanley Hotel is a majestic, colonial-style hotel just a few miles from the entrance to Rocky Mountain National Park. It was built by Freelan Oscar Stanley of Stanley Steamer fame. The hotel opened in 1909 as a resort for upper-class easterners and as a retreat for those suffering from tuberculosis. Today, the hotel is famous for having served as the inspiration for the Overlook Hotel in Stephen King's 1977 bestselling novel "The Shining." This particularly creepy novel was made into a very scary movie starring Jack Nicholson and Shelley Duvall.

Apparently, King stayed in room 217 (the most notorious room in the hotel) and was thus inspired to write his hair-raising novel. King's novels have been a guilty pleasure of mine for decades, and I considered "The Shining" to be one of my favorites. What a location to meet my new siblings!

We left Omaha filled with excitement and nervousness. I was lying awake at 5 a.m., looking at YouTube clips of the Stanley Hotel. I was so uptight I managed to drop an entire bowl of breakfast cereal in my lap before we headed out.

We broke up the uneventful eight-hour drive to Estes Park with an overnight stay in Fort Morgan, Colorado. We wanted to ensure nothing would make us late for our rendezvous. The atmosphere in our car was rife with anticipation, and my excitement and expectation was growing every mile we drew closer to Estes Park. We arrived early, had lunch, and looked around a bit before heading to the hotel to check into our room.

The Stanley Hotel is both beautiful and eerie. The imposing structure can be seen from many vantage points in Estes Park. When you approach the main entrance, a huge, stately veranda extends the length of the hotel with lounge chairs and couches affording a spectacular view of the Rocky Mountains with the city of Estes Park spread out below. The rustic interior features a fireplace with a round table surrounded by stuffed chairs. The reception desk has a rack of old-fashioned keys hanging from a board with numbered rooms on it.

When we arrived in the lobby, there was a small line at the check-in desk. Rita and I were looking around to see if Tyrone and Patra or Joe and Shirley, who were driving down together, were there yet. I glanced in every direction looking to see if there was anyone there who looked like me.

While we worked to resolve a reservation snafu, Rita turned to me and said, "I see Joe. He is in the back of the line and is looking around."

"Oh shit! Not yet! Where are they? I don't see anyone who looks like me!"

A minute later, we had our key and turned to look for Joe Sr. and Shirley. I had still not seen anyone. Just then, Rita spotted them leaving the lobby heading for the parking lot. That moment, while walking toward the lobby exit, I saw them as well.

In the instant before Rita yelled, "Hey, Joe!" I wondered what it could possibly have been like for him, married with children and grandchildren, to discover that his dad had fathered another child. It must have turned his world upside down. More family secrets revealed. I had been through this emotional rollercoaster before, and in a split second it was about to happen again.

At 68 years old, I was about to meet my new brother for the first time, in the most haunted hotel in America.

30

ESTES PARK - CASTLE ROCK - ARVADA
AUGUST 10-14, 2018

When Rita called to him, the man turned around. It was Joe. His image was instantly recognizable. For the first time, I felt I was staring at myself. I don't know if my mind was able to fully register exactly who I was looking at. For my whole life, I was never able to look at any other family member and see my own face looking back. It was mystifying to look at him and see my likeness staring back at me.

Shirley, who had driven with Joe, was also eagerly anticipating this most unusual family reunion. We all exchanged greetings and hugs. I wondered if any of the Stanley Hotel ghosts were looking on pleased.

We spent some time in the lobby. Joe explained that Cindy has problems with both of her knees and does not get around much, which is why she did not make the trip to Estes Park. We learned Joe and Shirley were not staying at the hotel. By the time they tried to reserve rooms, the Stanley was booked. They were staying at another hotel a short distance away.

Tyrone and Patra were supposed to arrive around 4 p.m. but were running late. He called, and I told him we had just met Joe and Shirley. Tyrone had worked that day, so he had a late start and finally arrived around 7 p.m. Rita and I were relaxing in the lobby with Joe and Shirley. We did not see when Tyrone and Patra checked in. They came downstairs about 30 minutes later.

I immediately knew it was Tyrone. Our eyes made instant contact, while we both tried to not stare at each other. There were pronounced similarities between us, but they were not as striking as between Joe and me. We had similar eyes, and it seemed certain facial expressions were similar. Tyrone was thin and appeared to be in great physical condition. I could tell this was a guy who works out regularly. Joe was tall, stocky, down to earth and struck me as the kind of fellow you would have a beer with while watching a football game. Since we had previously met Patra in Omaha, we were already acquainted. I was tense and anxious about meeting Tyrone for the first time, but the edginess wore off quickly.

We had a late dinner at the Stanley. The contrast between Joe and Tyrone could not have been greater. In one of Joe's jobs, he operated a limo service including driving VIPs from the airport who were in town for business consultations with Tyrone. Joe's auto accident occurred when another vehicle hit his limousine head on, leaving him near death. After a lengthy hospitalization, the resulting injuries forced Joe into early retirement. When we met Joe, he had been retired for many years.

On Saturday, we talked for several hours in the lobby, learning about each other's families. Patra decided to shop in Estes Park, so she was not with us. We began to learn about the Clark family. Tyrone owns a company called Broker's Choice of America, Inc. (BCA). By looking at the company website, I began to understand how successful his company is.

"Tyrone Clark is a nationally recognized annuity sensation! Essentially he has dedicated his life to the field of annuities. Brokers Choice of America (BCA) has been responsible for more than $8 billion in annuity premiums in its twenty-three years. In addition, Mr. Clark designed several successful annuity products. He has authored books on annuities and written numerous articles on the subject. Mr. Clark lectures on the subject of annuities throughout the nation. In fact, he is also known as the "Seminar King" and has given over two thousand consumer seminars to over fifty thousand consumers in forty-nine states."

Tyrone Martin Clark was even named after Hollywood royalty, the late actor Tyrone Powers and the late singer Dean Martin, who were among his mother's favorites. He and his family have lived in Castle Rock for many years with their 6-year-old son Raphie, whom we had previously met in Omaha, and two children by his first wife, 15-year-old daughter, Tyler, and son, Tyrone Jr., age 16.

Joe Sr. and his wife live in Arvada, a northern suburb of Denver. He has four grown children including his son, Joe Jr., whose DNA had matched my daughter Angela's. Joe Jr. works full time for Tyrone. Patra's sister, Kiki, works for Tyrone as his CFO. Kiki's husband, Jim, also a businessman, was a starting linebacker and center for Notre Dame back in the '80s. His son Taki is a talented football player and hopes to play college football as well. When we later visited his home, Jim proudly showed us his collection of Notre Dame and college football memorabilia. He had also worked for a time for the Democratic National Committee (DNC). I immediately liked this guy!

Tyrone and I bonded quickly. Patra commented about our mannerisms being similar in more ways than she could count. Patra is vivacious, friendly, and sincere. Getting to know her throughout our Colorado weekend did nothing to alter those impressions I had formed when we met in Omaha. She seemed eager to embrace Rita and me as her new family.

Joe Sr. seemed friendly but shy. He is an outdoors guy who owns a boat and fishes on a nearby Arvada lake. He is also an avid hunter and spends much time camping in the mountains. Joe comes across as genuine, friendly, and warm. The physical characteristics we shared were closer than with any of the other siblings I had found.

That afternoon, Shirley (the Clark family genealogist), provided Rita and me with a thoroughly researched book she had prepared, a documented history of the Clark family reaching back to the 1700s. Having a new brother appear must have been a delightful surprise to this amateur genealogist, as she had spent many hours learning about our family. It did not matter that Shirley was not directly related to me as her exuberance and enthusiasm about us was obvious. She had previously emailed Rita requesting information about our kids, grandkids, etc.

In the book she gave us, Shirley had added new branches to the Clark family tree to include my family as well. Shirley told us she did not learn Sam was not her father until she was 19 years old. She overheard comments about her lineage at a wedding she attended and the secret was out. But Sam had always treated her as a daughter. Shirley filled the role of older sister to Tyrone and Joe. She was 75 at the time of this writing, 15 years older than Tyrone and 13 years older than Joe.[1]

If people had observed us in the lobby, they might have thought it was a business meeting. I tried to learn as much as I could about Sam Clark. As with Pauline, there was frustratingly little to learn. Sam started out in Springfield, Missouri, wandering across the Midwest until finally settling in Colorado, where he became a successful businessman. He would have met Pauline during his early years when he passed through Iowa and Nebraska.

My birth father was described as a good man. Shirley related an early childhood memory of a hobo living in a shack near the parking lot Sam managed. Sam gave the man a job.

"Sam would often take in people and give them jobs. Sam trusted people," Shirley told us.

Sam had a brother, Reuben, whom he also set up in business. There was a mystery around Reuben, who would have been my uncle. He was a Korean War veteran who saw combat. Some of the men in his command were killed, and Reuben felt incredible guilt that remained after the war. No one knows what caused this guilt, but Reuben suffered a troubled life of alcoholism and depression that led to his early death. Today, he would have been treated for post-traumatic stress disorder.

Sam eventually expanded his parking lot business and married Corrine, Tyrone and Joe Sr.'s mother. At some point during the marriage, Sam began a relationship with another woman named Betty. Corrine and Sam had an understanding, and the relationship was allowed to continue. "It was like having two moms," Joe said. Shirley added, "Betty was part of the family."

At one point, I asked all three of them if they could attribute any negative traits to their father. There was a long silence. "Not really," Tyrone said. "Dad never hit or raised his voice to me, ever," he proudly stated. "He was very compassionate. He could have been a pastor or a priest."

This seemed incongruous since Sam had this relationship with Betty, yet the circumstances seemed almost natural to the brothers and it seemed to work for all parties. Corrine was at peace with the situation. Tyrone said his father was honest to a fault.

Tyrone reiterated that his dad loved to help people and often set them up in business. He had a great work ethic. He even paid for several people's funerals over the years. Shirley added that he never exhibited the slightest amount of racism during the turbulent '60s. Sam was not "a regular Christian church-goer," according to Tyrone. Shirley was quick to add, "Dad accepted Christ on his deathbed." To sum it up, Sam Clark was revered by his children.

Sam was six years older than Pauline, having been born in 1922. He died in 1994 at only 72 years old from cancer that had spread to his bones. He was also a heavy smoker. According to Tyrone, "Dad died a hard death."

Corrine had died only a short time before we discovered the Clarks. We will never know how she might have reacted to our "reunion," or what she might have told us about Sam's past. An opportunity lost.

In 2019, while staying at Patra and Tyrone's, Rita was examining several boxes of old Clark family papers Patra had given to her. These were papers Tyrone received from Shirley's house after her death. Neither Patra or Tyrone had ever examined these papers. Rita found several documents, including a divorce decree indicating Sam had been previously married to a woman named Leonora. The divorce decree was dated November 1951. It appears Sam and Leonora were married in 1945 in Hiawatha, Kansas.

The divorce decree states:

"... but that the Defendant has absented himself without reasonable cause for a period of more than two years last past, and to-wit, since on or about December 15, 1947."

The decree was from the court in Council Bluffs, Iowa. The reason for the divorce was recorded as desertion. Although the parties had been separated, Sam still would have been married to Leonora in 1949, although they apparently did not live together during the time of his affair with Pauline and at the time of my birth and adoption. When the final decree was signed, Sam was already living in Denver. I can only assume this was a youthful and ill-fated romance. It is interesting to note that Tyrone, Joe, and Shirley had no knowledge of this early marriage until they learned of it from us!

Based on the date of the divorce decree, Pauline was engaged in her relationship with Sam Clark while Sam was still married but separated from Leonora. Pauline had married Ken four months before my birth. Apparently whether Pauline knew about Sam's marriage to Leonora at the time of her affair with Sam is anyone's guess. Sam never discussed his first marriage to Leonora or his affair with Pauline with his sons or Shirley. One thing is certain. Pauline and Sam both kept secrets.

Rita also found a life insurance policy Sam had applied for in 1950. In recounting his medical history, he stated that he had been in an auto accident in Omaha in January 1950. He suffered a concussion but reported that he was fully recovered. In addition to all the evidence indicating Sam was my birth father, this insurance form is the only document we are aware of that placed him directly in Omaha in 1950, just a month after my birth. This means Sam would have been in Omaha at the time I was turned over to my adoptive parents in January 1950.

———

We spent all of Saturday getting to know one another and shared family stories. I felt comfortable with Tyrone and Joe. We felt mutual and immediate acceptance. As they learned the details of my long search, Tyrone expressed regret that it took so many years for us to connect. He felt emphatically that his father never knew he had fathered a child. "If he knew," Tyrone said, "he would have come looking for you." Pauline had told us she was not sure if he (Sam) ever knew she was pregnant, implying she never told him. It is most likely that Sam lived and died never knowing he had fathered another son.

Late Saturday afternoon, Joe and I took the Stanley Hotel ghost tour. We didn't have any close encounters with spirits, but we learned a lot of the hotel's haunted history. We even downloaded a ghost searching app on our cell phones, which amazingly never spotted any ghost activity. This did not speak well of the app, given we were in the most haunted hotel in America. I could not sleep late that night, so I got up and walked around the hotel. I wish I could report a close encounter, but alas, there was none.

Rita and I had decided that a gift was appropriate for the occasion. We had done this with the memory boxes ("New Beginnings") when we met Linda and Kenny back in 2002. This time, Rita helped me choose two pieces of art from an Omaha jewelry store. They were five-by-eight-inch handcrafted boxes made from copper, glass, and wood. Each box had an engraved picture with a quote from a famous author. We tried to select boxes with quotations related to "family." We wrote a personal message on the solid blank space on the back with a special pen.

Tyrone's had a quote from George Santayana, "The family is one of nature's greatest masterpieces." The picture on the front is of a nest with three eggs in it (I thought of three brothers). The box for Joe Sr. had a quote from Edward Abbey, "May your trails be crooked, winding, and dangerous, leading to the most amazing view." Since Joe Sr. was more of an outdoors guy, I thought this would be appropriate for him. On the back of both boxes, I first wrote their name with this below:

> *To*
> *Unexpected*
> *Blessings*
>
> *Bob*
> *August 9, 2018*

Actually, Rita wrote it since my handwriting is mostly illegible. We did not buy one for Shirley. We discussed this on the way to Colorado. Although she was not present when we presented the gifts to Joe Sr. and Tyrone, I came to regret the oversight.

After our two days at the Stanley Hotel, we went to Castle Rock. Tyrone and Patra had planned a family get together for Sunday night at their home. There would be many members of the Clark family present, all eager to meet the curious new family addition.

We arrived at the Clarks late Sunday afternoon. They lived in a spectacular mountaintop home with a magnificent view of Castle Rock. (They have since downsized to a smaller but equally beautiful home in Parker, Colorado, another Denver suburb). Walking into the double-door entrance, you come immediately upon a double-oval staircase leading to the downstairs. A beautiful abstract figurine of a woman, her arms extending to the top level, sets at the base of the stairs. First and second floor living rooms are visible from the entryway. To the right, an elegant dining room with a large table that can seat up to 14 people. Downstairs is a living room, a large bedroom en suite, a smoking room for Patra, and a gym extending over three rooms. The walls are lined with Super Bowl programs and many autographed items, including boxing gloves signed by Muhammad Ali and a seat from the old Yankee Stadium. A home theater is just to the right of the downstairs bedroom.

We met the entire Clark family that evening. Patra's mother and father were visiting from Greece, so we were fortunate to meet them as well. Rita and I were made to feel welcome and accepted every step of the way.

When we returned late and exhausted to the hotel. I contentedly drifted off to sleep. The search was over. Together, Rita and I had discovered all of the answers regarding my origins. I felt fortunate to have the six siblings in my life—my sister Jane, Linda and Kenny, Daniel, and now Tyrone and Joe. As sleep finally came, I thought of our first entrance into Tyrone and Patra's home. At the entrance was a decorative sign board that read "Welcome Uncle Bob and Aunt Rita." Below that, "We love you!"

On Monday, we visited Joe's home in Arvada. Joe and Cindy live in a lovely home in an older, quiet neighborhood. The first thing Joe said to us when we arrived was that his home was not like Tyrone's. I told him, "Neither is mine or anyone else's I know." He had nothing to apologize for. I was proud to be there.

Joe's garage is his workspace—his man cave. The 1969 Corvette he was rebuilding was his pride and joy. He has more tools in that garage than I would have known what to do with. The split-level house was well lived in and warm, their black Labrador playing in the backyard. Joe gave us several Clark family photos. He also presented me with a pocket knife that had belonged to Sam.

"Dad carried that knife with him everywhere," Joe said, with a glimmer of sadness on his face. He offered to clean the knife for me. I told him I would take it just the way it was, as it would have been when Sam carried it during his life. The pocketknife was a direct physical link to my birth father and today is a treasured possession. Joe has a camper he uses for camping in the mountains. He also said he occasionally enjoys alone time when he parks it in his backyard.

That afternoon, Joe drove us to a lake near his home. We left with a promise to go boating and fishing with him, something I have done only once in my life. We all went out to lunch and then back to Castle Rock for the evening. Our plan was to return to Omaha the next morning, but not before saying our goodbyes to Patra and Tyrone.

*****

1   Shirley passed away in 2019. She had been hospitalized for a heart procedure, had a stroke on the table, slipped into a coma, and did not recover. Although I knew Shirley briefly, I think of her often. Her exuberance and excitement over our reunion was infectious. Her genealogical research was both fascinating and useful as I wrote this memoir. Her online moniker was "Tokens of Joy." Tokens of joy, indeed.

31

"YOU SOUND LIKE JESUS"
CASTLE ROCK
AUGUST 14, 2018

Our last morning in Colorado began early on a radiantly beautiful day in Castle Rock with a sky painted sapphire blue. The Rocky Mountain air was clear, fresh, and exhilarating. We were invited to Tyrone and Patra's home that morning to say our thank-you and goodbyes. But most importantly, the visit would cap off the remarkable five days we spent with my new brothers and their extended families. As we left the hotel, we had a clear view of the Castle Rock, the butte that is now this affluent town's namesake, it sits just north of the town center and seems to tower over the entire city. The view was spectacular and unforgettable that morning— the butte jutting upward toward the cloudless sky. From the deck of the Clarks' spacious home, the rock is visible in all its splendor, overshadowed only somewhat by a distant view of Pikes Peak, about 25 miles to the west, looming over all.

Castle Rock looked to many 19th-century travelers like a castle on a hill. The rock is reminiscent of the famous Castle Rock in the 1954 novel and 1963 film "Lord of the Flies." The rock represented the special place on the island that was the center of control and power to the children trying to survive there. In some ways, Patra and Tyrone remind me of the symbolism of the rock, the seeming anchor of the extended family. Tyrone employed several family members. It does not seem coincidental that from the deck of their home Tyrone and his family can look into the distance and view this great edifice, their home resting atop gently rolling foothills that morph into majestic Rocky Mountain peaks.

Tuesday was a workday for Tyrone, so we wanted to be punctual. He had asked us to come at 8:30 a.m. as he would be leaving for work shortly thereafter. We were about two blocks from the house. It was

8:34 a.m. (I checked), when Tyrone called us in our car to make sure we knew exactly how to locate the house. Of course, we had been to the house for the "coming out" party the previous Sunday night. We wanted to arrive at the house on time, particularly since this was a workday. But we were running a few minutes late. Perhaps it was those few extra minutes we spent taking photographs of the Castle Rock bluff from the hotel parking lot.

We were still anxious to get to the Clark house. In addition to saying our goodbyes, we would be afforded a glimpse of the Clark household on a typical workday morning. From there, it was the long drive through the flat plains of Nebraska back to Omaha.

When we arrived, everyone was busy, especially in the kitchen. Gina, Patra's younger sister, is a petite young lady, vivacious, and a smoker like her sister. She made crepes in one area of the large kitchen. Patra prepared bacon and eggs. Andre, Tyrone's nephew and now mine as well, had apparently spent the night. Maria, Patra's mother, is a warm, cordial, smiling Greek woman. She moved about, observing and supervising every occurrence.

Within minutes, Patra brought me a Diet Coke with ice in a glass. (It was 9:00 am, a bit early even for me, a rabid connoisseur of Coke products). Everyone was obviously aware of my frequent intake of this not-so-healthy drink. Tyrone had long since broken his own Diet Coke addiction, while I had achieved only minimal success trying to break mine. Shortly thereafter, both Joe Sr. and Shirley called to check in with Tyrone, most likely to gather an assessment of the past five days.

While Rita chatted with Patra and her sister, I sat down at the kitchen table with Tyrone. The view of Castle Rock and its environs was just as spectacular in the morning as it had been the night of the party. Tyrone was dressed for work, meticulously. A sharp, clean white shirt with his full name, Tyrone M. Clark, monogrammed on each sleeve cuff—not your typical monogrammed shirt with two or three initials.

In addition to punctuality, Tyrone appears methodical and orderly. When I sat down, he had already filled one sheet of a short, white legal pad and was writing on another. We spoke while he continued to write. He had obviously prepared for our farewell visit this morning. Tyrone's handwriting could best be described as wobbly, quivery, but legible. The first sheet was titled "Anti-Aging." It included a list of various YouTube videos, websites, products, and books about fitness and anti-aging. As I am nine years older than Tyrone, I imagine the anti-aging materials were directed to me. The list included such titles as "Healing with Oxygen" (is there any other way? I thought), "Seeking Immortality," and "Bulletproof Podcasts." Websites included "Self Decode, TA G5" by Rev Genetics and "Alkaline Booster."

I had not the remotest clue as to what any of this meant. But it was impressive, and it has certainly worked for Tyrone. He was in great physical shape: lean, thin, and muscular. The last time I looked like that was, well, never. At one point I had asked Tyrone about maybe getting up and working out with him in the morning in his private gym (which just happens to be in his house). He told me he was usually up by 4:30 or 5 am. I took a pass.

Tyrone also does cryotherapy every Sunday morning. Cryotherapy treatment, also known as cold therapy, involves freezing or near-freezing temperatures. The science, as Tyrone explained, is that cold reduces inflammation, improves circulation, and cures various ailments. It involves entering a subfreezing chamber wearing only a bathing suit. We are speaking of temperatures like negative 200 degrees Fahrenheit.

"Yes, but you are only in the chamber for about three minutes," Tyrone explained, unconvincingly.

It sounded like a questionable technique used by a clandestine government agency to interrogate terrorists. I have to be coaxed into taking the dog out in the winter when it's 20 degrees, and I am wearing five layers. "CRYotherapy" seems just the right name for this endeavor. What's next? Maybe waterboarding to clear the sinuses. "Tyrone, I think I'm going to take a pass on the Cryotherapy." I am impressed with Tyrone's discipline and drive.

The second sheet was a summary of several future trips we had spoken of during the past few days. It included a trip to Nebraska to visit Rita and me in October and spending Thanksgiving with the Clarks and their extended family in Beaver Creek, Colorado, the home of an upscale Rocky Mountain resort. A trip to New York would be highlighted with a performance at The Metropolitan Opera. Tyrone had learned of my lifelong passion for opera, and he wanted to experience it firsthand. I was committed to making this happen. In addition, I never turn my back on an opportunity to visit New York and attend the Met—hallowed ground for me. Finally, there was a planned trip to Israel in 2020 when Rita and I celebrate the bar mitzvah of our grandson Edin followed by a trip to Greece, which would include the village where Patra was born and where many of her family still live. COVID-19 would put a halt to those plans.

Underlying this discussion was the sure knowledge that Tyrone was anticipating we would have a future together. This was even after I politely passed on pullups at 4:30 a.m. and sub-zero temperatures in some high-tech torture chamber with my new brother. In the past five days, we had established a chemistry, a strong bond, and a true sense of family through a common lineage: the birth father whom I would never know. These five days, spent with two brothers, their half-sister, and their families was deeply moving. At this moment, sitting across from Tyrone, I knew we were family. I could not have been happier. The fact this connection only came about through the DNA match of our daughter Angela and Tyrone's nephew Joe. Jr. simply added to the emotional intensity.

Rita and I knew it was time to begin the drive to Omaha. Tyrone had to go to work, and life had to return to normal. There was just one thing left to do. I had been asked several times to sing. When we were at Joe's house the day before, I had been asked to sing something for Joe Sr. and Shirley. I had done so, reluctantly, very reluctantly. I knew I had to "perform" for Tyrone and Patra as well. While some might consider this private performance as an ego trip, to me it was not. I was quite nervous and apprehensive, but I knew it just had to happen. And yes, I wanted to do it. The gift of a decent singing voice is a valuable gift I had treasured my entire life. I had performed dozens of times in many different venues ranging from an opera chorus, as a High Holy Day Cantorial soloist, other solo and group performances, and musical theater. No one else in my adopted or extended families (I checked) can sing at all.

As soon as I mentioned it, Tyrone immediately smiled. I think he was hopeful and expectant I would sing, but was too polite to ask. Apparently, Joe had already told him I had sung for them the day before. Tyrone left the room and returned with his son Raphie and his friend who had spent the night.

With the concert preparing to begin, Gina and Maria, Tyrone's niece, joined us in the room. I decided to sing the same John Denver song I had sung yesterday for Joe Sr. and Shirley. I figured what better choice than John Denver, a Colorado icon. I chose the same beautiful love song the late singer and songwriter had written for Annie, his wife at the time. The lyrics to "Follow Me" are particularly beautiful and felt somehow connected to our trip to Colorado and our new family.

As soon as I had finished, Raphie walked up to me and whispered, "You sound like Jesus."

After a moment of stunned silence, Tyrone smiled and said, "Where do you think that came from?" My initial thought was, "I never even knew Jesus was a singer." I thanked Raphie very sincerely. I knew it was heartfelt and was meant to be the ultimate compliment. I imagine that in his belief system, Jesus was his ideal, his protector, and the core of his developing religious belief.

Tyrone was puzzled that Raphie could come up with such a pronouncement, an intense and contemplative moment for all of us. Tyrone and Patra could probably look to themselves for the answer. They have provided their son the gift of religion, Christianity in Raphie's case, complete with a strong belief in God and a strong sense of Jesus as representing goodness and virtue.

I had been struck by the importance of religious values to this family, many of those values important in my family as well although we shared different faiths. Tyrone is a born-again Christian and deeply religious. He attends church every Sunday and appears to live his

Christian values. Patra is Greek Orthodox, and many religious icons adorn the master bedroom and other rooms in the house. During our weekend discussions, he told me about a lawsuit he had been involved in and the millions of dollars he spent to defend himself and his company. Years later, one of the respondents in the suit had been caught in a compromising position resulting in public embarrassment and did great damage to his career.

When I asked Tyrone if he had been glad to see that happen, he emphatically told me he was not. His Christianity taught him to forgive and not gloat in the defeat of an enemy and that he tries to live by that standard. This moving statement enabled me to better understand why Raphie would say such a thing. In spite of our religious differences, I felt a close bond with Tyrone. Perhaps we were not so different after all.

I took Raphie's statement as a supreme compliment, the perfect end to our Colorado sojourn. I saw Tyrone glance at his watch, and I knew it was time for us to go. The Colorado trip had been a phenomenal experience and, most importantly, a feeling that although this trip was ending, it was also a new beginning—a new chapter in my life.

As we left that morning, Maria came out with Greek cookies for us to take home—little snowballs of dough, like a wedding cookie with almonds in the middle, and a rich buttery taste throughout.

It is said that Greeks do not think of their family just as mother, father, and children; the families include the grandmothers, grandfathers, aunts, uncles, and cousins. We are all one large extended family. Rita and I had just become the newest members of that large Greek family. I felt proud as we left for the drive home.

Back in Omaha that evening, as we were getting in bed, I received a text. It was from Tyrone.

"We had one of the best times in our lives. We feel attached to you and Rita. We are looking forward to experiencing a great life together. It's God's hand. How else can this be explained?

Thanks, Brother"

God's hand indeed.

EPILOGUE

OMAHA
NOVEMBER 2022

Four years have passed since meeting the Clarks during the 2018 summer weekend in Castle Rock. My successful search to learn of my biological origins is complete. Today, I have learned the circumstances surrounding my birth and adoption. I know who my birth mother and birth father were and discovered the details of the torrid affair leading to my birth, relinquishment, and subsequent adoption.

The secrets were revealed painstakingly slowly over the years, uncovered and discovered like finding ancient coins during an excavation. As I write this epilogue, I am 72 years old. I realize, in one way or another I have been involved in this adventure for half of my life. In many respects, this book is as much an autobiography as it is a memoir. I have shared more of my personal life than I intended when I first conceived of chronicling this incredible story.

I realized that my personal life is directly related to the lengthy search process and the discoveries I made along the way. The search for my birth families, and the discovery of five siblings has been a dominant force providing both focus and meaning to my life these past 35 years. Rita and I have spent many months at home enduring, like millions of us, the COVID-19 pandemic, During most of 2020 and a good part of 2021 we did not leave town or visit anyone. The time at home has afforded me the time to reflect on my adoption journey, the siblings I have found, and the families I have become a part of.

LINDA AND KENNY

The secret Pauline so carefully kept from her children for so many years regarding her affair, my birth, and subsequent adoption are secrets that probably would never be created in today's world of open adoptions and Ancestry.com. Yet Pauline's secrets profoundly affected the family relations of the Sages and the Clarks, and especially the intricate relationship between Linda and her mother.

In "The Secret Life of Families," author Evan Imber-Black, Ph.D., discusses the varying types of secrets which can exist in families and their effect on family relationships. She writes about how secrets can shape and define relationships. Some of those secrets can be dangerous and even toxic in the most-damaging situations. *"Toxic secrets are secrets that take a powerful toll on relationships, disorient our identity, and disable our lives."* According to Imber-Black, "they handicap our capacity to make clear choices, use resources effectively, and participate in authentic relationships.[1]

I would classify Pauline's secrets as toxic. For as long as we have known the Sages and the Karnes, my presence must have been a continual reminder that I had initially caused a rift between Pauline and Linda by entering their lives. Kenny has told me he believes Linda's relationship with her mother was altered after they became aware of my existence. Shouldering the burden of this knowledge has never been easy, but the feelings have always been tempered by the strong relationship Linda and I developed over the years. My strong relationship with Pauline continued until the end of her life.

I cannot imagine the hammer blow Linda must have felt in 2017, while beginning the mourning process for her mother, to learn her mom had given up yet another child and never told her about either one of us, despite the closeness of their relationship. Was the discovery of Daniel yet another act of betrayal? Would Linda now question her mother's moral code if she already had not?

The second secret (Daniel) came at the very time Linda was mourning her mother's death. This may explain why she asked me to engage with Catholic Services to discover what was going on.

As of this writing, five years have gone by since we learned of Daniel. During all of this time, Linda has maintained a distant relationship with him, having seen and spoken to him only a couple of times. Kenny's relationship with Daniel has also been limited to a couple phone conversations. They have met only once or twice.

Linda and I have now shared a relationship for 20 years. Over those years, we have become close and she will always remain an important part of my life. As of this writing, we have only seen Linda and Bill a few times since my 70th birthday party in December 2019. This has been mostly due to the COVID pandemic. Before Covid, we met them on many occasions, often for lunch when they came to Omaha for Linda's doctor appointments.

Like most other family relationships, there have been ups and downs. There were disagreements, some over politics, and occasional disagreements over Pauline, including the Mother's Day dilemma. Much of our relationship with Pauline was largely filtered through Linda, especially when we were not communicating with Pauline.

In December 2019 there was an unfortunate situation. The month before, Rita and I had driven to Austin to visit my daughter Alicia and her family. They were temporarily living in Austin, the headquarters of Dell computers, for whom Alicia and her husband were working. On the way, we stopped in Dallas to visit Kenny and Dee. We had a lovely time there and enjoyed the time we spent with them. The problem stemmed from a conversation that took place while Linda and Bill were visiting Kenny and Dee in Texas a few weeks after our visit. The comments were unflattering, and I'll leave it at that. The conversation or a fragment of the conversation was inadvertently recorded and accidentally posted on Kenny's Facebook page along with vacation photos. As I was friends with Kenny on Facebook, I opened the attachment and overheard the conversation. The comments were hurtful and Rita and I were taken aback by them.

Perhaps I was naive not to have fully realized there was a certain emotional distance between us. This probably began at the very beginning, in 2002, when Linda surreptitiously obtained our phone number off her mother's refrigerator and initiated the first contact with us. This decisive action on her part represented an act of defiance to her mother's wishes and, in some ways, may have created a stumbling block in our future relationship. My father had warned me of such possibilities as I stood in my parents' kitchen lamely and ineffectively trying to explain why I had contacted my birth family. Revealing Pauline's deepest secret may have created a rift in what had been an unconditional love between mother and daughter.

None of us spoke for some time after the discovery of the unfortunate audio—call it a cooling-off period. Linda called me in early spring 2020. Since then, we have had periodic phone conversations. We have used these phone conversations to catch up on family and to discuss how the pandemic has affected our lives. It took some time for the number of phone calls to increase. We have only met in person a couple of times since, but as previously stated, this is largely due to the COVID pandemic. Linda and I, along with Bill and Rita, have shared many memories and a lot of good times over the 20 years since we discovered each other. We have shared sad times as well, especially the death of Pauline. My relationship with Linda is the most complex of any of the relationships I have with my other siblings. The secrets Pauline kept from her, the discovery of Daniel on the very heels of her mother's funeral, and my learning the identity of my birth father and his family made me both the bad guy and the good guy. We visited them in Atlantic in late June of 2021 and our visits have increased in 2022. I believe our relationship is solid and will remain so for the rest of our lives. I look forward to once again getting together more often with Linda and Bill as the pandemic gradually subsides, and our lives return to normal. I have an unbounding love and respect for Linda and Bill.

My relationship with Kenny has always been somewhat tenuous. Our religious and political differences may have created a chasm difficult to overcome, even though we both share military experience, law enforcement backgrounds, and other traits. Of course, the distance between Dallas and Omaha is significant, and coupled with the pandemic, have made visits more difficult. I like Kenny and relish the conversations we have had on a myriad of subjects. I still look at Jeff Gordon's miniature NASCAR when I am in my library and think of Kenny. I am certain our relationship will strengthen over time.

DANIEL

My contact with Daniel has increased severalfold since we met five years ago. At first, I was not sure of my feelings. Our lives and interests were divergent. His motivation for his search was, at least initially, for medical reasons only. This was only one of many reasons why I conducted my search. Yet after penetrating through his tough Marine Corps exterior, I found him compassionate, considerate, and benevolent. Daniel is one of those people who will come through for you in a pinch. He is that guy you would want to cover your back in a foxhole.

My respect for Daniel grew when I observed his incredible commitment to learning the Karnes family history. This included trips to the Jewish cemeteries and dozens of phone calls and lunches. Daniel has an almost obsessive need to ensure that his parents' graves are always maintained in excellent condition, even during the dead of winter. Daniel is somewhat of an amateur artist and as mentioned previously, has hand-carved Stars of David placed on their graves, sometimes running afoul of the synagogue's policies about what can and cannot be left on a gravestone. This has resulted in more than one heated argument with synagogue administrators, but his incredible commitment to keeping his parents' memories alive and respected is commendable and certainly worthy of respect and admiration.

Daniel's commitment to the granddaughters he adopted is beyond admirable. I am not sure I could have done what he has done. At 72 years old, I cannot imagine raising two teenagers under *any* circumstances. The past four years have not been without stressful situations involving the girls. Each time one of them runs away, Daniel and Peggy go through a living hell until she returns or is brought home by the authorities.

In June 2020, we were proud to see their oldest granddaughter graduate from Papillion-La Vista Senior High School. This was an enormous accomplishment for her, one that made her grandparents proud. Because of the pandemic, the graduation ceremony was shown by video conference. When her name and senior picture appeared on the screen, we felt pride in her accomplishment and the sense of achievement her grandparents must have felt.

In August, Daniel and Peggy threw a party at their home to celebrate her graduation. The house is easily recognizable by the Stars and Stripes and the flag of the U.S. Marine Corps, flying front and center in the front yard. The highlight of the event was watching family members (most of whom we did not know), taking photos of a smiling but somewhat embarrassed young lady posing in her cap and gown.

———

Late in 2019, Daniel came over for dinner and presented us with a wood carving on a piece of tree trunk which he had made for us. The bark of the tree forms the sides of the oval-shaped design. The highlight is a large Star of David with the word *shalom* (peace) written in English and Hebrew. Surrounding the star are designs of books with music and political titles as well as the title of this book, with a musical staff in one corner. He successfully captured my interests. In the lower-left corner, another book features the words "Book of Life" on one side and "Family" on the other.

Daniel and I have enjoyed frequent lunches (less so during the pandemic), and we speak regularly. In the fall of 2020 Daniel came over to our house armed with PVC pipe and plastic to create face shields for our daughter Abby to use in her classroom as barriers protecting her and the students from COVID. Recently, in a reflective moment, Daniel asked if I would speak at his funeral. He had just passed the date he had been told he could expect to live. My fervent prayer is that many years pass before I am called to honor that request. Perhaps he will speak at mine. Family is paramount in Daniel's life, and I am most fortunate to call him family.

TYRONE AND JOE

I have spent quality time with Tyrone and Joe over the past four years. In 2018, we spent an incredible Thanksgiving at Beaver Creek Resort, high in the Rocky Mountains. They rented a large multi-bedroom suite atop the Marriott Hotel. Patra's sister Kiki and her husband Jim joined them for the long weekend. All the kids were there as well. This incredible weekend was complete with excursions into the village and great games of "Family Feud" in the evenings. A huge Thanksgiving feast was the highlight.

We were back at Beaver Creek during the summer of 2019. This time, we brought our grandson Edin with us for another long weekend and a great time. We have made several trips to Castle Rock over the last two years and have enjoyed the hospitality of Patra and Tyrone each time.

On one Castle Rock trip, Tyrone gave us the tour of his offices at Broker's Choice of America. I could feel his pride as I was introduced to his employees as his brother. During our first trip to Castle Rock, we stayed at a nearby hotel. From that time on we stayed at Patra and Tyrone's home.

We seem to have a lot in common and share several physical traits. Patra has told us many times that Tyrone and I are nearly clones. I take that as a compliment each time although I'm not sure Patra always means it as one. I learned that I share characteristics with my birth father as well. Apparently, Sam had a habit of checking and double-checking doors each night before retiring, a habit I have had for decades, often to Rita's annoyance. Neither Tyrone or Joe could explain why Sam did this, and neither can I. Must be in the genes.

We differ about politics. It seems my fate is to be the only left leaning liberal in the field of new siblings. Tyrone will often open discussions with views he knows to be contrary to my own. I often get the feeling that he does this as a sort of tease. Most of our arguments are jocular and not serious. Our discussions intensified during the 2020 election, a year of divisive times in many families.

Rita has also developed an amiable and gratifying relationship with Patra. She speaks with her more than I talk to Tyrone or Joe. When we visit Castle Rock, we make the short drive to Arvada to visit Joe. Joe loves to talk about fishing and hunting in the mountains. On one trip to Colorado, he proudly showed us his boat docked on a nearby lake. Rita and I are looking forward to our first voyage. Joe and Cindy traveled to Nebraska in the fall of 2018 for the Nebraska vs. Colorado football game. They stayed with us and we went to the game together. Except for the score (CU 33-NU 28), it was a tremendous weekend. Joe and Cindy* also met our kids.

The next year Rita and I attended the NU-CU game in Colorado. It was the perfect weekend for a football game. Tyrone and Joe were decked out in Colorado gold and black and Rita and I in Nebraska scarlet and cream. This time Colorado won 34-31, but it was a splendid time for all of us.

An interesting side note: On one of Patra and Tyrone's trips to Omaha, he met Angela, who was visiting us. I found it serendipitous that the two of them would meet, since it was Angela's DNA test that enabled me to discover the identity of my birth father and his family. We also had a lovely dinner with Jane one evening. I was glad they got to meet.

My biggest regret is that during the first nine years of my search Sam Clark was alive. His name was on the back of that card in the JFS files. It was right there! Both Tyrone and Joe were emphatic in their belief that had Sam known about me, he would have welcomed a relationship. The fact that I might have had a chance to meet him but never did is painful.

During the summer of 2020, we traveled to Castle Rock, our first trip since the pandemic began. We stayed with Tyrone and Patra and met Joe for lunch, all of us careful to social distance with no inside restaurant dining. Our Colorado trips increased in 2021 as the pandemic subsided, and we spent a Greek Orthodox Easter weekend with the family in 2022.

Although we are all still learning about each other, we have shared family stories and family intrigues. The Clarks have moved to a new location in Parker, Colorado, and we spent time helping move furniture and other chores so the house could be properly shown. We have all grown closer together and are truly becoming family.

In conclusion

My parents always thought I was no different from a biological child. For many years, I grew up believing it as well. In 1949, birth parents and adopting parents rarely met, corresponded, or, as in my case, knew nothing about each other. According to Imber-Black:

"All parties were told by adoption agencies and courts that records were sealed. Adoption of an infant began with secrecy and was expected to remain secret. Laws were passed to prevent adoption agencies from giving out any but the most cursory information to adopting families, such as the birth mother's height or grade level in school. Birth mothers, in turn, received even less information about the people who would raise their children. They were simply expected to take their secret and disappear."[2]

The author calls this "a conspiracy of silence and denial of difference."

In the 1940s and '50s, this philosophy of dual-sided secrecy was the accepted doctrine that adoption was in the best interests of everyone involved. According to author Gabrielle Glaser in her 2021 book "American Baby," *"it gave birth mothers the chance to escape the stigma of unwed motherhood, spared the children the shame of illegitimacy, and offered infertile married couples the chance to become parents. Few invested much thought in the feelings of the adoptees who were brought up to think their birth parents hadn't wanted them, and that regardless of how cherished they were-they were their adoptive parents 'second choice' to biological offspring."[3]*

In the case of my adoptive parents, I was not a second choice because they never had a first one. I was indeed cherished by my parents and the respect and love that I have for them exists to this day and will for the rest of my life. Yet I, like so many other adoptees, could never shake the curiosity, the need to know my origins, the story of my existence. How could a woman forget the baby she carried for nine months and gave birth to? If she knew nothing about where I was sent or to whom I was sent or how I turned out, how could she just put it out of her mind like it never happened? Would the memory and knowledge of the child be eliminated, like a form of erasure? I needed and demanded to learn those answers. I was never a party to the agreement in 1949.

Three factors are vastly different today than they were in 1949, or even 1985 when my search began. Two involve changing societal norms and expectations. The first is the desire, indeed the right, for any individual to know his or her medical background. The second is the lack of stigma today with out-of-wedlock birth or the embarrassment of infertility. The third factor is technology. The mass availability of technology, and companies such as Ancestry. com and 23andMe, make DNA analysis readily available and can render a search for biological family as easy as spitting in a tube and mailing it off for analysis. In 1949, it would have been unthinkable that someday one could learn the identity of distant and close relatives they never knew existed, or wondered about for many years, like I did.

Neither Pauline nor my parents could have remotely foreseen this. The changes in our social fabric along with the burgeoning technology should render adoption searches such as mine a thing of the past. In my opinion, this is a good thing. A person should not have to spend more than three decades of their life trying to discover their origins, heritage, or their medical history.

Throughout my relationship with Linda and Kenny, I was always careful never to judge Pauline for her conduct and actions, especially after the surprising revelation about Daniel. Pauline was a product of her times. She had little education and lived in a strict Jewish orthodox environment where one can assume that premarital sex, much less pregnancy out of wedlock, would not be discussed or tolerated. In 1949, there was little or no sex education. Her father had died when she was eight years old, and she was raised with no father figure in her family.

It is doubtful she was educated about forms of birth control, which was pretty much limited to condoms. According to Glaser, *"Condoms were all but off limits to young people – they were kept largely behind the counter, and pharmacists, acting in loco parentis, often demanded proof of age. Access to the birth control pill, approved by the FDA in 1960, was prohibited even for married couples in some states until 1965, when the Supreme Court issued its historic ruling in Griswold vs. Connecticut,* (which ruled that the Constitution protects the rights of married couples to buy and use contraceptives without government interference or restriction). *And abortion, of course, was illegal—and risky—in most states until the landmark Roe v. Wade decision in 1973."*[4]

Pregnant girls were routinely removed from schools and often sent away to homes for unwed mothers, returning home from "vacation" after the child was born with the pregnancy and birth kept a secret from all but the most immediate family. Pauline spent time in a home for unwed mothers directly across the street from St. Catherine's Hospital. Years after I came into her life, Pauline still referred to the period of her pregnancy as "her shame." She told us she went to great strides to hide her pregnancy from the outside world. Based on all evidence, this would include in all probability, the father of the child she was carrying.

Adoption was the only real choice Pauline would have had to save her marriage. The period from the end of World War II through the early 1970's became known as The Baby Scoop Era, characterized by an increased rate of premarital pregnancies (Pauline was single in 1946 when she gave up Daniel), along with a higher rate of newborn adoption. The culture in which she lived would have encouraged her to place two unwanted children for adoption within a relatively short period of time. In coming to terms with Pauline's decisions, one must understand the moral climate of the mid to late 1940's as opposed to judging her by late 20th or 21st century standards.

The distinctive feature of the entire adoption process during that time was secrecy. It was a common practice, when a child was born to a single mother and then adopted to a new family, courts would seal the original birth certificate and issue a new document listing the adoptive parents as if they were the original mother and father. *"The falsified record would erase the perceived taint of illegitimacy from the adoptee, and protect the adoptive parents from the fear that birth parents might one day attempt to disrupt the happiness of the newly created family. This approach also made adoption a transaction in which the adoptee might never know the mother who bore them, or the father who begat them – or for that matter, their identity at all."[5]*

Pauline really had no choice but to give me up for adoption. Her mother and grandmother would not have wanted her to keep the child. Her husband would not raise a child of whom he was not the father. Sam Clark only offered her the option to run away and start a new life, which would have entailed leaving her husband, her grandmother, her mother, her young son, and her home. Being conflicted and deeply ashamed of the predicament she was in, receiving no support from her family or her religious community, she would have felt helpless to have come to any other decision but to give the child up for adoption. Even the State was complicit in helping to hide this mother's shame by legally altering the birth certificate. See photo section.

Finally, Pauline thought her newborn son had little to no chance of having a happy or a normal childhood, living in a home in which her husband did not want the child. She knew he would have a better home being raised by someone else. Yet she still had the temerity to insist the child be placed in a Jewish home. In that regard, her decision was both courageous and selfless.

Perhaps if my parents were alive today they would better understand why I could never accept the parental prerogative of "we know what's best for you to know." They might understand my desire to learn of my origins did not impugn my deepest love for them. Perhaps Pauline would have understood why Linda felt the need to make the phone call and discover the identity of her brother. These secrets altered all of our relations with our parents.

My story was an extraordinary journey through time, through false turns and personal desires to keep secrets. It is a simple fact: I would not exist but for a specific set of circumstances. In the end, I have been blessed with good luck. Many adoption searches do not end successfully or happily. Mine did.

There have been ups and downs, as there are in most families, but many more ups than downs. My faith in God and Judaism was the supreme gift Pauline gave to me at birth, enforced by my parents, and has helped to shape me into the person I am now. I am grateful to have found them all, and I hope they feel the same about me. Today, my extended family is stitched together like squares on a quilt. I feel a living, emotional connection to all of them. My life has been enriched for knowing them. I hope that in some small way, I have enriched their lives as well.

I could not have done this search without the ongoing and never-wavering support from my wife. November 2020 marked our 30th wedding anniversary, and she remains the supreme love of my life. She kept me going when I was ready to walk away from this long, arduous, and sometimes discouraging search. I hope this journey has enriched her life as much as it has enriched mine.

The journey, of course, never ends. Questions always lead to more questions. Once the pandemic ends there will, God willing, be many more trips and get-togethers. My fervent hope is that our relationships will continue to grow over the coming years.

*****

1   Evan Imber-Black, Ph.D. *"The Secret Life of Families,"* Bantam Books, 1999 pp. 15-16

2   *Ibid.,* p. 83

3   Gabrielle Glaser, *"American Baby,"* Viking, An imprint of Random House LLC, 2021 p. 7-8

4   ibid., p. 41-42

5   ibid., p. 130

*POSTSCRIPT 2022
On a tragic note, Cindy Clark passed away in January 2022, a victim of complications from COVID-19. I only met her on a couple of occasions, but she was a warm and kind hearted person, a perfect complement and a soul mate to my brother Joe. Rita and I will miss her dearly.

** On a happier note, Rita and I moved into a new home during the fall of 2021. It was a home we built together after 31 years of marriage. Daniel and Peggy gave us the perfect housewarming gift, a *Mezuzah* to adorn the doorpost of our front door. We all gathered together one cold but sunny winter afternoon, and Daniel, my brother affixed the *Mezuzah* to our door in accordance with Jewish tradition. It was an unforgettable moment Rita and I will treasure for as long as we live in our home. We aren't planning on moving anytime soon.

ACKNOWLEDGEMENTS

I have recounted my incredible journey to discover my roots as accurately as possible. It has been a defining and cathartic life experience. I have made incredible discoveries, some under unusual and almost stranger-than-fiction circumstances. I have gained new relationships that will remain with me for the rest of my life. I can't count the number of people who, as I would relate the story of my adoption and search, would tell me I should write a book. It's that interesting, they would say. Well, I've done just that, and as a first-time author, I hope I have been successful. I want to thank all those who have encouraged me these past years to tell my story. I want to thank my Wednesday lunch group (Romeo's, for Retired Old Men Eating Out) who not only gave me encouragement, but I am sure listened to my stories more times than they wanted to over many a Wednesday lunch.

I could not have written this book without the advice and help of many individuals. I am grateful to all those who offered support and confidence. I am truly blessed to have discovered my birth mother Pauline (of blessed memory) and all of my siblings: brothers Kenny, Tyrone, Joe and Daniel, my sisters Linda and Jane. I have learned and been inspired by each of you, and I hope I am a better person for knowing you. I thank each of you for welcoming Rita and I into your families and your lives. You have greatly enriched both of our lives, each in your own way. We hope that in some small way we have strengthened and enriched your lives as well. I deeply regret I never got to meet my birth father, Sam Clark.

I wish to thank my editor Robert Fraass **(www.robertfraass.com)**. He spent several months reviewing drafts of my manuscript, each time making the manuscript more succinct, readable, and hopefully entertaining. I was fortunate to work with such a skilled professional.

Proofreaders who reviewed various drafts of the book were extremely helpful in their efforts to enhance and improve the narrative. First was Melisa Wilzbacher, who edited a few early drafts of the first few chapters. My thanks to the other readers who provided valuable input along the way: Our friend Cathy Rosen, my daughter-in-law Caryn Scheer, my daughter Angela Abenaim (whose own DNA search led me to discover the identity of my birth father, Joe and Tyrone and their families). Special thanks to Meryl Ain, a friend and author in her own right (*The Takeaway Men, Shadows We Carry*), for reviewing the manuscript in its earliest stages and providing me both inspiration and encouragement. I particularly want to thank my good friend Larry Shapiro, a real stickler for grammar, and who constantly challenged me to put my deeper feelings, my heart and my soul into this narrative.

My deepest appreciation to Bill Smith, President of the Richard Wagner Society of Chicago. His insightful comments and grammatical suggestions helped to make this narrative a better read.

Thank you to Rabbi Steven Abraham at Beth El Synagogue in Omaha, Nebraska for providing me with Judaic sources and insights about adoption.

A special thank you to Jimmy James, a former colleague from my years in the Douglas County Attorney's Office. Jimmy is also an author (*It Was Never A Gamble*). He provided guidance in the publication and distribution of this book. His assistance was invaluable and it was wonderful to renew our friendship after many years.

Thanks to Teresa Drelicharz, MS, NCC, LIMHP, RPT from Jewish Family Services in Omaha. You will have to look up all those credentials! Among other responsibilities, Teresa is in charge of the adoption services for JFS. She allowed me as much access to my adoption files as she could allow, and made more than one trip to the basement to dig up information from decades old records long filed away. Teresa was also present and turned over that card during the dramatic meeting when we confirmed the name of my paternal father.

A huge thanks to our former neighbor and weekly lunch partner Nancy Chalupa, who read through the manuscript and assisted in the marketing of the book. Thank you Nancy.

Special thanks goes to Jay Shaw, Graphic Designer at Standard Printing Company in Omaha. He combined our thoughts, and his, to design an intriguing and thought-provoking cover.

I am grateful to Stacia Mann, the artist whose beautiful depiction of Castle Rock is found in the photo section. She graciously gave her permission to include her design in this book. Check out **staciamannart.etsy.com**.

Thanks to my sister Jane and her late husband Dorand for the hours they spent with Rita going through old World Herald obituary pages and other documents during the early years of my search.

Even with the great assistance I have received in writing this book, any remaining errors are my own and no one else's.

Finally, my wife and soul mate Rita. Not only would this book not have been written without her help and support, but there would have been no book to write. The search would never have been completed without her perseverance. I drew strength from her confidence that I should never quit, (and there were times when I was ready to) and keep working until we found the answers we were looking for. She was with me every step of the way – she lived this story with me. She was the one to make the difficult phone calls to Pauline. She provided the computer skills I lacked. I could go on and on. She has been the true love of my love for 32 years and will continue to be for the rest of my life. My story is equally her story. I could not have done this without her.

Robert J. Yaffe

June 2023

ABOUT THE AUTHOR

Robert Yaffe is a native of Omaha, Nebraska. He received his BA from the University of Nebraska-Lincoln and graduated from Creighton Law School in Omaha. His career took him from the U.S. Army Judge Advocate General's Corps, where he served as trial counsel and later chief of military justice to an 8-year stint as a deputy county attorney in Omaha.

He later served several years as an executive director of both Jewish Community Centers and synagogues.

Bob's interests include opera and classical music, and he was an opera history instructor for Elderhostel of America, as well as a noted opera lecturer and instructor in the Chicago area. He has served as a cantorial soloist for High Holiday services and as a soloist during religious services in various synagogues. Bob published an article "The Executive Director Facing Ethical Dilemmas" while serving as a Jewish Community Center executive director.

Bob lives in Omaha with his wife, Rita. They have a blended family of four children and nine grandchildren. This is his first book.

www.ingramcontent.com/pod-product-compliance
Lightning Source LLC
Chambersburg PA
CBHW051714020426

42333CB00014B/975